A QUEBEC JEW

From Bloc Québécois MP to Jewish Activist

Adapted and translated to English by
Lori Beckerman and Richard Marceau

Richard Marceau
A Quebec Jew

Cover: Cindy Shtevi
Cover Illustration: Cindy Shtevi and Richard Marceau
Layout: Cindy Shtevi
Editor: Natania Étienne
Review: Lori Beckerman, Deirdre Beckerman, Steve McDonald, Jack Shapiro
Translation: Lori Beckerman and Richard Marceau
Legal Deposit: Fourth Trimester 2011
Bibliothèque Nationale du Québec 2011
National Library of Canada 2011

Bibliothèque et Archives nationales du Québec and Library and Archives Canada cataloguing in publication

Marceau, Richard, 1970-

A Quebec Jew : from Bloc Québécois MP to Jewish activist

Translation of: Juif, une histoire québécoise.
Includes bibliographical references and index.

ISBN 978-2-923721-24-8

1. Jews - Québec (Province). 2. Israel - Politics and government - 1993- 3. Palestine - Politics and government - 21st century. 4. Marceau, Richard, 1970- . I. Title.

FC2950.J5M3713 2011   305.892'40714   C2011-942844-X

Les Éditions du Marais
5562 Glencrest Avenue
Côte-St-Luc, Québec
H4V 2L9 Canada
Tel.: (+1) 514 486-6456
Fax: (+1) 514 486-0764
Email: editionsdumarais.ca

Richard Marceau

A QUEBEC JEW
From Bloc Québécois MP to Jewish Activist

Éditions du Marais
Montreal, 2011

To Lori, Michel and Olivier

CONTENTS

Prologue

PART ONE: ME

1. The *p'tit gars* from Quebec City 17
2. Love at First Sight 22
3. Through Strangers' Eyes 27
4. Mourning and Politics 34
5. A Quebecker in Israel 46
6. Zionist 52
7. Conversion 62
8. My Coming Out 73
9. To Make a Difference 77

PART TWO: US

10. Quebec's Jews? 85
11. A Complicated Region 94
12. Holocaust: "Never Forget" and
    "Je me souviens" 116
13. Canada-Israel Relations: Deep and Solid 120
14. Panorama 125

PART THREE: LET'S TALK

15. Frankly Speaking 147
16. The Other Lobby 150
17. Jewish Anti-Zionism 167
18. The Red-Green Alliance 173
19. Anti-Semitism in Quebec 178
20. Reasonable Accommodations 201
21. Conventional Wisdom or Ignorance 210
22. The Middle East …in Quebec 220
23. Apartheid, You Say? 253

Conclusion 280

This book, while largely inspired by my French book Juif, Une histoire québécoise, is not a straight translation. It was adapted for an English-speaking audience.

Please note that in many cases, the quotations used have been translated from the original French to English, for ease of reference for the reader. While every effort has been made to accurately translate these quotations, the original is referenced and any discrepancy between them is inadvertent.

Introduction

This book was almost called "The Bad Jew". Why? Simply because according to a portion of the Quebec intellectual class, a good Jew is a Jew who is always critical of Israel, even an anti-Zionist – someone who seeks the destruction of the State of Israel.

That is the case for one reader of a prominent publishing company in Quebec. When we were introduced, he immediately spoke to me about his good, Jewish anti-Zionist friends. I immediately understood where he stood on the issue of the Middle East conflict.

Nonetheless, I sent him the manuscript for my book (in French). He judged it to be "marvellously well written", but too pro-Israel, which did not accord with his view of the world and so he indicated he did not want to publish it.

I am therefore, a bad Jew. And I am proud to be called so.

I am a partisan of the State of Israel. While I do not hesitate to criticize decisions made by whichever government of Israel of the day, I am of the view that the achievements of this young and tiny state are impressive.

I am of the opinion that the State of Israel is a near miraculous culmination of the long history of a people who have been the victim of discrimination, persecution and attempts to exterminate them throughout history. Which is what explains the centrality of Israel to the Jewish identity for the vast majority of Jews in the Diaspora, regardless of their level of religious observance.

I also believe that the State of Israel is an outpost of the Western free world in a region where our values (liberty, human rights, gender equality, minority protection etc.) are to this day, rare. And I believe that our civilization is intimately connected to this tiny democracy found to the east of the Mediterranean Sea.

Prologue: The Dive

Ottawa, September 2004

It was a beautiful day, that day. A sunny and cool September morning. A great day to be born. Or reborn. Accompanied by my wife Lori, I was heading for a transformation. I was about to undergo the most important change of my life.

I, Richard Marceau, 11th generation Quebecker, long-time agnostic, son of a practicing Catholic family, educated by priests in Quebec City, firmly rooted sovereignist, Bloc Québécois MP, was preparing, in good conscience and after deliberate consideration, to become a Jew.

I was at the local Jewish Community Centre, about to immerse myself in the *mikvah*, a ritual bath, in order to be reborn as a Jew. One has to go in as one entered this world: naked, without jewellery, contact lenses or, for women, make-up. And, in my case, recently circumcised.

Alone in the dressing room, I was intensely aware of each passing second. Undressing, many thoughts - some contradictory - were rushing through my head.

By changing religion, was I reneging on part of my identity? Or was I adding to it? How were my family and my friends going to see me? Were they going to see me as "the Jew"?

How was my father, a deeply religious and practicing Catholic, going to react? My head was reeling as I thought of my mother, my sister, my brothers.

Would my constituents from the riding of Charlesbourg, in Quebec City, accept being represented by a Jew? By converting to Judaism, was I putting my political career at risk? Was I going to be able to pursue the goal I had given myself of keeping René Lévesque's dream of an independent Quebec alive?

I remember. Yes I do remember that day. Clearly. It was the first of November 1987. That was the day of my political birth. A wave of sadness overtook me when I heard that former Quebec Premier and Parti Québécois founder René Lévesque was dead. Impossible! The dream could not stop there, with the passing of that man, both humble and proud, so small and yet so great. The idea of Quebec's independence could not die with him.

Although at 17 I was too young to have known Lévesque as Premier, I knew enough to realize that with his death, a great man had passed. A powerful symbol of national pride had left us.

The powerful feeling of belonging to a nation, the same emotional bonding that would later lead me to join the Jewish people, swelled deep within me. I felt it in my Quebec fibre, woven with a desire for national freedom, and a drive to make a difference.

When the announcement came that his would be a national funeral held at Quebec City's National Cathedral, I rushed to see the vice-principal of the private Catholic school where I was a student, the *Petit Séminaire de Québec*. I asked Father Pierre Dupont, with the candour one has at 17, if there was any way I could be a witness to this historic event. He answered, calmly, that it was highly unlikely but that he would see what he could do. I was to return to him the following day.

As agreed, the next day, I returned to his office. He asked: "Have you ever served mass?" I answered in the affirmative though, to be totally honest, my experience was somewhat limited. He then directed me to a priest in the cathedral. The priest estimated my size, handed me a pure-white robe and said: "There you go. Be ready to serve mass".

That is how, as a teenager, I played a role (granted a small role, but still a role) in a pivotal event in Quebec's history.

I vividly remember the fervour of the entire Quebec people. I also remember the feeling that there was a before and an after that fateful day. I remember telling myself that the dream of independence for a small but resilient French-speaking people could not be allowed to die with the passing of a great leader. Three days later, I acquired my membership card for the Parti Québécois.

But at the *mikvah*, I was now far from the mass-serving teenager. I had grown to become a Member of Parliament, a sovereignist in the House of Commons, thrice elected for the pro-independence Bloc Québécois.

I finished undressing and was entirely naked, like the day of my birth. Putting aside my natural modesty, I left the dressing room and walked towards the bath where three men were standing, the witnesses.

I entered the water and said the prayer in Hebrew. I then emerged from the water with a new name, a name I had chosen for myself[1]: *Yisrael ben Avraham*

My name was not chosen randomly, but was the product of much reflection. Of course, it is a reference to the people of Israel, the nation, not the state, of which I am now a member.

But indeed it is also the name of a state, only 63 years old today. The result of an unprecedented rebirth of an ancient people in its ancestral land, Israel is a small state to which I am spiritually and culturally, even organically, now connected.

But it is also, and I would even say mainly, a name with a very specific Biblical meaning: *He who struggles with God.*

I kissed my wife, who was very emotional and crying tears of joy, tears like the tears one sheds when a baby is born.

What had brought me to this point - a *p'tit gars* from Quebec City, born Catholic, educated by priests? How I had arrived at this moment, I don't know exactly. But to understand all the consequences of that fateful choice, I knew I would have to live them, to experience them. I had to dive in. And so I dove.

I dove and came out, still myself. Still Richard Marceau. Still the same man. But I came out fundamentally changed. Forever. I dove in and came out a Jew.

A Jew.

Me

1
A *p'tit gars* from Quebec City

In Quebec City, just in front of the cemetery where René Lévesque lies, on the other side of the street now named after him, there lies a Jewish cemetery. *Beth Israel Ohev Sholom* is the oldest active Jewish cemetery in Canada. So now, when I am in Quebec City, all I have to do is cross René Lévesque Boulevard and I find myself on either side of my two identities.

Despite the longstanding presence of Jews in Quebec City (since the 18th century), nothing had predisposed me to become a Jew. In fact, the cemetery as well as the presence of the Jewish community had been invisible to me throughout my childhood.

I was born in Quebec City to a Catholic family. I grew up in the suburbs in Charlesbourg: a place of backyard pools, hockey in the winter, baseball in the summer.

The roots of my family were planted in Quebec some 400 years earlier. My ancestor, Francois, arrived in New France in 1635, from the region of Poitou in France. My sons are therefore 11th generation "Marceau" in North America.

My father, who I was named after, was a civil servant with the government of Quebec. My mother Michelle, a secretary, had been a stay-at-home mom for many years, caring for the five children under her charge.

I was the first biological child born to the union of my parents.

But when I was only six months old, my parents decided to foster parent eight year old twin boys, Gaétan and Réjean.

I still ask myself today what could have motivated them to do so. Without question, when my sons were six months old, I would never have taken in two 8 year old boys at one time. But my parents did, and in doing so, gave me my first two brothers who also happened to be my first babysitters.

Two years later, the star of the family, my sister Karina, joined us. A world-class athlete, an unparalleled communicator, and a television journalist, I believe I can claim some credit for forging her tough character together with her other three brothers who "tortured" her as much as protected her.

At seven years my junior, Jonathan proved to be the family's most generous and kind. Gentle and playful, he is the family member that seeks to mediate and reconcile.

As you can see from the cast of characters, I was blessed to be raised in a traditional Quebec family.

My upbringing was also traditional, including my religious education. Naturally, that meant studying catechism at primary school. My parents were practicing Catholics and every Sunday I was obligated to attend Mass, a ceremony I still know by heart (unlike many Catholics and many Jews for their own service!).

As a skilled reader and the son of devout parents, I was one of two students chosen to read scripture at my First Communion in second grade. My confirmation was also a very important event for me and my family. I still have the photos of myself wearing a horrible polyester safari-style beige suit. My entire extended family was in attendance, including those who had made the trip in from other parts of Quebec.

I started secondary school in the public system where I had

attended primary school. Having always been a good student but lacking a challenge, my first year of secondary school (7th grade) was notably turbulent. I talked too much, was argumentative, and instigated others. I was, in general, a troublemaker. I didn't realize it at the time, but it was good preparation for my future in the House of Commons!

The school principal, however, saw it differently. Near the end of the academic year, he invited my parents in and strongly "suggested" that they send me to a private school to provide the necessary challenge to meet my academic ability. It was intended to provide a level of difficulty sufficient to ensure that I had to work in class.

Because my parents were not rich and had five children at home, private school required significant sacrifice. And so my father travelled to work by bus rather than by car, and I went to the *Petit Séminaire de Québec*, a school founded in 1668.

Every morning we took the bus together, my father sitting in the front and me in the back. My father was sensitive enough to leave me alone and allow me to avoid the embarrassment, understandable for an adolescent, of being accompanied by his father. This was especially crucial in front of all the students who attended the nearby girls' school, *les Ursulines*.

Le Petit Séminaire was the most prestigious school in Quebec City, located inside the walls and history of the Old City. The environment would fill me with emotions that would slowly cause my nationalist identity to grow.

Le Petit Séminaire was a boys' school run by Catholic priests. It had a strong academic program and there were also a vast number of well organized extracurricular activities and sports. I played, and loved playing, football for the school team. Our games were played on the Plains of Abraham, a scene charged with historic significance.

For the first time, I became socially active, realizing that life was much more than simply taking care of oneself. I became involved in the school co-op and was given responsibility for the graduates' yearbook in my final year of secondary school, something I am still proud of today.

To be expected, an important emphasis was placed on the spiritual development of the students. I therefore received an intense traditional Catholic education, both at home and at school.

I was a Quebec City boy, privileged in a number of ways but primarily just an ordinary boy from Quebec. My photo could easily have been featured in the dictionary beside the definition of young native Quebecker, not to mention francophone and Catholic - a *Québécois de souche*!

Having adored my experience at the *Petit Séminaire*, I decided to continue my CEGEP (college) there. While still situated in the incredibly majestic surroundings, I started to feel suffocated. Despite many social activities and numerous awards and nominations at the year-end celebration, I decided I needed to breathe fresh air.

So I decided to finish my CEGEP studies at a public school, François-Xavier-Garneau. That was when I became immersed in the two worlds that would become and remain my passions today: politics and international affairs.

The CEGEP Garneau was politically, intellectually and socially mixed; less rebellious than the CEGEP of Limoilou, but less restrained than that of Sainte-Foy.

At the time, the Parti Québécois (PQ) was far from the summit of its popularity and sovereignty seemed distant. Nonetheless, I founded a PQ group at the CEGEP. I started to become highly involved in the party, and soon served as an executive member of the local riding association. I helped raise campaign funds and organized demonstrations in favour of Bill 101, all at the time when the Supreme Court severely weakened the Charter of the French language. They were great years filled with political activism that would serve me well in the future.

It was also at that time that I developed the desire to explore the world, a passion that took me to France for the first time on an exchange program through the *Association Québec-France*. It was 1989, the bicentennial year of the revolution. I have since remained a great lover of France.

I worked at the Office of Tourism in Châtellerault, 80 kilometres south of Tours. I used the opportunity to quench my thirst for history by going to Colombey-les-Deux-Églises to see *La Boisserie*, the last residence of General Charles De Gaulle, as well as the cemetery where he is buried.

I tasted Paris, visited the European capital under construction (Brussels) and London. I absorbed everything that I saw and in so doing, peaked my desire to travel, promising myself to study overseas one day.

The little boy from Quebec was grown now. He had seen a bit of the world and had become hooked on politics. Looking back, in considering my childhood and youth, I must thank my parents. They always encouraged us, pushing us to realize our dreams and desires. I often think of them when I look at my own two sons. But I am getting ahead of myself.

While I was educated, had travelled a bit, and had been involved in politics, I had not yet met the love of my life.

2
Love at first sight

One day, I fell totally in love.

Just like in the movies, two incredible green eyes looked my way and love was thrust upon me. I couldn't resist the force that overtook me; it was both incredible and romantic. Shivers run down my spine even today when I think about that moment. I have never felt anything so strong. Corny, I know, but true. I was 21 years old when I met the love of my life, Lori.

Who would have thought that I would find the love of my life in, of all places, the middle of Ontario?

I remember it as if it were yesterday and yet this all happened in 1991. I had been studying law at Laval University and frankly, I was bored. I had worked hard at school through my teens and having entered my twenties, I was in need of some adventure. And so I applied to participate in the exchange program with the Faculty of Law at the University of Western Ontario in London.

Attending my first course there, while walking into the classroom, our eyes met and wow! Was she ever beautiful! Later, she would tell me that the girl who was sitting next to her had said: "That guy over there keeps looking at me." And Lori thought, "No, I think he is looking at me." Obviously I was looking at her!

Despite my immediate attraction, my first impression of

her was somewhat negative. When the labour law professor asked if anyone was against unions, she was the only person to respond positively. I later discovered that the company her father had founded and worked a lifetime to build had not long before been unionized after a bitter and mean campaign. The experience had been hurtful and left her with a negative view of unions.

Sometime later we introduced ourselves and from there, things moved quickly. Lori was older and more self confident than I was at that point. She asked me directly, "Would you like to go out for dinner with me?" Like a complete idiot I replied "Why?" She responded "To talk" and I, even more idiotically, asked "Talk about what"? She still reminds me of that conversation...

As luck would have it, for some reason she ignored my responses and we went out for dinner together. It was October 11, 1991, the Thanksgiving weekend. Everything clicked and when leaving the restaurant after dinner, we rented a movie. A bad movie, but we didn't really care. It was only the pretext to be together. No need to say more.

Lori was 29 years old and I was 21. She was a native English speaker, I was a francophone. She was Jewish, I was Catholic-born and saw myself as agnostic. She was from Toronto, I was from Quebec City. From appearances, we had little in common and our respective friends and family were not very optimistic about the likely duration of our relationship. But we disagreed with their assessment, and felt that our connection was becoming increasingly strong.

The first obstacle I thought I would face was Lori's family and its Judaism. She was a proud Jew, although secular and non-practising. The observance of Judaism in her family was essentially limited to a meal at the Jewish New Year (*Rosh Hashanah*), fasting at *Yom Kippur* (the day of Atonement), and *seders* (festive dinners) at Passover. Her observance was not unlike many Canadians whose religious practice is limited to Christmas and Easter celebrations. But culturally she was very Jewish and she was very committed to Israel, where she had lived for a short time in her early twenties.

Our relationship deepened and in order to get to know her and her origins, I turned to what I knew best: books. In English and in French, I read up on the history of the Jewish people and the State of Israel, the beliefs of Judaism, even Jewish dietary restrictions. I wanted to be ready when I met her family.

I shouldn't have worried about it. When I first met her mother, she served me shrimp, a food prohibited according to Jewish law. The family and Judaism were not going to be the obstacle I feared after all.

For a boy from Quebec City, dating a woman of another religion and language was like another world; it fulfilled my desire to discover the world in general. As it turned out, the age difference was not at all relevant.

When we decided to marry, I told Lori very clearly that I had no intention of converting to Judaism. While not practicing my own family's faith, and alternating between a rigid atheism and open agnosticism, I did not want to join another religious community.

If Lori wanted to transmit her Jewish heritage to our future children, it was fine with me. For me, what was essential was that their language of education be French. And that is the agreement we struck. Our children would be francophone Jews who were also able to speak English, and they would be exposed to the dominant Christian culture of Quebec, where we planned to live.

We were quite happy with our compromise. As a young couple we had our Christmas tree lit in addition to Hanukah candles. We ate *matzah* at Passover and chocolate eggs at Easter. We exchanged wishes for Christian and Jewish holidays in French and English. We enjoyed the cosmopolitan atmosphere of our ongoing cross-cultural exchange.

And naturally, it was what we wanted to pass on to our children. Consequently, it meant our children would go to French school, not be baptised, and, if we had boys, they would be circumcised in the Jewish tradition.

My first encounter with the Jewish civilization had come from the reading I did as a youth. I loved books and read constantly, devouring newspapers, magazines, dictionaries, encyclopaedias, biographies, and history books. But I was not particularly interested in Judaism, certainly no more than say, Hinduism, Greek history, or Latin America.

Of course, the information I gleaned was viewed through the prism of a Catholic Quebecker, for whom the Jews had erred spiritually in failing to recognize the divinity of Jesus Christ, had erred politically in being massively federalist and anglophone, and had erred geopolitically in preventing the creation of a Palestinian state.

Growing up, I paid attention to these questions out of intellectual curiosity, no more or less than other issues. It is also true that in Charlesbourg, I was not going to meet many members of the Jewish community. In sum, for me the Jews, Israel, and Judaism were all theoretical. Not that it stopped me from having very strong opinions. Strong, though as I would later realize, not particularly well-informed opinions.

The fact of living with Judaism, as it was an inherent part of my own wife, changed my perspective. If Lori wanted her whole extended family to attend a celebration, as I had for my confirmation for example, it was impossible. Lori's extended family had been decimated during the Second World War. On her mother's side of the family, only her grandparents, who had left Europe for Canada before the war, and one uncle who was found in Siberia after the war (where he had stayed after fleeing Poland), had escaped the horror of the Holocaust.

My perspective evolved as a new world opened to me. A world with thousands of years of history that are painful perhaps, but also exciting and fascinating. This new world I would discover with my wife Lori, because twenty years later, our love affair continues. We beat the pessimistic prognoses for our relationship.

3
Through Strangers' Eyes

When I arrived in London, Ontario in 1991, Canadian politics were at the boiling point. The failure of Meech Lake had provoked a political crisis and Quebec seemed to be headed for sovereignty. Robert Bourassa gave the impression that he was increasingly considering the sovereignty option, and polls suggested a strong majority of Quebeckers were ready to vote "yes" in an eventual referendum.

At the same time, Quebec flags were being burned and stomped on in Brockville, Ontario and the Charest Commission was attempting to repair the damage done by the death of the Meech Lake Accord. To make matters worse, the Oka crisis had occurred.

I was never a vengeful sovereignist. Nobody ever told me to "speak white!" an admonition familiar to many francophones in days gone by to speak English. My view of sovereignty was always positive, founded on the conviction that the Quebec nation could have its own state and govern itself if it so desired. I never felt or imagined that sovereignty was aimed against Canada or the anglophones.

But then, for the first time, I was confronted in certain circles with open hostility to Quebec and all the half-truths and ignorance about us. And that hurt - a lot. Most Quebeckers have felt that at one time or another. It was a feeling I would remember later on when it was my Jewish identity that was being attacked.

The best example is still the Oka crisis in 1990. The *Sûreté du Québec*'s (SQ's) attempt to re-impose law and order on and around the reserve had gone bad, and the Canadian army had intervened, causing immediate and inaccurate worldwide media reports of a chaotic scene.

As an example, the French newspaper *Libération* reported that an aboriginal had been killed - when in fact the victim was an SQ police officer. Certain international media gave the impression that the entire crisis could be summarized as a somewhat racist (and armed) Quebec against poor (and defenceless) aboriginals.

Even Reverend Tutu, hero of the anti-apartheid fight, arrived from South Africa to warn Quebec (and Canada) that the situation was comparable to South Africa during apartheid.[2]

However, the least attentive observer would have quickly realized that part of the aboriginal group was made up of heavily armed men who more closely resembled a group of thugs than anything else. Other than their ancestral rights, the trafficking of arms, alcohol, tobacco and drugs were also at the centre of the conflict. The famous "Lasagna", one of the armed activists, was not an aboriginal from Oka but indeed a resident of Brooklyn.

The citizens of Châteauguay were faced with a bridge that was blocked by a violent group of armed aboriginals, and had good reason to insist that the public powers be used to re-establish peace and order. That being said, the excesses of the angry mob that we observed remain inexcusable.

In Canada, the Charest Commission was trying to save the discarded Meech Lake Accord by hearing a range of viewpoints on Quebec. Some went as far as to oppose the "distinct society" clause out of fear that the government of Quebec would force women to have children!

I felt a strong sense of injustice listening to and reading the many critical and condescending declarations regarding my people. That too, I would later recall, when it was Israel being subjected to similar treatment: the caricature of the big bad Jewish wolf attacking the poor Palestinian lamb.

It did not however, stop me from throwing myself into the (Canadian) lions' den when I went to study in London, Ontario!

It would be the first of many occasions where I found myself, in a manner of speaking, the spokesperson for the sovereignist movement outside of Quebec.[3]

I must say that at university, I was very warmly welcomed. I even created a Bloc Québécois club, which was not as easy as it may seem. I first had to acquire a sufficient number of signatures which I did mainly with Quebeckers, but also with some English Canadians who were sufficiently open-minded. In doing so I managed to ensure the BQ was represented in the student parliament, even though the NDP was not, as they were unable to collect enough signatures to apply for club status.

My time in the heart of English Canada allowed me to get to know and appreciate this nation. Even today, I still feel comfortable wherever I am in Canada. If anti-Quebec prejudice persists, the great majority of Canadians I have met and been in contact with are highly respectful of Quebec.

Of course, the Quebec reality remains largely unknown among Canadians, and that is in large part due to the language barrier. But when Quebeckers take the time to explain themselves, as I did during my time at Western, they are, despite the odd display of intolerance, warmly welcomed.

Since those days in English Canada, I have taken on the task of showing that, far from being intolerant, Quebec on the contrary is a very open and welcoming society.

It is often difficult for English Canadians to understand the desire to defend the Quebec identity. For some, it seems odd to want this small nation made up of a majority of native francophones, to remain distinct and to preserve its linguistic heritage. This is not an exclusivist objective, but it is one that has been shared by all governments that have led Quebec, both federalist and sovereignist.

I have never hesitated to demonstrate that the sovereignist movement promotes generosity and a hopeful future. What I did then as a law student, I later did as a sovereignist Member of Parliament in the House of Commons.

The fact is that even Quebec federalists, who clearly do not share the goal of making Quebec a country, recognize that it is a legitimate project and a weighty argument, a position that is little known among English Canadians.

After my stay in Ontario and having finished my law studies, I dreamt of broadening my knowledge of other matters and completing my education, preferably out of Canada. I considered France, the UK, and the United States. After intensive research, two institutions were particularly interesting: the John F. Kennedy School of Government at Harvard University and the *École Nationale d'Administration* (ÉNA) in France. These two schools were very well recognized, attracted students from around the world, and guaranteed a solid education.

Having just completed two years in English-speaking Ontario, I decided to take a chance at ÉNA. I was accepted while working for a prominent law firm in Montreal. I decided to put my legal career on hold for the European adventure of attending one of France's *Grandes Écoles*.

Founded by Charles de Gaulle immediately after the Second World War, it was highly impressive. Former students included French Presidents Valéry Giscard d'Estaing and Jacques

Chirac, Prime Ministers Laurent Fabius, Michel Rocard, Édouard Balladur, Alain Juppé and Lionel Jospin, as well as numerous Ministers, highly placed civil servants, ambassadors, and managers of big corporations. In short, I was attracted to ÉNA by its reputation as France's top institution of higher education.

Quebecker and proud francophone, an admirer of Charles de Gaulle, fascinated by the history and grandeur of France and the legacy it gave to the people of Quebec, I was anxious to take in all that life in France had to offer. I had the opportunity to study alongside the most accomplished of French students, most of whom had been planning and working towards their entry to ÉNA from early adolescence.

In addition, I developed friendships with the other, approximately 30, non-French students in the same class, whose name was voted by the students to be "Marc Bloch", after a well-known French-Jewish historian killed by the Nazis.

My time in Europe allowed me to visit most of its countries, and to become knowledgeable on the subject of European integration and French public administration. I had occasion to observe and, to a minor extent, participate in French political discussions.

There was great curiosity regarding Quebec generally, all the more so as my time there coincided with the year of the referendum on sovereignty in Quebec. I was once again a spokesperson for Quebec and sovereignty, explaining without end the objectives and values of the movement.

My education at ÉNA included an internship at the prefecture of Chambéry in Savoie. For the internship, most foreign students were placed in symbolic positions without truly being integrated in an institution of the Republic. As a Quebecker, I was not however, considered a complete foreigner. As a result,

I had the great opportunity of working in the centre of the state administration, primarily dealing with security.

The autumn of 1995 was a particularly intense period, due to an Islamist terrorist campaign which hit France July 25 at the Saint-Michel metro station in Paris, causing eight deaths and wounding approximately 100. From July to October of that year, the French were suddenly faced with the reality of terrorism. In all, there were eight attempted attacks, 10 deaths, and over 200 wounded.[4]

I would start my internship at the prefecture shortly after these events and I saw from the inside, not only the threat presented by Islamist terrorism for Western societies, but also the consequences on the lives of citizens who wanted simply to live their lives in peace.

The anti-terrorist plan *Vigipirate* was initiated with a strong mobilization of police and military. This was even more so the case in an administrative region (*département*) that was on the country's border, as in Savoie, with the prefecture being the primary institution responsible for implementing state decisions.

To truly realize the impact of terrorism, one has to see the fear of the next attack and the threat of gratuitous violence that targeted innocent civilians - women, children, and the elderly - without discrimination. These were acts of pure terror, some six years before September 11, 2001.

In addition, the autumn of 1995 was filled with social unrest: strikes and enormous demonstrations were frequent.

In France at that time, there were two Ministers in Savoie (Hervé Gaymard and Michel Barnier) and their presence was like a magnet for the picketers. In addition, Chambéry was an important junction point for trains, and the resulting demonstrations by railroad workers were numerous and significant.

The CRS (anti-riot squad) was very active in the region. I was not only on the frontline watching, I was working in the heart of the response by the French government to the events.

In addition to a solid academic foundation, my time at ÉNA provided me with the opportunity to acquire a practical knowledge of the inner workings of state security and public safety. Having been confronted with Islamist terrorism in 1995, I found myself better prepared as a legislator to deal with the aftermath of September 11, 2001.

After an enriching time in France, it was time to return home. I knew more and more clearly what I was going to do. The flame that René Lévesque had lit had to be reignited in pursuit of the dream. I was going into politics.

The opportunity would present itself much sooner than I imagined.

4
Mourning and Politics

In November 1996, while still in France, I received a call. My mother was critically ill and her life was in danger. Shocked, I took the first flight home where I would spend many hours at the hospital with my family.

Over a period of months, I largely stayed at my mother's side as she fought for her life. However I also spent a few hours of each day out of the hospital, working in politics. If I leapt into a political battle quickly, it was because the Bloc MP Jean-Marc Jacob had, while an MP, thrown himself into the municipal election where he was roundly defeated. By refusing to step down from his position as MP, and losing the municipal vote, I believed that he had disqualified himself as a candidate for the Bloc at the next election.

I went to the National PQ Conference and reconnected with my sovereignist network to determine who had the necessary support to run against Jacob at the nominating convention. But nobody wanted to run, because confronting a sitting MP, who already has a team and significant support, is far from a sure thing.

And so, in December 1996, at 26 years of age, I decided to throw myself in and seek the nomination for the Bloc against a sitting MP. Despite my mother's encouragement to do so, it was very difficult to manage two fights at one time. I was winning one, but losing the other - the more important of the two.

My mother died at 49 years of age, the night of March 12, 1997, leaving our family devastated. Fourteen years later, we are still not the same. She was the anchor of our family, its centre of gravity.

When the nomination vote took place weeks after her death, there were 1,000 party members present and the atmosphere was charged. Suspense hung in the air, as everyone knew the result would be tight. However in the end I won, albeit by a small majority.

Some said I had to be rather full of myself, while others spoke of audacity and determination; Jews would call it *chutzpah*. No doubt, it was all of these. In the end, I was the Bloc candidate, a sovereignist representative, and pursuing my dream of following in the footsteps of René Lévesque.

A general election had been called by Jean Chrétien the day prior to the nomination vote, in an effort to benefit from the recent arrival of Gilles Duceppe (some three weeks earlier) as leader of the Bloc Québécois. The plan was to make inroads in Quebec with a surprise vote, and Chrétien almost succeeded. After a somewhat painful start, Duceppe managed to regain control, and we finished with a respectable 44 MPs out of a possible 75.

For me, the disappointment was that my mother wasn't there to share my victory. I would have so adored having her beside me when I was first elected.

There was a lot of work awaiting me. I inherited a riding executive that was divided and I had to rebuild the organization and the team. I was fortunate to have particularly devoted employees who supported me in achieving that goal. In the riding, my team was made up primarily of two political "old-timers" (Jean-Pierre Cyr and Vicky Fortier), who were later joined by Mara Aprile. In Ottawa, I had the extremely versatile, efficient, and original Patrick St-Jacques, whose competence made him one of the best parliamentary assistants on the Hill - and one of the funniest too! I have great appreciation and respect for those activists in political parties, and retain a warm and fond memory of my own years as a party volunteer.

Representing the people of my riding was one of the greatest honours I have ever been given. I will always be grateful that the citizens of Charlesbourg accorded me the confidence to represent them three times.

Clearly, an MP does not win an election alone. Much of the merit goes to his team. We would all like to say that we win on our own strength, but the reality of modern politics is that the party leaders and the national campaigns hold a lot of sway.

I still recall the hesitant Gilles Duceppe of 1997. He improved immeasurably through the campaigns of 2000, 2004, 2006 and 2008, when he attained the status of a first class political leader. In my view, the 2011 Bloc massacre was due to factors much more profound than Duceppe's performance during the campaign.

From the start, things clicked between Duceppe and me. While he is a political leader with a great sense of humour, Duceppe is essentially an unrelenting hard worker, disciplined, and with little regard for those colleagues who fail to bring the same rigour to their work.

His reputation as an iron fist leader is exaggerated. However, it is true that he has little time for laziness and superficial opinions. When he encounters them, he can be quite cutting. Seeing that I shared his philosophy on these points, he gave me an increasingly large arena in which to work and the confidence to grow into it. Over the years, we developed a great working relationship and collaboration that, over time, transformed into a solid friendship.

Despite his loss in the May 2011 federal election, Duceppe still has much to offer Quebec, in whatever position he chooses.

In addition to working in opposition, the Bloc directed by Duceppe also became a laboratory of ideas and we were strongly encouraged to bring fresh policies to the forefront. As critic for the Solicitor General, I was preoccupied by organized crime in Canada and I quickly concluded that one of the Achilles' heels of these organizations was money laundering. However, organized crime depended upon the $1,000 bill, which had become an indispensible tool for their major transactions. It was in fact, quite convenient to discreetly deal in large sums. It was almost as if the bill had been designed expressly for illegal transactions.

With my assistant Patrick, we mounted a campaign to eliminate the $1,000 bill. We worked hard for months and the evidence became so clear that the government had no choice. Eliminating the $1,000 bill cost nothing and would impede the functioning of organized crime. If today there are no longer any $1,000 bills in circulation, I am proud to say that it is due, at least in part, to our effort.

I also succeeded in having the House of Commons adopt the principle of a reverse onus of proof for individuals found guilty of gang-related offences. As a result, a member of a criminal organization convicted of a gang-related offence today has to prove that his or her belongings were not acquired through criminal activity. If not, they are seized by the government.

Encouraged by these successful projects, I tackled a more ambitious one: the integration of the North American economy. Although it was beyond the scope of my portfolio, the question had long been of interest to me. Having observed European economic integration up close, I sought to apply what I had learned to North America, a crucial issue affecting the Quebec economy.

I had discovered that the economic integration between Canada and the U.S. was more significant than between European countries. Still, Europe had adopted a common currency, the euro. In Canada at that time, we were faced with a currency valued at some 60¢ against the U.S. dollar, a fact that was working against our competitiveness. Businesses enjoyed an artificial advantage in the form of a weak dollar that ensured there was no need to innovate or excel in order to have a part of the marketplace. And when our dollar started to increase in value, it did so far too quickly, rising and dropping and destabilizing our export companies.

It seemed to me the time had come to discuss a common North American currency. I spoke with Duceppe about it and he was so enthusiastic that he started the debate on the issue during a press conference on the session, shortly before Christmas 1998. In doing so, he dropped a bomb on Ottawa and Bay Street. For many Canadians, the Canadian dollar is more than mere currency. It is a national icon, a symbol of pride and independence from the U.S.

And so I committed myself to furthering the debate, in the House of Commons and elsewhere. If the Reform Party at that time received it with some openness, the Liberals were totally opposed. For them, the issue was anything but rational. But of course, many experts, including economists, financiers, and industrial leaders, found the idea increasingly interesting. There was talk as far as the U.S. Senate.

The current economic situation might not be ideal for such a union but I still believe it is an option that Canada should explore.

After a few years as critic for Solicitor General, Duceppe showed great confidence in me by giving me the Justice file, one of the most important in Parliament. For five years, I had to deal with complex and highly emotional issues like prostitution, decriminalization of marijuana, and same-sex marriage.

The debate over same-sex marriage turned out to be fundamentally important for me, as well as for many Canadians. It forced me to carefully consider issues of individual freedom, the role of the state in their protection, the role of religion in the public sphere, and the importance of respecting one another's opinion when they are diametrically opposed.

I have to admit that I am fairly proud of the part I played in this debate. Despite my fairly young age, I succeeded in navigating the treacherous waters of the issue without error, for my party or for myself.[5] At the same time, I managed to defend deeply held convictions while demonstrating respect for opposing beliefs.

I also had my share of failures. The one that had the biggest impact on me was my failure, along with Liberal MP David Pratte and NDP MP Peter Mancini to sway Texas authorities to stop the execution of Canadian Joseph Stanley Faulder, even though he had mental health issues, was tried without his Vienna Convention rights being respected, and his legal counsel had been substandard. This episode reinforced my deeply held conviction against the death penalty.

Elected at 26, I represented youth in sovereignist circles. But I was not the only young MP. There were four others under the age of 30 elected for the Bloc: Bernard Bigras, Pierre Brien, Caroline St-Hilaire, and Stéphan Tremblay. Our presence illustrated that the sovereignist movement was not the cause of a single generation - our parents'. It also forced the movement to adapt to a new century.

We were very different in our outlook, from traditional left-wing sovereignist Bigras to centre-right nationalist Brien. It led to many heated discussions, held in our numerous tours around Quebec, but we were united by our deep commitment to Quebec's distinct personality.

Duceppe and the people around him quickly understood that

our generation has different interests and another way to tackle today's problems. He made use of our differences as a think tank for the Bloc on a range of important issues, such as globalization and identity in the 21st century.

The debate over Quebec's identity turned out to be a watershed event in sovereignist circles, as well as in Quebec as a whole. Quebec's identity, more diverse than ever, enriched by immigrants from around the world, is still hotly debated in Quebec. The debates around reasonable accommodations attest to this fact.

The Bloc was suited to lead this debate as it was made up of sound, well-respected, and hard-working MPs and first-class staffers.

Too often, people tended to forget about the selflessness and idealism of the Bloc contingent in Ottawa. They did not run to be in government or because they were power-hungry; by definition, the Bloc could not take power in Ottawa. They worked sincerely toward the realization of their values, and whether one agrees with it or not, to me it is something noble.

During my political career, I had the honour of being in close contact with three Quebec Premiers.

The first one was Jacques Parizeau, with whom I might have had some of the most interesting discussions of my life. While disagreeing with him on some issues, he always found a way to challenge me, my idealism and my enthusiasm. Now in his 80's, he remains one of Quebec's and I would even say Canada's, intellectually youthful politicians. I remember with pleasure his public compliments for me.

During one of the Bloc's general councils, in his inimitable style, in the serious and professorial tone he loved to use, Parizeau was explaining the necessity of Quebec's independence. At some point, while tackling the issue of the many monetary options available to a sovereign Quebec, he referenced the texts I had written on the subject of a North American monetary union, even calling me a 'prophet'!

Being quoted by a former Premier was very flattering. To be considered forward-thinking and original on economic issues by a world-respected expert in the field made me very proud.

Fortunately, it did not go to my head (too much...), as my colleagues turned it into a good-natured joke, one ceremoniously offering me a special edition of Khalil Gibran's *The Prophet*.

The few times I met Lucien Bouchard, far from being the serious, austere and severe man many believe him to be, I found him to be funny, considerate, and very attentive to me, the then-young politician. I hope his contribution to public life is not over, as he still has much to offer.

Finally, Bernard Landry occupied the top of Quebec's political ladder for too brief a time. He was destined for the position. We shared many ideas, including that of a North American monetary union. He too, in front of a Bloc general council, mentioned my work in this field and called me his 'disciple' which, once again, led my colleagues to tease me, some jealously. Unfortunately, in my opinion he made a major mistake by abruptly resigning as PQ leader in 2005.

After Landry's resignation, the PQ found itself leaderless while Duceppe was at his height of popularity. A few months before, every pundit had predicted that the Bloc would be destroyed by Paul Martin. However, Duceppe rolled up his sleeves and used the sponsorship scandal to triumph in Quebec. The 2004 election campaign was my best ever. The Party devised a fantastic slogan: *'Un parti propre au Québec'* - a play on words meaning both *'Quebec's own party'* and *'Quebec's clean party'*. Led by Duceppe at the peak of his form, the Bloc ran a magnificent campaign.

Duceppe was naturally pressured to succeed Bernard Landry at the helm of the PQ. He was certainly the favourite and many, myself included, thought he was going to make the jump to provincial politics.

The question of his successor as Bloc leader was obviously raised. I was somewhat bemused to hear that mine was touted as one of the most serious candidacies. I received many calls from colleagues, party activists, and journalists[6] and started to seriously consider the possibility. The idea of leading the Bloc was quite appealing. However, not everything was simple.

I had by then become Jewish. Was Quebec ready to have a Jew at the helm of a sovereignist party? Of course, the very fact that I was asking myself the question was somewhat troubling. In an ideal world, any citizen should be able to run for political office without his religion being a factor.

But I had a feeling that it would not be so easy. To complicate matters, my conversion was not yet public. Were I to throw my hat in the ring, it was bound to make a splash. Duceppe put a stop to my consideration of the matter by turning down the chance to go to Quebec City.

My life as an MP continued. Parliament can be a fairly collegial environment, where relationships can develop with people of other political parties when the language barrier is broken.

The fact that I was comfortable in English allowed me to meet interesting men and women from across Canada, from all walks of life. I could appreciate their convictions, their ideals, and their drive to make their community and their country a better place.

Stephen Harper is one of those people. Very smart, considerate and driven, the contact I had with him was always respectful and pleasant. Vic Toews, with whom I sat on the Justice committee, is light-years away from the doctrinaire image some have of him. Despite our differences of opinion, once a deal was struck between us, he stuck to it. I particularly appreciated his gentlemanly offer to help and his personal support, after my defeat.

I also valued my professional relationships with people like Jason Kenney and Stockwell Day, both principled and dedicated public servants - despite regularly holding different visions of society than myself.

On the Liberal side, I always enjoyed Denis Coderre, a man with energy and ambition unmatched across Canada. I also have fond memories of Jean Lapierre, both a ferocious fighter in the House and a gentleman politician who is today one of Quebec's most influential and well-connected men.

I have never been one of those sovereignists who despised Jean Chrétien. I obviously did not share his federalist passion, nor have I ever supported his Clarity Bill, but he was always very pleasant when I met with him on the floor of the House. The first time I met him, standing in line to vote for the Speaker on my very first day in the House, hearing I was from Charlesbourg he proceeded to ask me, by name, about a few Liberal activists he knew from my riding. I guess that sense of ease with others is the kind of thing that made him such a successful politician.

One time in 2003, when poll after poll was predicting a Bloc disaster in a battle against Paul Martin, I bumped into a group of journalists while walking on the Hill between the Centre Block and my office in the West Block. They proceeded to ask me if my résumé was ready, as I was sure to be looking for a job after the next election. To this I responded: "You'll see. As a politician, Paul Martin is not in the same league as Jean Chrétien. Martin will be easier to beat." The journalists all laughed, but for Paul Wells, who told me: "I think you're right."

I was right and, in 2004, won my third election.

My life in politics also gave the middle-class, suburban young man that I was, the opportunity to meet world leaders. I met and shook hands with U.S. Presidents Bill Clinton and George W. Bush, Nobel Prize winners Nelson Mandela, Shimon Peres, and the Dalai Lama. Having read about these historic personalities in books and magazines, I was stunned to find myself rubbing shoulders with them. I was far from the neighbourhood of Charlesbourg in which I had grown up.

It also gave me the opportunity to travel around the globe, encountering fascinating countries and people. One of the most memorable trips I participated in was the U.S. State Department's International Visitors' Program. Occurring a few short months after the September 11 attacks, it gave me the chance to see America up close at its most shaken, and yet most united and resolute.

The people in my group, all from Europe, were all up and comers in their respective countries. One, Danny Alexander, is even a Liberal Democrat Minister in Great Britain today.

A few weeks later, the European Union invited me to participate in a similar program. This allowed me to update my knowledge of this complex organization. It also led me to the conclusion that the European model was not one that could be adapted for the Quebec-Canada relationship. When I publicly stated my view on the issue, I knew PQ leader Landry would be displeased, as it was the bedrock of his public statements at that time.

Indeed Landry called to express his anger at my position. However, it did not have a big impact on my deeply held conviction and certitude to defend, respectfully but strongly, any idea that was mine.

Politics can be brutal. I found out the hard way when, in the general election of January 26, 2006, I lost by a little more than 1,000 votes. I had lost and, for the first time, tasted the bitterness of defeat. It was much more painful than I had expected. My political adventure was coming to an end with a lesson in humility.

However, I had fortunately developed another passion during my political career, one that was as captivating. I had become a passionate Zionist.

And I was about to have the chance to express this passion to its fullest.

5
A Quebecker in Israel

It was during my studies at ÉNA in France that I really took notice of the local political consequences of the Arab-Israeli conflict. It was the first time that I really understood that this conflict, despite occurring thousands of kilometres away, could be a hot political issue even in a country with no immediate interest in it.

I was in France when Yitzhak Rabin was assassinated by a Jewish extremist in November 1995. I was in France when Shimon Peres lost the following elections against Benjamin Netanyahu. And I was still in France when Palestinian terrorist attacks were occurring in growing numbers while Israelis and Palestinians were negotiating a peace agreement.

I could see that French opinion was solidly behind the Palestinians. Paradoxically, while supporting Palestinian independence, which would necessarily entail full ownership for decisions and their consequences, my French interlocutors kept trying to excuse the Palestinians from any responsibility for their situation. Every problem of Palestinian society was because of Israel. Every challenge - societal, political, economic, and even familial - was attributed to Israel. Palestinians were viewed too simply as victims and as objects of history, never as fully responsible participants in history.

This French view of the Arab-Israeli conflict, the prism through which the situation was analysed, was familiar as it was very similar to Quebec's. It is easy to understand why, as French media, French analysts, and French books were an important source of information on this topic for many Quebeckers, myself included. However, mastery of the English language (and thus my access to English-speaking TV, radio, and books) and my interaction with people who had lived or were still living in Israel - my wife Lori first among them - gave me another perspective from which to form a more balanced opinion.

As I said earlier, Lori is a strong Zionist. Like the vast majority of Jews around the world, for her the existence of a Jewish state is fundamental, and she is in no way willing to compromise on this. Zionism's very essence is the desire that an independent, national Jewish homeland continue to exist on the Jewish ancestral lands.

To be a Zionist is simply to live in today's world, where nation-states are still the most important actors in international politics. Zionism is no more racist than Canadian, American, British, Australian, French, or Chinese nationalism. This notion, by the way, I always thought should be easily understood and shared by Quebec sovereignists.

I knew Lori was closely following the events in Israel and the region. But for me at that time, it was not much more important than say, Europe, Latin America, or Asia.

In the spring of 2000, I received an invitation from the Canada-Israel Committee (CIC) to visit Israel. The CIC (now the Centre for Israel and Jewish Affairs) defined itself as "the official representative of the organized Canadian Jewish community on matters pertaining to Canada-Israel relations".

The CIC had an excellent reputation on Parliament Hill, one of expertise, efficiency, and political non-partisanship. It has always eschewed partisanship, both in Canada and in Israel, working with every political party to keep them informed of developments in the Middle East.

For more than three decades, it has proven to be a trusted source not just for Parliamentarians, but also for media, academics, civil servants and others. To its credit, the CIC had been the catalyst for many important breakthroughs in the relationship between Canada and Israel.

What was essential for me was that, from the time the Bloc was founded, the CIC had considered it a legitimate and important political player, one with which it was worthwhile to develop good relations. This was certainly not the case with many other organisations at work in Canada. The CIC respected the Bloc, and thus I had no difficulty accepting its invitation to visit Israel.

I was far from expecting that this trip would literally change my life. And that turned out to be the case on so many levels. It would ultimately alter my politics, my professional career, and my religious affiliation.

Accompanied by Lori and MPs from other parties, I hopped on the plane for the Holy Land. Having briefed myself beforehand, I felt I had a relatively strong knowledge of the politics of the region. I was about to find out that I held many preconceived - and I now know - superficial ideas.

As soon as we landed, we were swept up on a whirlwind of meetings, briefings, discussions, conferences, and discoveries.

What struck me early on was the normalcy. I was expecting to land in a war-torn country, with soldiers everywhere, and scores of stressed and fearful people. That was certainly the image presented by the media around the world. It was not at all like that. Despite security precautions, I found myself in a Western and modern state like many I had previously visited.

But it is a minuscule country. Indeed, Israel is only 0.2 percent of the territory of the Middle East. The rest, 99.8 percent, is made up of Arab-Muslim states.

Just to compare, Israel's territory is 21,671 km², Quebec's is 1,667,926 km² and Canada's is 9,984,670 km². In other words, Israel can fit into Quebec 80 times and into Canada 460 times.

In Jerusalem, the holy sites impressed me, even if the Holy Sepulchre left me fairly cold while the *Kotel* (the Western Wall) dazzled me. The Old City, with its tangle of religions, histories, and civilizations, cannot leave one indifferent. The light that envelops Jerusalem at sunset has no equivalent in the world. It is simply magical. The mix of the very modern and very ancient, of secular and holy, is unique to the city.

That Jerusalem would leave a deep impression did not surprise me. Who hasn't heard of Jerusalem in one way or another in his life?

The surprise was Tel Aviv, one of the world's most interesting, open, and colourful cities. Before going to Israel, one usually thinks of Israel as a homogeneous country essentially inhabited by Jews. But one tends to forget that Jews come from everywhere: from Eastern, Central, and Western Europe, from North Africa, from North and South America, even from Ethiopia, India and other countries in the Middle East. Moreover, more than 20 percent of Israel's population is not even Jewish.

This blend gives Tel Aviv a very special vibe, one I had not felt in any other city I had been in, other than perhaps Montreal on a good day. The well-known tourist guide Lonely Planet has named Tel Aviv one of the three best cities in the world,[7] praising it for its art and music scenes, and relaxed, liberal culture. It has also won acclamations for its tolerant attitudes and thriving gay culture, which makes it "a kind of San Francisco in the Middle East."

Imagine Montreal with beaches that are kilometres-long, lined with palm trees and basking in quasi-constant sunshine beside the Mediterranean Sea (instead of snowstorms) and you get an idea of Tel Aviv.[8]

The Dead Sea, on which one can lie like a mattress, Masada the fortress where the Jews took their last stand against Rome, the Galilee where most of Christ's ministry took place, the meetings with first-class Israeli analysts, Ethiopian immigrants, and Members of the Knesset - all this and more would make my first visit to Israel an unforgettable experience.

Obviously, political realities would necessarily catch up with us. The Canadian government, in collaboration with the CIC, had organized a meeting for our group with the Palestinian Authority's main negotiator, Saeb Erakat, in the Palestinian-controlled city of Jericho.

Climbing aboard armoured diplomatic vehicles, we sped towards this millennia-old city in the Jordan Valley. Surrounded by armed men - some even masked - we were received by a charming, well-spoken, and obviously bright man. Erakat is used to speaking to Western audiences and is a regular commentator on CNN and the BBC.

The Palestinian negotiator welcomed us with a violent verbal attack on Israel. All of us were somewhat puzzled by this as peace negotiations were being held between Israelis and Palestinians. We did not expect to be met with such an attack or even an aggressive tone. That being said, while negotiations were taking place, a murderous terror campaign was being waged against Israeli civilians by Palestinian terrorist organizations.

What surprised, even upset us the most, was being told by Erakat that he was a virtual prisoner in Jericho. He told us he could not travel around the Palestinian territories as Israel had forbidden him from doing so. We thought: "How can Israel even pretend to negotiate in good faith while it forbids the main Palestinian negotiator from travelling?"

I remember thinking that the Israelis had played us. That the dizzying sites we had seen and the fascinating meetings we had attended were intended to pull the wool over our eyes. In political terms, I felt they were blatantly spinning us.

But that was not the only surprise. The following day, with the caption LIVE FROM GAZA at the bottom of our screen, who did we see on CNN speaking about the latest developments? You guessed it: Saeb Erakat himself!

Erakat was thus not in Jericho anymore. And when you consider that one must cross Israeli territory to go from Jericho to Gaza, it was clear that not only was Erakat not a prisoner of the Israelis in Jericho, he had a good enough rapport with them that he received permission to travel through Israel. Erakat had lied to us, straight to our faces. I felt I had been had, not by the Israelis as I had initially thought, but by Erakat.

Two thoughts crossed my mind. First, that the Palestinians had become masters in the art of political propaganda. Second, that the Palestinian message that Palestinians=victims and Israel=oppressor, is an easy one for everyone to remember. And it is very effective.

Humans are naturally predisposed to want to support and help the victims, the weakest, in any situation. This is especially the case for Canadians. But I had seen with my own eyes that the situation was much more complex than the slogans. Complex, and yet fascinating. On the flight back to Canada, I was still excited by what I had experienced on the trip. I had discovered a new interest, one that would soon turn into a passion.

6
Zionist

Before leaving for Israel, I expected to see a country filled with rabbis with side locks and black hats, Uzi-armed soldiers, and besieged cities. In other words, I was expecting a religion-dominated country at war.

Reality turned out to be very different. My strongest impression was that of a certain resemblance between Israel and Quebec. I found Israel to be an inspiring country and its citizens warm and welcoming.

Contrary to many people, I more readily identified with Israelis than with Palestinians.

A few parallels between Quebec and Israel came to mind.

René Lévesque once said, and rightly so, that "French Canadians and Jews have quite a bit in common."[9] His words are proven true even in the basic institutional icons of the two peoples.

Both Israel and Quebec officially adopted their national flags in 1948 and both are blue and white. The fleur de lys is a symbol of both peoples. It is of course on the Quebec flag, but it can also be found on many antique Jewish decorations and on the one shekel coin, the Israeli currency.

Like Quebec, Israel is facing an incredible linguistic challenge. If Quebec is a French island in an English-speaking sea, Israel is a Hebrew island in an Arabic-speaking sea.

Not only must Israelis work hard to ensure that Hebrew remains vigorous, Israel resurrected Hebrew, a language that not so long ago was used only in prayer - similar to Latin for the Catholic church - and was totally inept for the modern world.

Israel's efforts to make Hebrew its national and everyday language are very impressive. For example, new immigrants must take intensive Hebrew lessons - paid for by the state -to facilitate their integration. Quebec would be well advised to follow this example.[10] René Lévesque underlined the example of Israel when he said that:

> *"[t]he difficulties faced by French Canadians are practically nothing compared with what some people went through to accomplish the miracle of Israel. In Palestine, there is new life after 2,000 years. Hebrew, which had been dead, has become a living language again. We can accomplish what we want - a future that is basically and more progressively French - if we work hard enough and if we push. We don't need a major miracle."[11]*

Today, Hebrew is both Israel's national language and its common public language. Yet, as in Quebec for its English-speaking minority, the Arab minority has rights, including linguistic ones, well-respected and protected by the Israeli Supreme Court.

To see the modest building in which Israel's independence was declared is very moving. Barely 40 years before this historical event, Tel Aviv was only sand dunes. By the time of Israel's accession to the concert of nations, it had become a bustling metropolis.

Israel is a true economic miracle.[12] A bit like Quebec, it decided to diversify its economy and invest in the high tech sector. This is the case such that Israel today is the country that invests the most, in proportion to its GDP, in research and development. In the 1950's, 70 percent of Israeli exports were agricultural. Today, 2 percent are agricultural exports.

As Quebec Finance minister Raymond Bachand said in October 2010: "Israel is similar to Quebec in many ways. There is the size. There are Israel's sectors of the future, which are similar to Quebec's: biotechnology, pharmaceutics, information technologies. And Israel is a world leader in both the technological sector and venture capital."[13]

Israel has truly become a world leader in technological developments. There are more Israeli companies quoted on the NASDAQ than any other country in the world, other than the United States. That includes Canada and Canada has four times Israel's population.

There is more venture capital in Israel than anywhere else in the world. Israel invests 4.86 percent of its GDP (in 2008) in research and development, compared with 2.63 percent for Quebec (2007) and 1.9 percent for Canada.

In 2008, the investments in venture capital per capita were 2.5 times that of the U.S., 30 times that of Europe, 80 times that of China and 350 times that of India. In fact, in the same year, in the middle of the economic crisis, more than $2 billion in venture capital was invested in Israel, more than France, Germany and Britain taken together.

Israel has the highest rate of computers per capita in the world. It has a high ratio of university educated people: 24 percent. In fact, 12 percent have PhDs, which puts Israel behind only the U.S. and the Netherlands.

Israel has the highest ratio of scientists and technicians in the world: 145 per 10,000, ahead of the U.S. at 85, Japan at 70, and Germany at 65. Israel also publishes more scientific research papers than any other nation at 109 per 10,000 inhabitants.

These massive investments and technology have yielded impressive results – and the entire world has benefited. Israeli engineers developed the first cell phone in Haifa, at the Motorola research lab. Intel's Pentium MMX was invented in Israel. Even something as common today as telephone voice mail was invented in, you guessed it, Israel.

The majority of Windows NT exploitation systems were invented by Microsoft-Israel. The only research centres outside of the U.S. for both Microsoft and Cisco are in Israel, where they knew they could find great engineers.

A Ben Gurion University scientist has developed a biological form of control for mosquitoes and black flies that cause malaria and a type of blindness, thus saving the sight and the lives of millions.

Velcade, a very effective drug against cancer, was created by two researchers at the Technion, the Technological Institute of Israel. The pair received a Nobel Prize in Chemistry for their groundbreaking work.

An Israeli company developed the first pill-sized camera that may be swallowed. It allows doctors to see the inside of the digestive system, enabling them to diagnose cancers and other digestive problems without invasive surgery.

It is an Israeli doctor who leads the team at Merck that created a vaccine against cervical cancer. And it was an Israeli company that created a blood analysis technique able to diagnose heart attacks by phone.

All in all, some 46 percent of Israeli exports are in the high tech industry.

In 2006, the average per capita income in Israel was $31,561, right behind France at $31,825 but ahead of Germany at $31,390, Italy at $31,051 and...Quebec at $30,910 (Canada without Quebec stands at $36,849).[14]

Since its (re)creation in 1948, Israel's exports grew 11,250 times, from $6 million to $67.5 billion. Between 1998 and 2009, they more than doubled, from $33 billion to $67.5 billion.[15]

And along with this growth has been an ever-rising quality of life. Israelis have a life expectancy of 80 years, on par with Norway. Israel's population has grown by 900 percent since 1948, and its growth is 1.8 percent - higher than all other developed countries.

All the above led to Israel being admitted to the OECD, the 'rich countries club' on May 27, 2010, confirming its arrival in the first world.[16]

From both necessity and innovation, Israel has made great strides in environmental stewardship. Israel recycles 70 percent of its used water, more than any other country in the world and three times the second place, Spain. For used water coming from homes, 80 percent is recycled, four times the second place country.[17]

Indeed, Israel resembles Quebec in more ways that I think residents of either one would assume.

René Lévesque did not hesitate to say that: "What the Parti Québécois is trying to do in Quebec resembles what Zionism meant for the creation of the State of Israel [...] Just like you have your own Jewish identity, we have our own Quebec identity and we are going to make it true."[18]

Lévesque often drew comparisons between Israel and Quebec: "Mr. Levesque evoked comparisons between the State of Israel and the preservation of Jewish culture and traditions, with Quebec and the preservation of French culture and traditions in North America",[19] notably when he "referred to Israel as a national home very similar to the one French Canadians are trying to set up."[20]

But instead of René Lévesque-type statements, today's so-called progressives are calling for boycotts against Israel like there were against South Africa. Yes, as ridiculous as it is, the Jewish state is accused of being an apartheid state.

To the contrary, Israel is a liberal democracy with the rule of law. For Israel, this makes it an anomaly in the Middle East.

Israel's gays are protected. Its women are guaranteed equality with men. It is a modern economy, based on the high tech industry and a people fighting to keep its distinct identity. Like Quebec.

Quebec is often misunderstood in the English-speaking world (Canada included), too often judged not on what it does but on preconceived ideas. Israel too is often misunderstood, judged, and condemned in advance, on the basis of ideology or a simplistic understanding of the world (and sometimes both).

There is of course a huge difference. If Quebec is sometimes the subject of "Quebec bashing", its existence is not contested and no country or organization has as its stated objective a desire to wipe it off the face of the Earth.

For one Desmond Tutu who compared Canada to apartheid-era South Africa during the Oka crisis, there are thousands who reserve their hate and slander for the Jewish state. For one Jan Wong who accuses Quebec society of harbouring racism[21] that caused the Dawson College shooting, there are thousands who accuse Israel of genocide or crimes against humanity.

Indeed, the unfair standards Israel faces are all too apparent. When criminal elements of a First Nation armed with assault weapons choose to block a bridge, everybody thinks it is normal for the army to step in, protect the public, and restore order. But when Israeli civilians are the target of missiles and rockets, even of suicide bombings, Israel's self-defence is condemned by some from the outset.

I have to admit to being somewhat baffled by the fact that Quebeckers in general, and sovereignists in particular, tend to identify more with the Palestinians than with the Israelis.

I could not clearly understand why public opinion in Quebec was so much in favour of the Palestinians. What I was learning about Israel through seeing, reading, hearing, and personal discovery, was light-years away from what I thought I knew based on media reports and discussions in Quebec. It reminded me of the many misconceptions I had heard about Quebec in the rest of Canada. So many things were divorced from reality.

Taking the example of what I had done - on a small scale I know, but still - for Quebec outside its borders, I set out to try to explain this little country to my fellow citizens. In other words, I had become a Zionist.

The word "Zionist" has become, for some, a charged word. It is even used as an insult by Israel's enemies and by anti-Semites. For me, it simply means a belief that the Jewish people too have the right of self-determination. Or even more clearly: Israel has the right to exist, period.

Back in Ottawa, I decided to be an active friend of Israel. But this in no way meant that I was going to be an enemy of the Palestinian people. It is not a zero-sum game, even if many anti-Israel groups try to make it so. I believed then - and believe now - that both Jews and Palestinians have a right to live in their own states, peacefully, side by side.

Thus, I joined both the Canada-Israel Parliamentary Friendship Group and its Palestinian equivalent.

At the time, I paid special attention to the Camp David

negotiations in July of 2000, under the leadership of U.S. President Bill Clinton. Israelis and Palestinians came close to an agreement. But Yasser Arafat was not willing to give up playing the role of the 'freedom fighter' for that of statesman. Taking care of taxes, schools, garbage collection and hospitals is much less glamorous than seeing yourself as a liberator.

Some revisionists have attempted to blame the Israelis for the failure to reach an agreement at Camp David and have even tried to convince the world that the generous offers by Israeli Prime Minister Ehud Barak were a myth. But the players that were actually privy to the negotiations all agree that Israel offered the Palestinians an independent state on 100 percent of the Gaza Strip, 95-97 percent of the West Bank, and parts of Jerusalem - as well as a $30 billion fund to help the Palestinian refugees.

Saudi ambassador to the U.S., Prince Bandar, called Arafat's refusal of Barak's offer 'criminal'. As Bandar was one of the main facilitators during the negotiations, that says a lot.

Under Bill Clinton, no world leader was received as often as Yasser Arafat in the White House. Clinton provided all the prestige of the office of the President of the United States to help the belligerents reach an agreement. But Arafat turned down any compromise. For his part, Clinton was not duped, and he put blame for the failure squarely on Arafat's shoulders.

Unfortunately, as I will review in a later chapter, Camp David was not the first time the Arabs turned down the chance for a two-state solution. Nor will it be the last. It is obviously not because they do not want a Palestinian state. Might it be because they do not want a Jewish one?

On this subject, one should note that a survey[22] was done by the pro-peace organisation One Voice and published on April 22, 2009. This study shows that it is '*essential*' for 71 percent of Palestinians that their state correspond to the land of the disputed territories and... all of Israel's territory! If we add the percentage of people who think that this is *'desirable'*, it goes up to 82 percent. Another survey[23] conducted by the Ramallah-based Arab World for Research & Development shows results along the same lines.

The heart of the issue is that, from the beginning, the Arabs have believed that one way or another they will vanquish the Israelis in the end. If that is the case, they must think, why compromise today if we can get all that we want later on?

This is what led 'New Historian' Benny Morris to write:

> *The secular Palestinian leadership... express[es] a readiness for a two-state solution but envision such an outcome as intermediate and temporary. They speak of two states, a Palestinian Arab West Bank-Gaza-East Jerusalem state and another state whose population is Jewish and Arab and which they believe will eventually become majority-Arab within a generation or two through Arab procreation (Palestinian Arab birth-rates are roughly twice those of Israeli Jews) and the "return" of Palestinians with refugee status. This is why Fatah's leaders, led by Palestine National Authority President Mahmoud Abbas, flatly reject the Clintonian formula of "two states for two peoples" and refuse to recognize the "other" state, Israel, as a "Jewish state." They hope that this "other" state will also, in time, be "Arabized," thus setting the stage for the eventual merger of the two temporary states into one Palestinian Arab-majority state between the River and the Sea.*[24]

Arguing for a more balanced position on the Arab-Israeli conflict for the Bloc was not always easy. The majority of my colleagues who paid any attention to the issue tended, while being open to discussion, to have a pro-Palestinian reflex, like a majority of Quebeckers. I could however, count on Duceppe's willingness to strike a just balance and not be pushed into a radically critical position of Israel by some members of the caucus, like foreign affairs critic Francine Lalonde.

I will get back to this later, but few nations have faced tragedies like the Jews have in their history. Still today, Israelis live under constant threat from terrorist organizations (Hamas, Hezbollah) at their borders, a nuclear-building Iran and others. But what an incredible willingness to build, to prosper, and to live on their ancestral land!

Every time I have gone to Israel, I have returned impressed by this tenacious and intelligent people. And I decided to be a counterweight, with the modest means at my disposal, to the clearly slanted narrative that was presented to Quebeckers.

Throughout my discovery of the Jewish people, in deepening my historic, political and cultural knowledge, the question of religion has always been present. I was intrigued by the Jewish faith and by the connection that it created between Jews across continents, observant or not, in Israel and in the Diaspora.

I was a lawyer in two provinces, a Member of Parliament, married to an extraordinary woman, and father of twins in good health. But even if I was successful in both my personal and professional worlds, something was missing. There was an empty space in my life, a space that was initially small, but was growing larger.

7
Conversion

My conversion to Judaism, while the final step in a long and complex process that I took very seriously, was not an end but rather a beginning. A beginning of what, however, I couldn't say.

I am still unable to entirely explain why a Quebecker, born and raised in a practising Catholic family, who later became agnostic or at least cynical, would later turn to God not as a Christian, but as a Jew.

When I returned to Israel in September 2003 (my third such trip), I felt like something was going to happen, but I wasn't sure what.

I was with a number of other Members of Parliament in a new program organized by the Canada-Israel Committee that twinned young parliamentarians with young leaders from the Jewish community.

I connected with Israel as never before. I felt more comfortable. I had the impression I was returning home in a certain sense. As though Israel was my place and I belonged there.

After a particularly special Sabbath, I experienced an exceptionally moving *havdalah* ceremony.[25]

The prayers - even in Hebrew - moved me, as did the melodies. The centuries-old rituals awakened something primordial in me, something that had been sleeping. Something I thought had died.

The fact that the ceremony took place in Jerusalem, outdoors and with a magnificent view of the Old City, could only add to the powerful emotions.

And so I decided not to convert to Judaism, but to explore the possibility of conversion. Once home, I took advantage of the absence of our twin boys to discuss my decision with Lori. She was of course already aware of my growing interest in Jewish civilization. But she was very surprised by my news. She was so happy she cried.

I was preoccupied by a number of considerations, some theological, others practical.

First, I didn't know when exactly my agnosticism was put aside or when my belief in God returned. At 17 years of age, able to liberate myself from my parental obligation to attend Mass every Sunday, I had quit the Catholic Church, its theology, and practice. I felt freed. Free of a religion that I didn't feel was mine. Free to profess my own beliefs, or more precisely, my lack of belief. Now I was preparing to return to religion.

Fundamental existential questions were bouncing around in my mind. Does converting to Judaism mean rejecting my family, my friends, my history, my people, in other words, a part of myself?

How would my family, and especially my father, a fervent Catholic, react? Was my father going to view my rejection of Catholicism as a rejection of him? And what about the political consequences? Although Quebec is not a Catholic state, it remains a fact that the Catholic Church is an integral part of Quebec's history and society.

The church had had such a profound influence on Quebec

that the question of the Catholic personality of the province had arisen. Even more, I was an elected representative of a party whose first mandate was the defence and advocacy of the uniqueness of Quebec, its identity and its values.

Coincidence or not, shortly after my return from Israel, I met my first Jewish spiritual guide at Parliament during an important event. At the time, I was the spokesperson for the Bloc on the same-sex marriage issue. As a result, I had been invited to a press conference of the Canadian Coalition of Liberal Rabbis[26] for same-sex marriage. One of the principal speakers was Rabbi Steven H. Garten.

Immediately after the press conference, I approached Rabbi Garten and asked for a private meeting with him to which he immediately agreed.

A few days later, I went to his synagogue, Temple Israel, a Reform congregation (the liberal branch of Judaism) in Ottawa. He welcomed me very warmly. I spoke to him about my interest in the possibility of converting to Judaism. He posed a number of questions regarding me, my family situation and my religious beliefs. He asked me to do two things: register in an introduction to Judaism course offered by the synagogue and attend Sabbath services.

And so I registered for a course that can, if it is the student's desire, lead to a Reform conversion. It was also open for the student to decide at any time during or after the course, not to convert.

While still non-practicing, Lori participated in the course which was incredibly interesting. Rabbi Garten is one of the best teachers I have ever met and from whom I have had the pleasure of learning. He is funny, very knowledgeable, modern and consistently pushed me further in my thinking.

For the most part, my class colleagues were young people who wanted to marry someone who was Jewish and who had already decided to convert to Judaism. I was in a different situation, as I had not yet decided to convert and I had already been married to a Jew for almost 10 years.

I should clarify one point. Judaism is a religion that does not encourage proselytizing; it does not look to convert non-Jews to Judaism.

Rabbi Rivon Krygier in a conference at Notre-Dame Cathedral in Paris on March 21, 2010 said:

> *Rabbinic Judaism - that is often accused of ethnocentricity - starts from a point of view more universal because early on and globally it admitted that there exist paths to salvation other than conversion. Of note, the Talmud provides for the righteous among the nations, which applies to all men of good will acting righteously, notably those among the Christian and Muslim world.*[27]

This attitude is radically different than Christianity and Islam. Those religions consider themselves the bearers of the absolute and exclusive truth. Their adherents will be compensated after death, and those who do not follow their beliefs will not obtain eternal salvation.

This fundamental belief gives these two major religions each a missionary characteristic. Practicing Christians and Muslims want to convert the non-believer to their religion with an ultimate goal of having their religion accepted by all of humanity. The history of Quebec is filled with stories of Catholic missionaries, initially with the First Nations people and later in Africa, Asia, and Latin America.

In contrast, Judaism does not teach that only Jews are loved and saved by God. Jews have no obligation to convert non-Jews. In this sense, Judaism is more universal than either Christianity or Islam.

An important dictate of Judaism requires that a candidate for conversion to Judaism be rejected three times before being accepted. As well, conversion to Judaism includes two aspects: 1) becoming a member of the Jewish people; and 2) accepting the Jewish religion.

The most well-known example is that of Ruth who was a convert and, according to Jewish tradition, the great-grandmother of King David, and therefore also (in the Christian tradition) an ancestor to Jesus. Ruth, a Moabite, when required to choose her destiny, and whether to join the people of Israel, responded to her Jewish mother-in-law Naomi: "Your people will be my people and your God will be my God."[28] This reflects the dualistic character of Judaism: the requirement of joining the Jewish people and accepting the Jewish religion.

The process that I followed included almost a year of intensive study, courses, analysis and critique of books and even a written exam. It also included regular synagogue attendance for Sabbath and religious holidays. These were merely the prerequisites to the conversion process and not the process itself.

While a part of the Reform services is conducted in Hebrew, which at the time I did not understand, read, or speak, I quickly got the feeling for it and began to feel comfortable. Hebrew, a Semitic language light-years from French, resonated with me. And the melodies seemed strangely familiar.

By May 2004, I had finished the first steps toward conversion. But prior to appearing before the religious tribunal (*beit din*) to formally undertake the process of conversion, I decided to take the summer to reflect on the decision. I wanted to fully consider the matter as I recognized that it had the potential to completely change my life.

I wanted to weigh the pros and the cons, the professional, familial and personal implications and of course, the spiritual.

Because this was not a decision I was going to take lightly.

Becoming a Jew in Quebec meant becoming the member of a community that an important part of Quebec society viewed with suspicion and undoubtedly ignorance.

I didn't want to reject any part of what made me a proud Quebecker. To the contrary, I wanted to add something marvellous. I did not want to put aside any part of myself, but rather I wanted to embrace a new and different element that I felt corresponded to my beliefs from the deepest part of my soul. I intended to add something that I felt would complete me.

In Quebec, religious conversion is a rare phenomenon. The rarity of this can likely be explained by the crushing force of the Catholic Church. It is much more frequent in the U.S.

In fact, according to a study published by *The Pew Forum on Religion and Public Life* on February 28, 2008,[29] 44 percent[30] of Americans leave the religion in which they were raised for another, or are totally unaffiliated religiously. My decision to convert is quite rare among Quebeckers, but quite common from a North American perspective.

I wanted to become a Jew and adopt the tradition mixing particularism and universalism, the religion that gave the world monotheism. I wanted to be a part of this ancient religion that had given birth to Christianity and Islam, this philosophy that had attracted me by its emphasis on the family, helping one another and asking questions and reasoning.

After a number of years of religious indifference, spent somewhere between a curious agnosticism and militant atheism, I was ready to reconcile myself with God. I needed spirituality. I needed a reason for being. And I had found these in Judaism.

My rediscovery of religion took place at a much more profound level than my years of Catholic education when I had been a child, adolescent, and young adult.

The idea of basing my beliefs - my life - on the Torah, attracted me. The fundamental belief of Judaism on this sacred text and its interpretation, on a discussion between God and man through the study of the text, filled a need in me for spirituality and intellectual debate. I was also attracted by the practical side of Judaism.

Some religions offer ways to avoid the suffering and limitations of a physical existence. Others offer hope of a better life after death. Judaism puts the emphasis on living one's life, here and now, on the importance of living a moral life, according to the rules enunciated for so doing.

Judaism requires more than belief. It requires one to question the texts and to discuss and argue the views submitted, even questioning those who explain or teach the texts. Doubt is not only accepted, but encouraged.

It is for that reason that when it came time for me to choose my Hebrew name, I knew well in advance what I would choose: *Yisrael ben Avraham.* Israel, son of Abraham.[31] Israel signifies "he who struggles with God".

While I had found my religious home and I had chosen my religious tradition, I knew I would spend my life doubting, questioning, and arguing. But I now belonged to a religion that encouraged it.

As Ruth in the Bible, I could now say to my wife, my children, and my community: "Where you go, I will go, where you live, I will live; your people will be my people, and your God will be my God."[32]

That said, I never believed, and I still don't today, that human beings necessarily require God. An individual can easily live well as an agnostic, even an atheist, and be happy. One can completely reject the notion of the existence of God and be a very good person, a moral individual. Believing does not make one better.

My decision was finally made and there remained three tests to pass. First of all, the religious tribunal, the *beit din*. Normally, this is composed of rabbis or occasionally learned leaders in the Jewish community.

The goal of the hearing is not to verify one's level of knowledge. That is presumed based on the earlier tests. The purpose of the *beit din* is to consider the motivation of the applicant. Does he know what it means to be part of a group that has been persecuted over time? Does he understand that certain things he previously did would no longer be permitted? Does he appreciate the consequences of this decision? Overall, does he understand what he is getting into?

These very personal questions made me uncomfortable. I had always been a very private individual, guarding my personal life, my feelings, and thoughts.

Why have you chosen to do this? What does your family think? Given that your father is a practising Catholic, is he going to be hurt by your decision to become Jewish? Are you afraid of the effect this will have on your relationship with him? What about your friends? What will living in Quebec be like where in most areas, interaction with Jews is fairly limited? As a Member of Parliament, have you considered the professional consequences? Will your constituents want to be represented by a Jew who is also openly Zionist? What will you practically change in your life when you become a Jew?

After approximately an hour of questions, I was excused. I waited some 10 minutes and was then told that I had been accepted. I was so relieved and happy!

A few days later I undertook the next test for which I was terrified: surgery. To become a Jew requires that a man be circumcised, and I was not. I quickly came to believe that it is better to undergo the surgery at eight days old than at 34 years...

Finally, I was required to go to the *mikvah* or ritual bath. This is a symbolic manner of representing the rebirth as a convert. One has to enter the bath as one is born: completely nude, without jewellery, without contact lenses or makeup.

After immersing myself, I recited the required prayers. My immersion symbolically cleansed me of my earlier beliefs and I re-emerged a Jew. I entered the *mikvah* without a religion, and emerged attached to a 4,000 year old tradition. I came out Jewish.

Is Judaism a question of faith? Of belief in God? Of tradition? Of history and heritage? The response is yes to all of these. There are many ways to be a Jew. Judaism of faith and of heritage are both valid.

While from the outside the Jewish people appear united, it is a somewhat fragile unity. Jewish society is found in many different groups, whether religious, philosophical, or political. And those groups can fight one another fiercely.

There is in fact a great deal of tension between the different branches of Judaism. Many Orthodox Jews do not consider non-Orthodox movements (i.e. Conservative, Reform, Liberal), to be authentically Jewish. And many non-Orthodox Jews consider Orthodox Judaism to be a fossil from a distant time.

Judaism is divided into four broad groups, from three main movements.

Orthodox Judaism (itself divided into *hassidism, mitnagdism* and modern-Orthodox), is the strictest movement and most closely tied to literal Jewish law (*halacha*), as developed over the centuries.

With the enlightenment and the exit from the ghettos where they had been confined, the Jews were exposed to new and different ideas. As a result, in the 19th century, many decided to adapt Judaism to modern society, to reform it, from which Reform Judaism (also called Liberal Judaism) was born. This theology postulates that Jewish law is more suggestive rather than obligatory, notably with respect to the role of women, the obligation to eat only kosher food, and the use of cultural objects.

Later, Jewish thinkers - not wanting to return to Orthodoxy, but uncomfortable with the breadth of the changes made by Reform Judaism - created the Conservative movement. Also known as the *Masorti* movement, Conservative Judaism sits partway between Orthodox and Reform Judaism. Conservatives see themselves as bound by *halacha* or Jewish law, but an evolved and evolving *halacha*.

There is also a movement which is found principally in the U.S. called Reconstructionist Judaism. Its founder, Rabbi Mordechai Kaplan, saw Judaism more as a civilization than religion in the traditional sense.

The majority of the global Jewish population today is not Orthodox. In North America, the most important denomination in terms of number of adherents is Reform Judaism, followed by Conservative Judaism.

My conversion was liberal. I was thus not considered a Jew by the Orthodox movement. For them, while I had quit my earlier religion, I was not Jewish because my conversion was not completed according to the strictest criteria of Orthodoxy, and the rabbi who presided over my conversion was not Orthodox. I was therefore in an uncomfortable limbo.

As the synagogue in Quebec City that I regularly attended was Orthodox, it was becoming increasingly frustrating for me to participate. This was due to the fact that I was not counted as part of the required quorum of 10 men (called a *minyan*) necessary to pray, which is essentially done collectively in Judaism.

As well, I was becoming increasingly traditional in my practice, and so I decided to look into the possibility of converting according to the Orthodox criteria.

After months of study and especially discussions with Rabbi Sultan of Quebec City, Rabbi Bulka from Ottawa, and Rabbis Joseph and Poupko of Montreal (truly a group effort), I appeared before an Orthodox *beit din* in Montreal. I was symbolically circumcised (which is practically fetishism, to borrow from the converted Jewish comedian Yisrael Campbell in his hilarious show[33]), and I re-entered the *mikvah* or ritual bath. In so doing, I became Jewish in the eyes of all Jews.

Many people over the years have asked me if I was welcomed by the Jewish community. They have wondered if, given that I was a born Quebecker of French-Canadian origin, my background caused me any difficulty being in accepted. Not at all, none.

To the contrary, many born Jews have commented on my passion for Judaism, a passion that I exude from every pore of my being.

8
My Coming Out

Until November 2005, I had kept my spiritual journey for myself and my really close friends and family. I had not in any way publicized my conversion, figuring it was a strictly private matter.

But a religion is not practised in a vacuum. I had been attending services in both Quebec City and Ottawa. And, as an MP, I was a public personality, in Quebec but also in the rest of Canada as the Bloc's main English-language spokesman.

The editor of the editorial pages of *The Ottawa Citizen*, Leonard Stern, a member of the synagogue I was then attending, approached me to write a text for the Ottawa Holocaust Education Week, a yearly event in the federal capital.

I was torn between the desire to keep my private life entirely private and the opportunity to help advance Holocaust commemoration, something dear to me.

After a lot of thought I concluded that public interest should come first, and that if I could make a difference in the fight against anti-Semitism and racism, even a small one, I should do it. I was committing to my coming out.

Of course I knew that there would be consequences. But I was not expecting to be attacked as I was, simply because I had joined the Jewish faith.

On November 9, 2005, *The Ottawa Citizen* published my column, *The Evil Lives On*. In it, I mentioned my conversion to Judaism and tackled head on the issue of anti-Semitism with concrete examples in Canada, the U.S., France, and in the Muslim world.

Knowing it was bound to create controversy in some circles, I outlined a strong - yet moderate - defence of the State of Israel. What I had decided to do was clearly state my position on the Arab-Israeli conflict: I am a pro-Palestinian Zionist. And I am unabashedly a supporter of the Jewish State:

> *Of course, the State of Israel is not perfect, and should be criticized like any other country. I define myself as a pro-Palestinian Zionist. I take strong issue with the continuation of the settlement process in the West Bank and the location of the security barrier. In fact, similar criticism is often voiced in the Israeli press. I have also been a consistent supporter of an independent Palestinian state side by side with the Jewish state.*

> *However, I believe Israel is consistently held to a higher standard than other countries. Why is Israel the only country being threatened by academic boycott while many other countries have a human rights record much, much worse than Israel's?*

> *As the New York Times columnist Thomas Friedman wrote: 'Criticizing Israel is not anti-Semitic, and saying so is vile. But singling out Israel for opprobrium and international sanction - out of all proportion to any other party in the Middle East - is anti-Semitic, and not saying so is dishonest.'*

As one can see from the above excerpt, it put my position squarely in the mainstream on this issue. There was nothing extremist or anti-Palestinian in it.

But I was clearly saying that Israel should not be subjected to a double standard - nor should any other country. Every nation in the world should be judged by the same criteria. And when we do so, Israel has nothing to be ashamed of and rather the contrary is true. All the more so when it is compared to the other states in the Middle East.

Neither did this column contradict my political party's positions on the subject. Of course, there were many Bloc MPs with a more pro-Palestinian perspective. But I was well within the Bloc's parameters: two states, one Jewish and one Arab, living side by side with secure and recognized borders.

Moreover, it was not the first time I was taking a public stance on the issue. On Tuesday April 9, 2002, in a speech I had made in the House of Commons during an emergency debate on the deteriorating situation in the Middle East, I had outlined four principles I believed had to be followed to reach peace in the region. These were: a) recognition of the inalienable right of Israel to exist within borders that are safe and recognized; b) the right of Palestinians to a viable and independent state; c) there would be no military solution to this conflict; and d) terrorism is unacceptable.[34]

That is why the attack that followed took me by surprise. Of course, I was expecting the anti-Israel crowd (disguised as pro-Palestinian) to take shots at me. For them, any defence of Israel is anathema, unthinkable. They are blinded by an irrational hatred for Israel.

But a rebuke came within the Bloc's own ranks, from a candidate (and later MP) named Maria Mourani.

Mourani took the unheard of action of publicly attacking me, a well-known Bloc MP and a fellow candidate on the sovereignist website Vigile.

Her attack was personal, low and demagogic. She implied that before my conversion, I did not care about racism. Had she checked, a quick internet search would have provided speeches I had given and columns I had written in my local newspaper, *Le Charlesbourg Express*, on the very subject.

She would have seen my comments about Islam in the tense period following the September 11, 2001 attacks on New York and Washington. She would have seen that, of all the elected officials (municipal, provincial, federal) in the greater Quebec City area invited to celebrate *Eid al-Fitr* at Quebec City's only mosque, I was one of only two who showed up. She would have seen that my yearly best wishes for the holiday period included mentions of Christmas, Hanukah, and Ramadan.

But for Mourani, all of this was unimportant and irrelevant. For her, to stand up for Israel seemed to constitute some kind of crime that erased everything else. She put Zionists (who simply believe that the Jewish people, like every other nation in the world, has a right to its own state) in the same category as the anti-Semites. She concluded her column by defending French comedian and stand-up comic Dieudonne, a man who is now *persona non grata* in France because of his numerous condemnations in court for anti-Semitic declarations.

It was the beginning of a steep learning curve, one which led me to the conclusion that, in some circles, it was easier to promote Quebec's independence in Canada than debate in favour of Israel.

The anti-Israel/pro-Palestinian supporters have managed to surprise even me, somewhat a cynic, with the toxic tone they adopt every time the subject comes up.

9
To Make a Difference

In 2006, despite strong organisation and fundraising, a good campaign and, I deeply believe, a solid and respectable record as an MP, I lost my bid to be elected for a fourth term.

I lost to an unknown Conservative candidate - who had previously been a candidate for a Parti Québécois nomination - who did not live in the riding. I found this to be a cruel event, but there was some personal solace in the fact that every Bloc MP in Quebec City but one, lost his seat. And so I knew I had not been personally rejected. Still, it hurt.

With this election, Stephen Harper's Tories had made a bridgehead in Quebec – which had caused my unemployment.

After nine years in political life, nine active, fascinating, demanding but oh so rewarding years, I was a free agent so to speak. What a humbling experience.

Only a few months before, when Duceppe was musing about a run for the PQ leadership, I was considered by many as a credible successor to the helm of the Bloc. And now I was without a seat and without a job.

The passage from political to civil life is always difficult. It is obviously even more so if this passage is...um... involuntary. I quickly set out to find a job. At 35, I was too young to retire and (contrary to popular belief) I could not touch my pension for another 20 years.

Rapidly, however, offers were extended to me – some from the political sector and some from other fields. I thought I needed to take a break from politics - however short - to do something else, especially as I was considering running for the PQ in the next provincial elections.

I needed some distance, something that political life does not really allow.

Each individual is looking for something different in his professional life. It might be a high salary or flexible hours or prestige. For me, what is important is the feeling of being able to make a difference. To work for what I believe in.

For that reason I started to do some punditry and to work with two well-known organizations: the above-mentioned Canada-Israel Committee (CIC) and the Simon Wiesenthal Centre.

I had previously dealt with the CIC. Not only did the organization have an excellent reputation (I knew it from my time in the House), it seemed to be a great place to work (which turned out to be true). As well, the fact that it was led by Shimon Fogel, a man who had had a huge impact on my life on so many levels, could only encourage me to work with them.

As I was aware, there is, in Canada's political sector, a very broad consensus on the Middle East.

Of course, there were some noticeable exceptions, like the Bloc's Richard Nadeau[35] and Maria Mourani, as well as the NDP's Libby Davies.[36] In taking radical positions on the issue, these MPs and others tend to only marginalize themselves.

Generally speaking, Canada's position is to the effect that: a) Israel is a democracy, a close friend and ally of Canada and it has the right to exist with defensible, secure and recognized borders; and b) the Palestinians have the right to an independent, viable, democratic and peaceful state side by side with (and not instead of) Israel.

This has been Canada's position for decades now and the Conservative Party, the Liberal Party, the NDP and the Bloc have all been in agreement.

Still, it is quite evident that Harper's Tories have been, in terms of clarity, tone, and a principle-based approach, the strongest supporters of Israel. Be it during the 2006 Lebanon war, during the *Francophonie* summit following it (where a motion deploring only Lebanese victims - not Israeli victims - was blocked by Canada), during the debate surrounding Durban 2, or during the Gaza conflict of 2008-2009, Israel has been able to count on Canada.

As a result, the Jewish state is very appreciative and pays much more attention to Canada, giving it much greater influence than it has had in the past.

I believe that, contrary to conventional wisdom, Canada now carries more weight than it used to. Adopting a principle-based approach instead of always attempting to find the middle of the road just for the sake of being "balanced" has given Canada a more powerful voice. Before, countries in the region were not really paying attention to what Canada was saying. Now, they do. This was confirmed to me personally by people in the Arab lobby and by Palestinian contacts, though they would never admit it publicly.

This position by the Conservatives has led to the new fact that, for the first time in a very long time, the Liberal party no longer has a lock on the Jewish vote. The Conservatives, spearheaded by Stephen Harper, Jason Kenney and Stockwell Day, have made important headway with this segment of the electorate.

That being said, and contrary to the simplistic image given by some to the Conservatives, they have in no way adopted an anti-Palestinian position. For example, they offered the Palestinians a $300 million package over five years, an offer without precedent in the history of Canada's relationship with the Palestinians.

In fact, during his May 2009 official visit to Canada, Palestinian President Mahmoud Abbas reiterated his appreciation for Canada's support of the peace process and its generous contributions in humanitarian aid through the U.N.

Moreover, on all of the above-mentioned subjects, the Harper government has always had the support of at least one opposition party. The Liberals have a very active and influential group of 'Liberal Friends of Israel' whereas the NDP has principled and fair-minded MPs and provincial politicians among its ranks. While the NDP also has a radical and noisy fringe which can be detrimental for their party, the NDP under Jack Layton always tried to take a balanced position. I can only hope that the new leader will stay the course.

I have always said that there is absolutely no need to adopt a Manichean position on the Middle East, a zero-sum game. Canada can be both a solid ally of Israel and build a strong relationship with this country with which we have so much in common, while being strong friends and supporters of the Palestinians and their quest to realize their legitimate national aspirations.

I also worked with the Canadian Friends of the Simon Wiesenthal Centre (SWC), which is based in Los Angeles with offices in New York, Florida, Paris, Toronto, Buenos Aires and Jerusalem. It is an international Jewish organization focused on the fight against anti-Semitism, racism, and terrorism, in support of human rights around the world. The SWC is accredited with many international bodies like the U.N. and the Council of Europe.

The Centre in Los Angeles has the superb Museum of Tolerance, dedicated to harmony between ethnic and national groups, mainly in the U.S. The museum plays an important role in the movie Freedom Writers, starring Hillary Swank. It is visited by 350,000 people per year, including 130,000 students. The SWC also has a division, Moriah Films, which has won many prizes, including a number of Oscars.

The SWC wanted me to present their annual report on hate on the internet in French, and I was happy to oblige.

The internet is a wonderful thing, a tool we could not live without today. But it also has a dark side: it is an efficient vehicle for racism, intolerance, anti-Semitism, and terrorism. There are many examples, such as: video games whose goal is to kill as many gays or blacks as possible; instructional videos on how to make a bomb; historical revisionism of Martin Luther King Jr. and his legacy; anti-Muslim pages; neo-Nazi websites, many eerily well done.

Having always placed great importance on the promotion of the rights of minorities, I was pleased to conduct those press conferences, which were well covered by the media.

My new engagements led me to explore the Jewish world, here and abroad. I remained involved in politics, internationally and locally here in Canada. I was still in a position to make a difference.

Us

10
Quebec Jews?

My conversion automatically turned me into a member of the Quebec Jewish community.

I had not thought too much about it. I had converted for spiritual reasons, without having had many contacts with the community which I did not know very well.

In fact, like many Quebeckers, I had many preconceived notions about the Quebec Jewish community. I imagined it to be entirely English-speaking, allergic to Quebec's French fact, wealthy, insular, and detached from Quebec's specific history.[37]

I did not know of the extraordinary contribution by Quebec Jews to their society and their connection with it.[38] In 2011, Montreal's Jewish community is celebrating its 250th anniversary, which is obviously an important milestone.

I know today how right former Premier René Lévesque was when he said: "Today's modern and dynamic Quebec has not been exclusively built by francophones, but also by other groups, in particular by the very creative Jewish community."[39]

The Jewish question was already present at the beginning of the colony. In fact, New France's first historian, Pierre Lescarbot, who landed in Quebec with Champlain in 1608, believed that the aboriginals he met were descendants of the 10 lost tribes of Israel. He conducted research based on this premise, meeting and interviewing members of the First Nations. He obviously had to admit that, no, the Israelites that were exiled in the 6th century BCE, did not become North America's aboriginals.

It was not under the control of France that the Jewish population in New France was going to grow. In fact, in 1627, a royal proclamation forbid all non-Catholics from settling in New France.

For example, in 1752, a Jewish businessman from Bordeaux, Abraham Gradis, despite being one of the most valuable allies of New France and having made the perilous crossing of the Atlantic (which took six weeks), was not allowed to debark because he was Jewish. He had to return to France without ever touching the ground in New France.

The legal arrival of Jews began with the British. In 1758, Samuel Jacobs was the first Jew to settle in Quebec. He settled in Saint-Denis (close to Montreal) and married a French Canadian. While he remained loyal to his religion, his five children were raised as Catholics. His was not, therefore, a seed that sprouted.

The foundation of the Quebec (and Canadian) Jewish community was laid in 1760. That is when Aaron Hart, who is considered by many as the 'founding father' of the Jewish community, entered Montreal with British general Amherst and his troops. He then moved to Trois-Rivières, the region in which the Hart family was to make its mark both in business and in public life. The second post office to be opened in Canada was in Aaron Hart's house.

Another example of the Jews' early social implication in Canada: the first leader of Quebec City's fire department, from 1790 to 1799, was a Jew named John Franks.[40]

However, without a house of worship, without a synagogue, it is impossible to ensure a Jewish community's perpetuity. The first synagogue, the *Spanish & Portuguese Synagogue* (whose Rabbi Howard Joseph, converted me) was established in 1768. Not long after, in 1777, the synagogue *Shearith Israel* opened in Montreal, at the corner of Notre-Dame and Saint-Lambert (today called Saint-Laurent). From that point on, the small Jewish community was more solidly established.

The community was also becoming politically established. In 1807 Ezechiel Hart[41] was elected to Lower Canada's legislature. However as a Jew, according to British law, he could not take his place in the House.

Only in 1832, and because of the Patriot leader Louis-Joseph Papineau, was full legal equality for the Jews confirmed by law. The importance of this event must not be underestimated. Lower Canada (later to be called Quebec) was the first jurisdiction in the entire British Empire to emancipate its Jews, 26 years before Great Britain itself!

This open and progressive attitude of the Patriots helps explain why one of the most fervent supporters of the Rebellion in Lower Canada was Louis Marchand, whose real name was Levi Koopman, a Dutch Jew who had immigrated to Lower Canada.

Later, Marchand/Koopman would be one of the founders of the *Société Saint-Jean-Baptiste* with another Jew, Joseph Olivier Joseph. Moreover, when the first rebels were imprisoned, a Jewish lawyer, Adolph Mordecai Hart, took up their defence.

It was during this period that one of the most important Jews in Quebec history entered the scene: Moses Judah Hays. In 1832, he established the first aqueduct in Montreal. In 1835, he and Benjamin Hart became the first Jews to be appointed Judges. In 1845, Moses Judah Hays became Montreal's chief of police and, in 1848, went on to build Montreal's first theatre.

Other Jews also played important roles in Quebec's history.

In 1836, brothers Jesse and Jacob Joseph were prime movers of Canada's first railroad, the St. Lawrence and Champlain, from La Prairie to St-Jean. In 1861, Jesse Joseph inaugurated Montreal's first public transportation service. The same Jesse Joseph would later become the president of the *Montreal Gas Company*, a company that later became the *Montreal Light, Heat & Power* and later still, Hydro-Québec.

In 1858, Abraham Joseph was one of the founders of the *Banque Nationale* and in 1876, Sigismund Mohr, a German Jewish engineer, brought the telephone to Quebec City and, in 1885, used Montmorency Falls near Quebec City to make electricity.

The first Jew to become mayor in Canada was William J. Hyman, in Cap-des-Rosiers in 1858, a position he held for some 20 years.[42]

In 1887, Emile Berliner, a Jewish immigrant, created the gramophone in Montreal, thus establishing the basis for the modern record industry. In 1888, an Alsatian Jew, Jules Helbronner, became *La Presse*'s editor-in-chief.

All those individual achievements are accompanied by collective ones. In 1863, the creation in Montreal of the Baron de Hirsh Institute marked the establishment of Canada's first social services agency, a model for such organizations today. In 1896, Talmud Torah was established, giving birth to a network of schools of the same name in 1917.

Important Quebec Jews also appeared on the scene around this time. In 1903, union leader Lea Roback was born in Montreal (she grew up in Beauport), and in 1915, Nobel Prize winner (for literature) Saul Bellows, was born in Lachine.

Quebec Jews also made their appearance in the culinary arts: in 1908, they invented the famous Montreal smoked meat.

The Jewish population was growing, which was not without political and social consequences. In 1901, there were only approximately 7,000 Jews in Montreal. Ten years later they were more than 30,000, and by 1931 this figure had risen to 58,000, representing 7 percent of Montreal's population.[43] In 1913 alone, 20,000 Jewish immigrants arrived in Montreal. In the 1920's, Yiddish was the third most common language spoken in Montreal.

In other words, between 1901 and 1931, Quebec's Jewish population grew by more than 800 percent!

In 1916, this important community sent Peter Bercovitch to Parliament, the first Jew to be so elected. The expanding Jewish population also required more services and a voice so the Canadian Jewish Congress was established in 1919.

Jews were also strongly represented in the manufacturing sector to the point that, in 1935, 35 percent of Montreal's Jewish community was employed by this sector, namely in the clothing, leather, and fur industries.[44]

Many Jews, coming from a socialist environment, were very active in Quebec's union movement.[45] Jewish-French Canadian relations were positive: "In the relationship between Jews and French Canadians, the group of Jewish workers is certainly very open and regularly contributes to the organizing of French Canadian workers, like in the clothing sector."[46]

An author went as far as writing that "Montreal Jewish workers showed exceptional activism at the turn of the century. Their leaders have the merit for having organized the clothing unions."[47]

In 1921, the Baron Byng High School was established on Saint-Urbain Street in Montreal, a school that would have as students the poet Irving Layton, writer Mordechai Richler, NDP leader David Lewis, Quebec Justice Minister and Judge

Herbert Marx, and even the famous *Star Trek* Captain Kirk - William Shatner himself.

In 1934, the Montreal Jewish Hospital opened, serving a majority of non-Jewish patients. Today, 70 percent of its patients are non-Jews.

In 1916, Samuel Bronfman started his career in the alcohol sector, laying the foundation for Seagrams. In 1934, singer Leonard Cohen was born and, in 1943, Canada's only Communist MP, Fred Rose, was elected to the House of Commons, with the help of Jacques Parizeau!

The Second World War had an immense impact on Jews worldwide, including Canada's Jewish community. Between 1944 and 1946, about 40 Montreal Jews fought in the Jewish Brigade, attached to Britain's Eighth Army. This Brigade, which would later give 35 generals to the Israeli Army, would thus help to build the future Israel Defense Forces.

Canada became an important refuge for Holocaust survivors. In terms of percentage, 35 percent of Canada's Jews are direct descendants of Holocaust survivors, compared with only five percent of American Jews.[48]

Speaking of the Holocaust, René Lévesque, then a war correspondent in the U.S. Army, was one of the first Allied soldiers to enter Dachau.[49] This largely explains the strong antipathy the future Premier would develop towards anything smacking of anti-Semitism. This worldview would reveal itself further in the excellent relationship he later established with Quebec's Jewish community.

Quebec's Jews would leave their mark here and abroad. In 1948, Montreal's Dov Joseph became the first Israeli military governor of Jerusalem. In 1949, the University of Montreal became the first institution of higher learning in Canada to hire a Jewish Studies professor, with Rabbi Chaim Denburg.

It is also important to note that until the 1960's, McGill University had a 10 percent quota on Jewish students whereas the University of Montreal had no such restrictions.

The Jewish community changed the face of Quebec at the same time it experienced its own internal changes. Nineteen-fifty-seven marked the beginning of the arrival of French-speaking Moroccan Jewish immigrants to Montreal.

Expo 1967, which opened Quebec's doors to the world, also had an important impact on Quebec's Jews. They hosted the *Pavilion of Judaism* while Moshe Safdie, today one of the world's most famous architects and a Jew, designed Habitat 67. Moreover, with money amassed by a film processing laboratory during Expo 67, Harold Greenberg established Astral Communications, an important player in today's media sector.

In 1970, Alan B. Gold was appointed Quebec's chief justice. That same year, Victor Goldbloom became the first Jew to be a member of Quebec's cabinet.

In 1988, Montreal's Sol Simon Reisman negotiated the Canada-U.S. Free-Trade Agreement.

In 1999, Charles Bronfman, with American Michael Steinhardt, established Birthright, an initiative with a world-wide impact on the Jewish community. This special program, targeted at 18 to 24 year old Jews, might very well be the most successful Jewish community project ever. It brings young Jews from the Diaspora to Israel, strengthening their Jewish identity and their connection to Israel.

The enormous impact Quebec's Jews have had on Canada and around the world is evident. They can be proud of their exceptional contribution, especially to Quebec itself.

But who are they today?

Today's Quebec Jewish community is very concentrated. It is 93,000 strong, 98 percent of which live on the island of Montreal.

Twenty-five percent of the community have French as a first language and 62 percent are bilingual. Moreover, the younger the Jew, the stronger is his bilingualism.

Hassidic Jews, the most visible of all Jews - whose image fills every stereotype here and abroad - represent only 12 percent of the Quebec Jewish community. It is also a community that, contrary to popular belief, has problems with poverty. Eighteen percent of Quebec's Jewish community lives under the poverty line. Twenty-five percent of Jewish children under the age of five are poor, suffering the consequences (school problems, health issues, etc.) that accompany poverty.

Seniors represent about 20 percent of Quebec Jews, and more than 20 percent of them live below the poverty line. Thirty-two percent of Jews living below the poverty line are single mothers. As a whole, the Quebec Jewish community is getting older and faces demographic decline. Therefore, despite its numerous successes, Quebec's Jewish community also faces important challenges.

Unfortunately, Quebec Jews are often accused of being too self-centered and caring only about their own, despite all evidence to the contrary.

One single illustration is sufficient to dissipate any doubt. On January 12, 2010, a terrible earthquake hit Haiti, leaving up to 300,000 dead. Israel - even though it is more than 10,000 kilometres away - was the first country to establish a field hospital there, and according to many reports it was the best care[50] ('*the Rolls Royce of medicine*'). The Canadian Jewish community also showed its extraordinary generosity.[51] Montreal Jews collected and sent approximately $400,000 to Haiti, while Toronto's (larger) Jewish community amassed

$800,000 for the cause.

Far from being insular, Jewish Quebeckers are active in many areas of Quebec life, have been part of Quebec society for a very long time, and contribute to many important causes here and abroad.

I want people to know about Quebec's Jews' contribution to their society because in general, it is not known.

But it is important to remember that this extraordinary contribution would not have been possible if Quebec had not been the outstanding society that it is, a society that is the envy of many around the world.

Yes, Jews have given a lot to Quebec. But Quebec provided the Jews with an exceptional environment in which to grow and prosper politically, economically, and spiritually.

11
A Complicated Region

"Towards the complex Orient, I was flying with simple ideas."
This is how Charles de Gaulle began recounting his stay in the
Middle East, when he was being posted there by the French
army.

A lot of people around the world, including so-called experts,
view the Middle East situation through a simple lens. Such a
framework has led to an understanding, as stated by Lysiane
Gagnon - columnist for *La Presse* and *The Globe and
Mail* - "to which subscribes, in a disconcerting unanimity, a
very large part of the French Quebec population."[52] At one
time I too was included in that assessment. To be clear, this
is not from a lack of TV reports, newspaper and magazines
articles, or internet sites.

Indeed, the Middle East occupies a lot of space in Canadian
media. Canadian journalists are not the only ones to focus
on this region. In fact, besides Washington DC, Israel has the
highest number of accredited journalists in the world.

My premise on the Middle East, which might not receive
unanimous support but which I believe is the correct one, is the
following: despite its importance, the Israeli-Arab conflict does
not have the centrality that some people give it. Many analysts,
diplomats and politicians argue that if the conflict between
Israel and its neighbours was solved, there would essentially
no longer be tensions between the West and the Muslim world,
and peace would reign from Indonesia to Morocco, through

Afghanistan, Iran, Iraq, Algeria, and elsewhere.

As David Ouellette so justly noted in Sherbrooke's *La Tribune*:

> *The Taliban, for example, who are attempting to establish a fundamentalist emirate in as far a region from the Israeli-Arab conflict as Afghanistan, an Asian country chronically destabilized by the geopolitical national and tribal interests of its Muslim neighbours, would be the first to be surprised and unhappy to learn (…) that their theocratic and jihadist fervour would cool down, as if by magic, come an Israeli-Palestinian peace agreement.* [53]

Indeed, for many in the Muslim world, their opposition to the State of Israel is not only because it is a Jewish state. It is also because they consider Israel, with its democracy, its freedom of religion and association, protection of minority rights, and acceptance of gays and lesbians, to be the incarnation in their own backyard of the hated West. In other words, the creation of borders between Israel and a Palestinian State would in no way disarm the jihadists active in so many countries.

An Israeli-Arab peace accord would not cause the Muslim fundamentalists' hostility towards the West to disappear. It would not stop Iran's attempts to become a nuclear power. It would not solve the centuries-long schism between Sunnis and Shiites. Nor would it put an end to the laboratories of terror plaguing North Africa and the Arabian Peninsula, through Central and Southeast Asia.

The latest evidence that the Israeli-Arab conflict is not as pivotal as some would like us to believe is found in the recent demonstrations across the Arab world. The thousands of Arab protesters of what some called the Arab Spring did not march to solve the Israeli-Arab conflict. They marched for more freedom, greater economic opportunities, and democratic rights in their own countries.

In other words, an Israeli-Palestinian peace agreement in and of itself would not guarantee the security of the two nations (Israelis and Palestinians), appease the Islamists, or stabilize the wider region.

Let me be clear: I passionately hope for a peace agreement between Israelis and Arabs, and strongly believe we must do everything we can to help them reach that goal. What I am saying, however, is that to give this conflict the centrality that some do, is a mistake that can only lead to dashed hopes.

Jewish history: a very, very, very short summary

The modern Zionist movement was born at the end of the 19th century. However, the connection between the Jews and the Land of Israel dates from ancient times and runs very deep.

Before a historical summary, a few words on the Jews' spiritual and religious attachment to the Land of Israel are *de rigueur*, because this attachment is much deeper than a simple nostalgia for a homeland after 2,000 years.

I acknowledge that it is difficult for Canadians, living in a secularized world and not being all that familiar with Judaism, to really understand the connection that a Jew can have with the Land of Israel. For a devout Jew, God gave the Land of Israel to the Jewish people, through Abraham. This gift was given so that the Jewish people might fulfill their divinely assigned mission: to spread to the entire world a vision of morality and justice. And this mission, it is conceived, can only be accomplished from the crossroads of civilization that is the Middle East.

The Land of Israel is considered sacred by observant Jews as being directly connected to God. This sacredness requires its inhabitants to behave in a holy manner.

But the right of the Jewish people to live in the Land of Israel is based not only on the Biblical promise made to Abraham. It is conferred by an uninterrupted Jewish presence on the land, the historical connection of past Jewish kingdoms, the purchase of land at fair market value, and the international law with the Balfour Declaration, League of Nations resolution, and the U.N. Partition Resolution of 1947.

According to tradition, every Jew is the owner of part of the Land of Israel. His title deed is, so to speak, his heritage from Abraham.

Let us not forget that from the beginning of its exile from the Land of Israel, the Jewish people have prayed for a return. Still today, synagogues in the world face Jerusalem. Spiritually, Jews are very attached and connected to the Land of Israel.

But this connection between a Jew and the Land of Israel is not only of a religious nature. A non-observing, agnostic or atheist Jew is not indifferent to the Land of Israel. He sees it as his own heritage, rooted in history.

The history of the Jewish people is a long one, which goes back millennia. It is a rich, diversified, fascinating, tragic, heroic and incomparable history. And it is a history that is difficult to summarize.

The Jews (or Hebrews as they were then known), entered history almost 5,000 years ago. Their origin is somewhat mysterious and archaeological evidence somewhat rare, but historians believe that they came from Mesopotamia.

After many years of wandering and divisions, in approximately 1020 BCE they built a state, and territorial institutions. Saul became their first king. He was followed by David, who established his capital in Jerusalem. David's son, Solomon, then built the First Temple.

At King Solomon's death, in 932 BCE, his kingdom was

divided in two: the Kingdom of Israel in the North and the Kingdom of Judea in the South. In 721 BCE, Israel was destroyed by the Assyrians; the 10 tribes were lost to history. In 586 BCE, it was Judea's turn to be conquered, this time by Babylonian king Nebuchadnezzar. Jerusalem and the Temple were destroyed and the elites deported to Babylonia. It is the beginning of the Jewish Diaspora.

In 539 BCE, the Persians conquered Babylonia. The Persian emperor Cyrus allowed the exiled Jewish population to return and reconstruct the Temple in Jerusalem. Many, however, decided to stay behind in Mesopotamia.

After having been under Persian then Greek domination, the Jews regained their independence following the Maccabee Revolt (which is celebrated today with the Jewish holiday of Hanukkah). But this independence is quickly put to the test and eroded by Rome's growing strength.

King Herod, a Roman vassal, reigned from 37 to 4 BCE. He was a builder and most famously rebuilt, in a grandiose manner, the Second Temple in Jerusalem. The Western Wall, today Judaism's holiest site, is a remnant of Herod's work. Estimates today are that Jews constituted up to 10 percent of the entire Roman Empire population.

In 70 CE, after a Jewish revolt against the Roman domination, the Second Temple was destroyed by Roman troops. Still, Jews did not give up on the idea of independence. In 132-135 CE, the Jews rose up once again, under Bar Kohba's leadership.

After Bar Kohba's revolt, in order to erase all Jewish traces in the region, the Romans renamed the land 'Palestine' after the Philistines, a people that had much earlier disappeared. As well, Jerusalem was razed and was rebuilt as *Aelia Capitolina*.

From then on, Jews were forbidden in Jerusalem. Even though an important Jewish population stayed in the Holy Land, the majority of the Jewish population would reside in the Diaspora. The territory, after being controlled by the Romans, became Byzantine. It later came under Arab control, following which it came under Crusader control, and then back to Arab hands before being conquered by the Ottoman Turks in 1517.

Centuries of exile, persecution, pogroms and forced conversions followed. Jews were not actors of history but objects of history. Different ideas arose and took root (hassidism, Liberal Judaism, Orthodoxy and others), but these debates were internal to the Jewish community. Still, the Jews dreamt of and hoped for a return to Jerusalem.[54]

At the end of the 19th century, the Ottoman Empire grew weak. Pogroms became more and more frequent in Eastern Europe, often condoned if not supported by the local authorities. Jewish emigration, at first a trickle, grew stronger. The majority left for North America, but a few left for their ancestral land in the Middle East and built proto-state institutions. In other words, they built the embryo of a Jewish country.

European anti-Semitism led to different reactions in the Jewish communities scattered across the continent. One of those reactions was the realization that for the Jews to become a normal nation once again, they must stop living as a minority in other peoples' countries. That is, the Jewish people must dwell in their own country once again and on the land on which they were born: the Land of Israel.

That is how the modern Zionist movement was created, proposing the return to Zion (i.e. Jerusalem) of Jews scattered around the world. Following the Dreyfus Affair,[55] the first Zionist Congress was held in Basel, Switzerland in 1897, under the leadership of Theodor Herzl. What was once a mere idea became a political movement.

In 1917, during the First World War, the Zionist movement won its first diplomatic battle when the British government released the Balfour declaration, in which it called for 'the establishment in Palestine of a national home for the Jewish people'.

The Declaration, which was at first only a British document, became international law when the League of Nations (the precursor to today's United Nations) integrated it into the Mandate it gave to Britain over Palestine.

Map 1 –British Mandate[56]

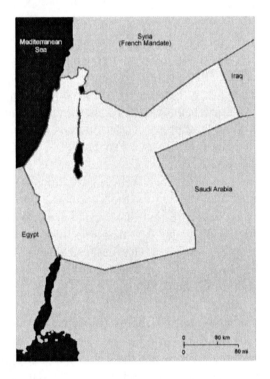

In 1937, Great Britain attempted to find a solution to the growing tensions between Jews and Arabs, an illustration of which is the 1929 Hebron massacre which lead to the deaths of 60 Jews and the expulsion of its entire centuries-old Jewish community. The Arabs tried everything they could to stop

Jewish immigration, including massacres.

The British government established the Peel Commission to study the problem and suggest solutions. Even in 1937, the commission proposed partition between two states, one Arab, one Jewish. While the idea was accepted by the Jewish community (worried by Hitler's growing persecutions of the Jews of Europe), it was violently rejected by the Arabs.

Under Turkish domination since the 16th century, and then under British control for 20 years, the Palestinians had never had a state of their own. If they had accepted the Peel Commission's recommendations, by now they would have had a state for more than 70 years.

Between 1939 and 1945, as we know too well, the Nazis implemented their genocidal plan to exterminate the Jewish people. More than six million Jews were massacred while the rest of the world – including Canada – closed its doors to Jewish immigration.

It is important to note that while the democratic world was fighting the Nazis with all their force, the leader of the Palestinian Arabs, Mohammed Amin al-Husseini, Mufti of Jerusalem, was openly supporting Hitler and collaborating with his regime.[57] American documents declassified on December 10, 2010, once again confirmed the close relationship between the Mufti and the Nazis.[58]

The Holocaust did not create the Jewish state. Prior to the Holocaust there was already the foundation of a state, with a functioning democracy, schools, ministries, a free press, etc. What is of note is that the Holocaust would not have happened (or at least to the same extent) had the State of Israel existed at the time.

After the Second World War, Great Britain was tired and broke. Lacking the strength to keep its empire, it decided to put the destiny of Mandatory Palestine in the hands of the newly created United Nations.

The U.N. established the Special Commission on Palestine, a body which included representatives from 11 countries, notably Canadian Justice Ivan Rand. The majority proposed the creation of two states, one Jewish, and one Arab.[59]

The Commission's proposals were confirmed by a vote in the U.N. General Assembly (Resolution 181) on November 29, 1947. The result was 33 in favour (including Canada, France, the Soviet Union, and the United States), 13 against, and 10 abstentions.

The premise of this decision was that the claims of both Jews and Arabs over Palestine were valid but irreconcilable. Partition was seen as the most realistic and practical solution. The resolution itself made express mention of both an Arab state and a Jewish state, which is an element that Israeli Prime Minister Benjamin Netanyahu insists be part of any peace deal between Israelis and Palestinians.

The partition decision had nothing to do with any form of Israeli 'colonialism' or 'imperialism'. It had everything to do with the realization of the right of self-determination for two peoples. This is all the more true as the areas given to the future Jewish state had a Jewish majority.

Jews were not satisfied with the size of the area allocated to them. They were disappointed by the fact that Jerusalem was to be internationalized, and thus not a part of their state. However, despite those heart-breaking disappointments, they still accepted the U.N. plan.

The Arabs, however, refused it. For the second time, the Arabs turned down the idea of two states for two people.

The territory under British control after the First World War

(Mandatory Palestine) included Jordan, Israel, the West Bank, and the Gaza Strip. By 1922, 80 percent of the territory of Mandatory Palestine and of the 'Jewish National Home' was divided by the British, who thus created Transjordan (Jordan).

Map 2 - Separation of Transjordan (1922)

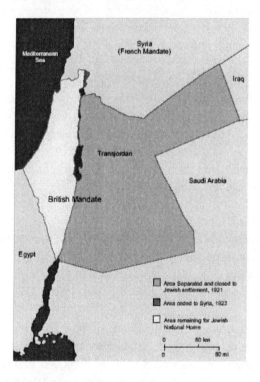

With the 1947 partition vote, the U.N. was partitioning the 20 percent remaining of the Mandatory Palestinian territory into two states.

With Jordan's annexation of the West Bank in 1948, the Arabs were in control of 80 percent of Mandatory Palestine, with Israel controlling 17.5 percent and the rest being Egyptian-occupied Gaza.

If the U.N. partition plan had been accepted by the Arabs,

today the Palestinians would have had their state for more than 60 years.

Unfortunately, instead of the peaceful solution offered by the U.N., the Arab states decided to do all they could to stop the creation of a Jewish state in the Middle East. On May 15, 1948, just one day after declaring independence, Israel was attacked by Egypt, Transjordan, Syria, Iraq, and Lebanon, with help from Saudi Arabia, Yemen and Libya.

The goal of the Arab states was not only to stop the implementation of the two-state U.N. plan. Their stated objective, less than three years after the Holocaust, was much darker. The Arab League's General Secretary, Azzam Pasha, said then about the coming conflict: "This will be a war of extermination and a momentous massacre which will be spoken of like the Mongolian massacres."[60]

At that point, there was no doubt as to who should be blamed for the war. U.N. Secretary General Trygve Lie clearly laid the blame on the Arab side: "The invasion of Palestine by the Arab states was the first armed aggression which the world has seen since the world war."[61]

Against all predictions, the State of Israel, while waging a defensive war, ended up at the cessation of hostilities with more territory than was allocated to it by the U.N. partition plan. Israel was of course trying to acquire the territory necessary in order to defend itself in the next war. A war that everybody knew was only a question of time.

Egypt (with Gaza) and Transjordan – now Jordan (with the West Bank) swallowed the rest of Mandatory Palestine. Already then, the neighbouring Arab states were more interested in acquiring territory than helping the Palestinians.

The Arab-Israeli conflict has seen many violent flare-ups since 1947. There was the Sinai conflict of 1956. There was the dramatic Six Day War in 1967, during which, in a defensive war, Israel captured Gaza, the West Bank (or Judea/Samaria) and the Golan Heights. It is noteworthy to recall that, in 1967, Akhmed Shukeiry, then head of the Palestine Liberation Organization, clearly threatened genocide and destruction by declaring: "Those native-born Israelis who will survive will be permitted to remain in the country. But I don't think many will survive."[62] That was followed by the 1973 Yom Kippur War, when Israel was the victim of a surprise attack by Egypt and Syria on Judaism's holiest day, and subsequently the 1982 Lebanon war.

Despite all this violence, peace would have been possible… had the Arabs truly wanted it.[63] But their actions throughout have shown an interest in perpetuating war.

In 1937, the Arabs refused the partition proposed by the Peel Commission, which would have created two states for two people.

In 1947, the Arabs refused the solution proposed by the U.N., which too would have created two states for two peoples. Had the Arabs accepted the U.N. partition plan, there would have been two independence days celebrated every year: Israel's and Palestine's.

In 1967, after the Six Day War, the Arabs refused Israel's offer to return the territories it captured while in a summit in Khartoum. In what is famously remembered as the "Three 'No's", the Arab League passed a resolution vowing "no peace with Israel, no recognition of Israel, no negotiations with Israel." Had the Arabs accepted Israel's olive branch, it would have led to two states for two peoples.

In 2000 at Camp David, Yasser Arafat refused to sign an agreement that would have created a Palestinian state in all of Gaza and on 95-97 percent of the West Bank. This Palestinian rejection was qualified as being 'criminal' by the Saudi

Ambassador to the US, Prince Bandar. After refusing to sign an agreement, the Palestinians launched the murderous second intifada.[64]

In September 2008, Israeli Prime Minister Ehud Olmert made an even more generous offer[65] to Palestinian President Mahmud Abbas. The deal consisted of a Palestinian state on 100 percent of Gaza, the equivalent of 100 percent of the West Bank (with swaps here and there on a 1:1 ratio), the division of Jerusalem (Jewish areas to Israel, Arab areas to the Palestinians), a special regime (without sovereignty) for the city's key holy sites that would involve international control, and the admission within Israel proper of a limited number of Palestinian refugees. Israel is still waiting for Abbas' official answer.[66]

Of note, Israel's withdrawal from the Sinai, the Gaza Strip, and from certain parts of the West Bank already constitutes withdrawal from 94 percent of all the territory that Israel seized in 1967.

Israel has shown its desire and willingness to exchange territories for peace on multiple occasions.

On the other hand, the Palestinians have been opposed to a peace of compromise, the only kind of peace possible. Consider the numbers, which speak for themselves. On November 9, 2010, the *Arab World for Research and Development*, a Ramallah-based research institute, published the results of a survey[67] of Palestinians in Gaza and the West Bank. The survey included a lot of interesting data, but two points stand out:

a) In answer to the question: "If Palestinian negotiators delivered a peace settlement that included a Palestinian State but required compromises on key issues (right of return, Jerusalem, borders, settlements, etc.) to do so, would you support the result?", 84 percent of Palestinians responded that they would oppose while only 12.7 percent would support it.

b) Sixty-five percent of Palestinians surveyed said that it was 'essential' that any peace agreement arrived at include, for the Palestinians, 'historic Palestine – from the Jordan River to the sea' while 18.3 percent answered that this was 'desirable'. In other words, for more than 80 percent of Palestinians, it is 'essential' or 'desirable' that the State of Israel disappear, in order to achieve peace.

Ex-Israeli Foreign Affairs minister Abba Eban was painfully accurate in saying that the Palestinians never missed an opportunity to miss an opportunity.

Abbas at the U.N.: Wanting a state without peace

Many people in Canada applauded the Palestinians' decision to eschew direct negotiations with Israel and go to the United Nations in September 2011.

The enthusiasm is misplaced. In doing so, Abbas' goal was to obtain a state and the land to constitute that state without peace with Israel, which is a prescription for permanent conflict.

The Palestinian Authority's move at the U.N. avoids direct negotiations between Israelis and Palestinians, in violation of international agreements. Under U.N. Resolution 242 (1967), the formula for the peace process is based on "land for peace". That formula essentially requires Israeli withdrawal from territories (such as the West Bank) in exchange for the Arab world providing Israel with full recognition, security guarantees, and lasting peace. In separating the legitimate needs of Israelis and Palestinians, the Palestinian bid at the U.N. removes any incentive for the Palestinian leadership to make the necessary compromises.

Therefore, any support for the Palestinians' efforts at the U.N. undermines international law and contravenes four decades of cross-party Canadian diplomacy. It also supports the violation of previously signed agreements between Israel and the

Palestinians.

Peace in the Middle East is possible only if the aspirations of both sides are bound together as core elements of a peace agreement. This can only be achieved through direct negotiations between the parties, something Israel has repeatedly stated it is ready to resume, without preconditions. Despite the urging of the international community, the Palestinian Authority has refused to enter into direct talks since the fall of 2010, effectively abandoning peace negotiations.

By going to the U.N., the Palestinian leadership said no to negotiations, no to mutual compromise, no to recognizing a Jewish state, and no to ending the conflict. In other words, the unilateral steps taken by the Palestinians move the process further away from negotiations and reconciliation, the only way to secure a peace accord and Palestinian statehood.

The most significant and revealing part of Abbas' speech in the U.N. General Assembly in September 2011, was one that was unfortunately overlooked by many. He said:

> *I come before you today from the Holy Land, the land of Palestine, the land of divine messages, ascension of the Prophet Muhammad (peace be upon him) and the birthplace of Jesus Christ (peace be upon him), to speak on behalf of the Palestinian people in the homeland and in the Diaspora, to say, after 63 years of suffering of the ongoing Nakba: Enough.*

Notice: the Jews were absent. In other words, according to Abbas, the Jews have no legitimacy in the land. THIS is the root cause of the conflict.

Indeed, the refusal of the Palestinian leadership to recognize Israel as a Jewish state underlines their intolerance and rejection of the sovereign rights of the Jewish people. Tragically, this rejectionism prevents the establishment of a genuine solution based on the principle of two states for two peoples.

As mentioned previously, Abbas' rejection is only the latest in a long line of rejections of peace agreements, based on the principle of two states for two peoples. The most recent example of this rejectionism is Abbas' refusal to negotiate in 2009-2010, despite Netanyahu's unprecedented decision to freeze building in the settlements for 10 months in order to re-launch the negotiations.

The acceptance of any of the offers previously mentioned in this chapter would have led to an independent Palestinian state and the disappearance of basically all Jewish settlements, making the point that, while the settlements are irritants, they are NOT the reason why a peace deal has not been reached.

As Pulitzer Prize winner Charles Krauthammer put it:

So why did the Palestinians say no? Because saying yes would have required them to sign a final peace agreement that accepted a Jewish state on what they consider the Muslim patrimony.

The key word here is "final." The Palestinians are quite prepared to sign interim agreements, like Oslo. Framework agreements, like Annapolis. Cease-fires, like the 1949 armistice. Anything but a final deal. Anything but a final peace. Anything but a treaty that ends the conflict once and for all — while leaving a Jewish state still standing.

After all, why did Abbas go to the United Nations last week? (…) to get land without peace. Sovereignty with no reciprocal recognition of a Jewish state. Statehood without negotiations. An independent Palestine in a continued state of war with Israel.[68]

The forgotten refugees

As a quick aside, I should raise an issue that is too often obscured in discussions over the Arab-Israeli conflict: that of Jewish refugees from Arab lands. Any resolution of the conflict requires that a just and equitable solution be found for the issue of refugees. But, by definition, to be just and equitable, the solution needs to take into account not only Palestinian refugees, but also Jewish refugees from the Arab world. Why is it that we never hear about the latter?

All those who follow the debates about the Middle East know about the demands of the Palestinian refugees, but too few know that there is a Jewish equivalent.

At the end of the Second World War, there were more than 870,000 Jews in Arab countries. Between 1945 and 1950, the situation worsened for these Jews, with persecution, anti-Jewish riots, and confiscation of property. It became such a difficult situation that nearly the entire Jewish community left those countries, where they had lived for more than 2,500 years.

If some took refuge in Canada, France or the United States, the vast majority, some 600,000, went to Israel. They arrived there penniless and with nothing.

But Israel did all that it could and more to integrate them, despite the lack of means at the disposal of the newly established state. So, while Jewish refugees from Arab lands became full-fledged citizens of Israel, the displaced Arab refugees from the Arab-Israeli conflict were left to languish in refugees camps. The Arab states, despite their rhetoric, have done next to nothing for the Arab refugees. Worse, they decided to use them and their misery for political purposes. In 1959, the Arab League passed Resolution 1457, which states as follows: "The Arab countries will not grant citizenship to applicants of Palestinian origin in order to prevent their assimilation into the host countries."[69]

In fact, Western governments pay for more than 95 percent of UNRWA's budget, the U.N. agency in charge of the Palestinian refugees.[70] For their part, the Arab states contribute approximately 1 percent. Moreover, these same Arab states refuse to integrate them.[71] If this is not hypocrisy, what is?

It is essential to note that UNRWA was supposed to be a temporary agency. Its number of personnel has now reached 27,000 people. That is four times the number of employees working for the United Nations High Commissioner for Refugees, an agency that is responsible for refugees from all other conflicts on the planet!

What we are talking about is a transfer of population between the Arab states and Israel. This is similar to that which occurred between Turkey and Greece at the turn of the 20th century, between many European countries after the Second World War, and between India and Pakistan after their accession to independence in 1948.

If we do not really hear about Jewish refugees, it is because Israel made sure to put its money where its mouth was and integrate them into Israeli society. This was very onerous for the nascent Jewish state. The Arab states, which had confiscated Jewish property, did nothing to help their former citizens resettle, nor did they offer any kind of compensation.

And so I return to this key point. While we need to find a solution to the problems of Palestinian refugees, a just and equitable resolution of the Arab-Israeli conflict also requires reparations for Jewish refugees from Arab lands.

Supporting hate

It will require more than leaders and signatures on a piece of paper to establish a true and enduring peace in the Middle East. Real peace means peace between the peoples. It is for this reason that incitement against Jews and Israel is such a big problem, and might very well be the stumbling block to this long-term vision.[72]

Here is an example of what incitement can lead to. On March 6, 2008, a terrorist entered into a Jewish religious school in Jerusalem, killing seven young men[73] (aged 16 to 26) and injuring some ten others, including a Canadian.[74]

The very next day, Hamas claimed responsibility for the attack. An attack such as this, against a school, is a terrible act. But what makes this episode especially vile is the reaction of joy, outright celebration, in the Palestinian territories.

It illustrates the toxic, hate-filled theology that is so widespread in Palestinian society. How can one celebrate the deliberate, premeditated, cold-blooded killing of young men in their school?

On March 19, 2008, *The New York Times*[75] published the results of a survey of Palestinians completed by Khalil Shikaki, a Palestinian whose organisation, the *Palestinian Center for Policy and Survey Research*, is the leader in this field and with whom I have had the occasion to meet a few times over the years.

The survey of 1,270 Palestinians revealed that 84 percent of those surveyed supported the attack against the Jewish school – 84 percent!

Nothing can better illustrate the chasm between where Palestinians truly are and the will necessary to live in peace with their Israeli neighbours. No piece of paper signed by a Palestinian leader can provide the necessary security assurances that Israel needs to solve the conflict. This is even truer when one considers the wider regional situation.

Israel encircled

To achieve peace, an agreement between Israel and the Palestinians is essential, but not sufficient. A peace agreement must include other actors in the region because the reality is that Israel is a very small country, surrounded by entities who seek only its destruction.

In the north, Hezbollah, the major player in Lebanon, has rearmed itself since the 2006 conflict. Many trustworthy sources report that Hezbollah is now in possession of long range SCUD missiles and other modern weaponry (provided by Syria and Iran).

In the south, the Gaza Strip is controlled by Hamas' Islamists who are also armed by, and under the influence of, Iran.

To the northeast, Syria, still technically at war with Israel, has allied itself with Iran, and arms and trains both Hamas and Hezbollah.

And right beside Israel is the weak Palestinian Authority. Its capacity to truly resist a disciplined and fanaticised Hamas is doubted by most analysts in the region. In passing, it is interesting to note that WikiLeaks revealed that Fatah, the party of Palestinian president Mahmoud Abbas, asked Israel to attack Hamas in 2007.[76]

And behind all of this, one finds Iran.[77]

Iran

Iran is a great country and civilization which is, unfortunately, governed today by a group of extremist religious zealots.

Today, Iran does not respect women's rights, or basic human rights for that matter. It persecutes religious minorities and executes gays. And let us not forget Iran's torture and killing of Canadian photojournalist Zahra Kazemi in a Tehran prison in 2003.

Iran has, as its president, a man who denies the Holocaust while hoping and preparing for another one, through the acquisition of nuclear arms.

Iran has embarked on a program of uranium enrichment, in violation of International Atomic Energy Agency protocols and U.N. Security Council resolutions. Iran's acquisition of nuclear weapons constitutes a grave menace to peace and security, not only in the Middle East but around the world as well.[78]

This threat is compounded by Tehran's desire to acquire the technology for long-range missiles, by its flat out refusal to negotiate in good faith with the international community and its aggressiveness towards the West in general and Israel in particular.

The threat is not only against Israel. Europe is worried, as are the U.S. and Canada.[79] Even more telling, the internet site WikiLeaks revealed in October of 2010, that it is neighbouring Arab states that are most in favour of attacking Iran, in order to stop it from going nuclear.[80]

Let me touch briefly on the current Iranian President Mahmoud Ahmadinejad. However, I would caution that the problem and the danger are not limited to Ahmadinejad; he is but one element of the Islamist regime. It is the regime itself that constitutes the greatest threat.

In October 2005, Ahmadinejad made a speech on Israel's right to exist, calling for the State of Israel to be "wiped off the map".

Ahmadinejad called the Holocaust a myth and proposed the creation of a Jewish state in Europe, in the U.S., or in Canada.

He also criticized European laws against Holocaust denial, called Israel a cancerous tumour, and asked Germany and Austria to cede a portion of their own territory to establish Israel there.

For a Jew, it is disturbing to hear such statements from the mouth of the leader of an important nation, as it should be for everyone. It is even more disturbing to hear people around the world saying that we should not pay him any attention, the argument being that he is 'only playing to his base'.

Haven't people learned the lessons of history? When the leader of an important power states his intention to annihilate the Jews - and is working towards acquiring the means to do so - the world's duty is to listen and pay attention. And ultimately to stop him before it's too late.[81]

The real issue

There is only one conclusion to draw from the above. The real issue in the Arab-Israeli conflict is neither Israel's withdrawal from conquered territories, nor Jerusalem, nor the 'return' of the refugees. The real issue is Israel's existence - its very legitimacy. Once this is understood, the way forward to reach peace will become much clearer.

12
Holocaust: "Never Forget" and "Je me souviens"

Back from my third trip to Israel, I decided to work on a project that was dear to my heart: the commemoration of the Holocaust (*Shoah* in Hebrew). I like studying history, in particular the period of the Second World War, and by extension, issues related to the Holocaust.

I am not a fan of victimization. I much prefer accounts in which the Jews fight back. I have read every book I have been able to find on the Jewish Brigade and on Jewish partisans, in particular Aba Kovner and the Bielski brothers - on which the movie *Defiance*, starring Daniel Craig of James Bond fame, was based.

However, the great majority of Jews were caught by the Nazi machine of death and did not have a real chance of fighting back. They were tortured, gassed, and massacred.

The lessons from the *Shoah* are obviously important for today's world. There are two distinct dimensions to the Holocaust, which may seem, at first glance, to be contradictory: a universal dimension and a particular dimension.

The universal message is that any identifiable group (ethnic, national, religious, sexual or other) can be the victim of an intense and ferocious hatred, even to the point of unspeakable acts. The Armenian genocide after the First World War, the massacres in Cambodia in the 70's, the Rwandan genocide in

1994 and today's situation in Darfur show time and again what man can do to a fellow human being. The Jews do not have a monopoly on persecution - and have never so claimed.

The specific aspect of the Holocaust is however, that for millennia, the Jewish people have been the subject of a special hatred, one that has been called 'the longest hatred'.

This hatred seems timeless. It infected the pagans of the Hellenistic world, and later on the Roman world that rejected monotheism, the very basis of Judaism. It infected the Christian world, which could not accept the Jews' refusal to recognize Jesus as the long awaited Messiah.

Of course it infected Germany, which put its immense resources and talents towards the destruction of the Jewish people.

And today, the virus of anti-Semitism is carried by the numerous Islamist movements throughout the world.

I had long been considering an initiative that would enable me to leave my sons a tangible memorial and a unique testimonial to one of the greatest atrocities in history, and serve as a powerful reminder of the murder of six million Jews.

On December 1, 2001, the death of Albert Rudolph, the father of my friend and brother-in-law Howard Rudolph, was the catalyst that led me to table and push a bill through Parliament establishing a Holocaust Memorial Day – *Yom ha-Shoah* in Canada.[82]

The life of Albert Rudolph makes for a compelling story in itself. Having survived the Holocaust, he arrived penniless in Halifax in April of 1950 at the age of 24. He worked all his life as a butcher and was able to provide a university education for each of his five children: Allan, Howard, Dina, Karen and Corry. He had the satisfaction of seeing eight of his 14 grandchildren before he died.

Born in Bendzin, Poland, near the German border, he was interned at the age of 16 in the Buchenwald concentration camp.

When Mr. Rudolph died, I realized as never before, that as time moved inexorably on, there would soon be no one left alive to bear witness to that dark period in the history of humanity. At the same time, I saw that my position as an MP enabled me to contribute in a unique way to the preservation of the memory and lessons of that terrible Nazi atrocity.

And so, supported by my assistant Patrick St-Jacques and my intern Steeve Azoulay, I conceived the idea of a private member's bill (that is, a bill not introduced by the government) to commemorate the Holocaust in Canada's body of legislation.

It should be noted that it is rare for a private member's bill to make it through the entire legislative process. I needed to find support among all the political parties in order to succeed. I got that support from Judy Wasylycia-Leis from the New Democratic Party (NDP),[83] Scott Reid from the Canadian Alliance, Scott Brison - then a member of the Progressive Conservative Party and Art Eggleton from the Liberal Party.

These colleagues not only undertook to get their respective caucuses' support, but to co-sponsor the bill with me. With the additional help of Liberal MPs Jacques Saada and Anita Neville, I knew we were in good shape to make it happen.

The problem became one of timing. With the arrival of Paul Martin at the helm of the Liberal Party, there was a persistent rumour that the House was going to be prorogued, which would have killed any chance of having the bill adopted quickly. We were in a race against time.

Despite all that, on October 21, 2003, the *Holocaust Memorial Day Act* was unanimously adopted by the House of Commons in a fast track procedure, and passed in a single day.[84]

After the short statements following the adoption of the Act and the Speaker's official word that it had passed, the importance of what had just happened dawned on me. I was very proud. Emotions were running high on Parliament Hill, both in and out of the House.

Shortly after, the Senate followed suit and, on Friday, November 7 of 2003, the Governor General gave the bill Royal Assent. Bill C-459 had become Chapter 23 of the 2003 Statutes of Canada.

Now, every year, party leaders, MPs, senators, ambassadors from many countries and officials, join together in Ottawa to take part in an official ceremony to remember.

I had played a role in making sure that Canadians, by themselves and through their democratically elected leaders, never forget. Because we cannot afford to forget.

13
Canada-Israel relations: deep and solid

Working for the Canada-Israel Committee and now for its successor, the Centre for Israel and Jewish Affairs, I am often asked what type of relationship Canada has with Israel and how close it is.

In fact, when I am invited to participate in conferences, I am asked to talk about this subject as often as I am asked to talk about the Arab-Israeli conflict.

For that reason, I think it worthwhile to include a few paragraphs on the subject in this book. Particularly given that the media usually focuses solely on the conflict, while the Canada-Israel relationship is much stronger, deeper and broader than one can appreciate from reading the newspapers. And it is the relationship that is at the very heart of my job.

The year 2009 marked the 60th anniversary of diplomatic relations between Canada and Israel. Looking for original ideas to celebrate this important milestone required research to truly understand this bi-national relationship. Thus, the anniversary gave me the opportunity to learn a lot of what ultimately unites the two countries.

Of course, there is a great deal of common ground. There's the fact that the two countries share values based on democracy and human rights and both have built advanced economies. Canada and Israel share a history of mass immigration, have similar legal systems based on the British common law,[85] and are both parliamentary democracies.

This tight relationship is evidenced in a myriad of subjects and goes to the very beginning of the modern State of Israel. Indeed, in April of 1947, Canada was one of eleven countries on the United Nations Special Committee on Palestine. In August of that year, Canadian Supreme Court Justice Ivan Rand drafted the U.N. Partition Plan calling for the creation of a Jewish state alongside a Palestinian state.

Logically, then, in November of 1947 Canada voted in favour of creating a Jewish state at the U.N.. From that moment on, Canada has always been in favour of two states, one Jewish, one Arab, as the solution for the Jewish-Arab conflict in the Middle East. As early as 1948, Canada granted Israel *de facto* recognition and, the following year, *de jure* recognition after Israel's admission to the U.N.

This recognition was but the starting point for an increasingly fruitful relationship, on many levels.

Trade

Canada and Israel have strong economic links based on numerous agreements, the most important being the *Canada-Israel Free Trade Agreement* (CIFTA). Indeed, the CIFTA caused trade between the two countries to more than triple. The agreement, completing the 1977 *Memorandum of Understanding strengthening bilateral trade and economic relations between Canada and Israel* and the 1997 *Co-operation agreement between the Manufacturers Association of Israel and the Alliance of Manufacturers & Exporters of Canada*, led to the fact that, in 2008, Canadian exports to Israel were worth $582.78 million, and Canadian imports from Israel were $1.22 billion.

As both countries were becoming high-tech powerhouses, it was natural to arrive at the creation in 1994 of the *Canada-Israel*

Industrial Research and Development Foundation (CIIRDF), which promotes collaborative R&D partnerships. CIIRDIF has been an important factor for technological developments in both countries, whether in nanotechnologies, wireless, or health sciences. In fact, based on CIIRDIF's success, the government of Canada created similar cooperative programs with India, China and Brazil.

It is not only with Ottawa that Israel entered into important agreements. In 2005, Ontario and Israel signed a *Memorandum of Understanding to promote industrial and technological development* between them. This was followed by a 2008 agreement between Quebec and Israel to develop economic and technological cooperation.[86] This agreement was renewed during the most important trade mission ever organised in Canada[87] to Israel, a mission led by the Quebec Minister of Economic Development.

Culture

However, for a strong relationship between two countries, the dynamic cannot be one of a commercial nature alone. Culture, a nation's very soul, is also an essential domain through which societies become acquainted with one another and ultimately grow. Cultural agreements between Canada and Israel are many, as exemplified by: the 1*980 Agreement on film relations between Canada and Israel, the 1985 Agreement on film and video productio*n, the *1999 Cultural and Educational Memorandum of Understanding between Canada and Israel*, and the *2007 Cooperation Agreement in education, science/ technology and culture between Quebec and Israel.*

Those agreements led in 2009 to *Les Grands Ballets Canadiens* being one of only two international performers to be invited to participate in Tel Aviv's 100th anniversary celebration, and Israel's innovative Batsheva Dance Company, which has performed in cities across Canada, being invited to Vancouver for the first time as part of the Cultural Olympiad festival.

Sports are also, I would argue, culture, but of a different kind. Sports can help build bridges between societies, even societies separated by thousands of kilometres. For example, the Canada Centre in Metulla is home to Israel's national ice hockey team and its only Olympic-sized skating rink, whose walls are adorned with tributes to Canadian hockey greats Jean Béliveau, Roger Nielson and Sydney Crosby. In 2005, with the benefit of a number of Israeli-Canadian dual citizens and ex-Montreal Canadians Jean Perron as head coach, Israel won the gold medal at the International Ice Hockey Federation Division II, Group B, World Championships.

Peace Process & Security

Canada is, and has for a long time been, committed to the goal of a comprehensive, just and lasting peace in the Middle East, including the creation of a Palestinian state living side by side in peace and security with Israel.

Canada's important efforts towards that goal are illustrated in a range of areas. In 1957, Lester B. Pearson won the Nobel Peace Prize for his leadership in deploying U.N. peacekeepers to the Sinai Peninsula. Canada has participated in the United Nations Disengagement Observer Force in the Golan Heights since its creation in 1974. Canada served as chair and Gavel holder of the Refugee Working Group, supporting efforts to reach a just, comprehensive and durable settlement of the refugee question. And Canada's 2007 commitment of over $300 million in aid has supported the Palestinian Authority in its efforts to improve Palestinian security, governance, and prosperity.

Legal

The law is also a fundamental issue which can bring peoples closer together. This is surely the case with Canada and Israel. Canada's Charter of Rights and Freedoms, for example, is often cited in Israeli legal interpretations and court decisions.

According to Canadian-born Israeli professor Allen Zysblatt, the Canadian Charter is the most influential non-Israeli document on Israeli law. It is often used and cited by Israeli courts, in particular the Israeli Supreme Court, for comparative law and human rights cases.[88]

But there also exist many agreements of a legal nature between Israel and Canada, like the 1969 *Extradition Agreement between Canada and Israel,* the 1992 *Canada-Israel Legal Cooperation Program* (founded to share Canadian expertise in human rights law), the 1999 *Mutual Legal Assistance Treaty to facilitate information sharing in investigating and prosecuting crimes*, and the 1999 *Declaration of Intent on Cooperation in the Field of Law to promote the exchange of legal officials.*

It is worth noting as well that both Canadian and Israeli Supreme Court Chief Justices are women.

As is evident from this very brief review, the relationship between Canada and Israel is both deep and mutually beneficial.

My everyday job is to help develop it, nourish it, and enrich it. It is, for me, an important and fulfilling job. It might not be as spectacular a job as being a Member of Parliament, but I would argue that I still have an impact on public policy, albeit of a different nature.

14
Panorama

The different jobs I have held throughout my professional life have always required a certain amount of travel. Wherever and whenever I travel, I make time to visit Jewish institutions, meet Jews, and exchange with them.

I cannot help but be struck by the fact that, despite the vastly different situations in which they find themselves, there is a strong sense of common fate, of solidarity between Jews from around the world. Here is a small sample.

Jews can be found on every continent. In fact, today, the majority of Jews live outside of the State of Israel. There are about 15 million Jews in the world living in 100 countries. Of those, 41 percent live in Israel. A similar number, 40 percent, live in the U.S. The other numerically important Jewish communities are found in the countries of the former Soviet Union, France, Canada, Argentina, and Great Britain.

As the home of the world's largest Diaspora Jewish community is just south of the border in the U.S., I often have the opportunity to visit. Its diversity, its creativity, and its dynamism are truly remarkable.

For our 10th wedding anniversary, Lori and I went to San Francisco. If there is a place where the hippie culture and/or counterculture is still alive, it is certainly the Bay Area. After a few days spent walking around this charming and beautiful city, we went to synagogue to have a few hours to rest and refresh ourselves. The service we went to felt like a 1970's folk concert with a guitar, long-haired men and people dancing. We had found ourselves in a Temple where a very Californian form of Judaism was practiced.

In Washington DC, Temple Micah, the synagogue where Lori, the boys and I went while spending a few days in the American capital, surprised us by its ethnic composition. Between a quarter and a third of the congregants were African-American. The melodies used during the service were either Black spirituals or strongly inspired by them. A few times, it felt like we were at a gospel music concert. It was very different from what we were used to but it was, at the same time, also very inspiring and meaningful.

In New York, the biggest Jewish city in the world, my family and I went to the biggest Reform temple in the world: Temple Emmanu-El. This synagogue, built just across from Central Park, was founded by German Jews in 1845. The building itself, dating back to the 1920's, is magnificent and grandiose. One can sense the desire that New York Jews seemed to have had to compete with or outdo their Protestant neighbours. Inside, this synagogue had the same ambiance as a Protestant basilica: an organ, an almost entirely English-language service, minimal Hebrew, clergy (male and female) dressed like Protestant ministers and hardly any prayer shawls or *kippot* (head coverings) visible.

One of the events I love attending is the annual convention of the American Israel Political Action Committee, known by its acronym of AIPAC. AIPAC is the main pro-Israel lobby in the U.S. and its conventions are a site to behold. Think about it: more than 7,000 delegates from across the U.S. (with a few foreigners from Israel, Europe, and Canada) gathering to show their support for Israel.

Contrary to what conspiracy theorists say, as well as what so-called experts affirm when they draw an unrealistic portrait of the American pro-Israel community, the delegates are regular people. Year after year, they attend the convention to listen to very high-level speakers, to dialogue among themselves, and to exercise their very basic democratic right to meet with their elected officials.

There is nothing sinister or secret going on. In fact, AIPAC delegates remind me of the more serious delegates I met throughout the years at the numerous political conventions I attended in Canada.

It is very impressive, to say the least, to be a part of a convention with such a huge number of delegates together in one place. It is also an indication of the depth of the relationship between the American people and Israel. Note, I did not say the American Jewish community, but the American people.

The strength of the relationship between the U.S. and Israel is not reliant on any individual who may occupy an elective office - which is, by its very nature, temporary - in either the U.S. or Israel. The relationship is much more than that and the AIPAC convention is a visible demonstration of this fact.

Paris is another great Jewish city. The political, economic, administrative, and cultural heart of France, Paris is also the heart of French Jewish life. As it is a city where I have lived, a city that I love, a city in which I have fond memories, my latest Jewish experience there saddened me.

After a few meetings in Paris, I was to stay in town over Shabbat. Looking over the internet, I chose the closest synagogue to my hotel. However, going into the synagogue turned out to be much more difficult that I had expected.

As the majority of the French Jewish community is now Sephardic, coming from North Africa, with my blond hair and blue eyes I stuck out like a sore thumb. Add my Quebec accent to the mix and I was the subject of a very tough interview process, including aggressive questioning and a manual search, before being allowed inside.

I knew that security was a major and troubling issue for French Jews, but I did not know the extent of it before experiencing it myself. Going through an examination before attending service put a damper on my pre-Shabbat peaceful mood.

France has seen a rise in anti-Semitism in recent years. It took a few unfortunate assaults against Jews and Nicolas Sarkozy's dynamism on this issue to force French authorities to put in place the necessary measures to fight this phenomenon.

I cannot say that I know Hassidic Jews well. They are often considered, at least in Quebec, as archetypical Jews and are frequently the subject of conversation. Primarily this is because they are the only Jews that are so obviously Jewish. And secondly, because they live among themselves, they are harder to get to know.

It is important to note that Hassidic Jews are divided among themselves into different sects, the most important of which are Chabad-Lubavitch, Satmar, and Breslov (the names signify the East-European towns from which they originate). Contrary to what one who hasn't spent time with them might think, they are generally very happy and warm. They love life, singing, dancing, and drinking!

Even though I have no desire to become a Hassid, I was interested in getting to know more about this community and its adherents, if only to rid myself of any preconceived notions. Such an occasion arose in 2009 and I jumped at the opportunity.

I was invited to spend the Jewish New Year – *Rosh Hashanah* – in the town of Uman in the Ukraine. Why Uman? A famous Hassidic rabbi, Rebbe Nachman, is buried there. This rabbi, dead for more than 200 years, is the founder of the Breslov branch of Hassidism and is the great-grandson of the founder of Hassidism himself, Rabbi Israel Baal Shem Tov. Shortly before his death, Rebbe Nachman expressed his desire to see people pray on his grave on *Rosh Hashanah*.

Breslov Hassidim believe that during *Rosh Hashanah*, it is possible to attain a heightened spiritual level, which will be even more elevated if the prayer is said on the grave of a Hassidic master. Indeed, their belief is that if one prays on Rebbe Nachman's grave on *Rosh Hashanah*, the Rebbe will intervene in the pilgrim's favour when he dies and comes to his time of judgment by God.

It is not an exaggeration to say that the experience took me to an entirely different world - a parallel universe.

Uman is a small city a four-hour drive from either the Ukrainian capital of Kiev or the famous port of Odessa. Every year, 30,000 Jews from around the world converge on this small town for a brief period of time. And Uman does not have the necessary infrastructure to welcome that many people.

People sleep in tents, in the streets, or rent the apartments and houses of Uman inhabitants. That is what I did, having joined a group of young French-speaking Jews who had been to Uman before. I was surprised by the size of the Montreal Jewish delegation. In the house we rented, we were 28 men (8 to 10 per room) with…one bathroom and one shower.

The Ukrainians who rent out their lodgings either sleep with their families elsewhere, or in their sheds and garages. Doing so, in about one week they make more money than they usually make during the rest of the year.

It was a unique experience: Jews from Canada, Israel, the U.S., France, Australia, Great Britain, religious and secular (yes, secular), Sephardim and Ashkenazim, all getting together once a year to celebrate the Jewish New Year.

I was surprised to note that the majority of the pilgrims were not Hassidic. Hassidic Jews formed about 40-45 percent of the total number of people there. I was not the only curious one.

Despite the numerous differences, a mix of Hebrew, French, and English assured a fairly easy means of communication. The intensity of the prayers and the other activities will forever be engraved in my mind. I am not sure if I will ever return, but it was a once in a lifetime experience that I am happy to have had.

While I earlier discussed the dynamism of the many Jewish communities I visited, I must also mention a concern of many Jews of the Diaspora: assimilation.

I think a parallel can be drawn between the situation of French-speaking Canadians outside of Quebec and that of Jews in minority situations.

When one thinks about francophones living outside of Quebec in Canada, one thinks of their very high assimilation rate.

Having lived exclusively in English for a while in Ontario, I remember that after a period of studying, working and socializing in English only, I found myself looking for my words in French. And I had grown up exclusively in French.

Having been born and raised in an English environment, the fact that francophones outside of Quebec have been able to keep their French is incredible. It is a testimony to their desire to preserve their heritage.

Obviously, it is a tough battle; some would even say a losing battle. It is, in any event, an effort that starts at home.[89] If a francophone marries an anglophone and English is the main language in the home, their children will likely be anglophones. It is a widespread phenomenon in English Canada and one that I encounter even in Outaouais, the Quebec region situated just across the river from Ottawa.

The same thing happens to Jews in minority situations. The likelihood that the children of a mixed couple (Jewish-non Jewish) have a Jewish identity is much lower than the children of couples where both parents are Jewish. That is aside from the fact that the majority of Jews do not recognize as Jewish, a child whose father is Jewish but whose mother is not. This is one of the main reasons Jewish parents prefer that their children marry Jewish partners. It has nothing to do with racism; the issue is that of parents wanting to transmit their heritage to their children.

Nonetheless, my children's former complementary Jewish school class in a Reform synagogue looked much more like a mini-United Nations than any school in, say, Trois-Rivières, Quebec City, Moose Jaw, or Fredericton.

The Jewish intermarriage rate is more than 75 percent in the ex-Soviet Union, more than 50 percent in the U.S.[90], more than 40 percent in France and Great Britain, and 35 percent in Canada. Many experts are of the opinion that, if today only 41 percent of world Jewry lives in Israel, in a quarter of a century the majority will be living there, mainly because of the high assimilation rate of Jews living in the Diaspora.

Seeing the decline of French in North America outside Quebec - or even in Europe - is always disheartening for me. In the same way, it is sad to see the decline of the Jewish population in the world.

In addition, contrary to conventional wisdom, the Jewish people's unity is fragile. Movements within the Jewish world are engaged in terrible battles: Orthodox Jews against liberal Jews (i.e. Reform and Conservative), religious against secular, Diaspora-focused and Israel-centric, etc.

With the high assimilation rate of Diaspora Jews, I cannot help but think that should the State of Israel disappear, the entire Jewish civilization would be at risk of disappearing.

The State of Israel is increasingly central to Jewish survival, while at the same time it faces grave existential threats. This is the main conundrum facing Jews today.

While attending CEGEP, here I am at a demonstration I had organized with others, to defend Bill 101.

Not more than a few months after my election at the age of 26, I am pictured between Lucien Bouchard, Premier of Quebec and Leader of the Parti Québécois, and Gilles Duceppe, Leader of the Bloc Québécois. I was far from the suburbs of Quebec City where I grew up.

During a visit by Jacques Parizeau to my riding, the ex-Premier had
succeeded in bringing out hundreds of people despite the snow storm
in Quebec. I always found my discussions with Mr. Parizeau to be
fascinating.

During my third and last swearing in as a Member of Parliament in 2004. I had just completed my best election campaign.

As a Member of Parliament, I had the opportunity to meet some fascinating people. Here I am with the Dalai Lama when he visited Ottawa.

Richard Marceau

**Here I am with the legendary Nelson Mandela, Prime Minister
Jean Chrétien and some Bloc colleagues.**

At a visit by Nathan Sharansky in Montreal, March 14, 2004.
Sharansky, a human rights activist, is one of the most celebrated Soviet
dissidents and the personification of the persecution of millions of Jews
by the Communist authorities.

Richard Marceau

During a working session in 2003 with Shimon Peres, Nobel Peace Prize winner and current President of Israel.

140

During the annual Holocaust Memorial Day on Parliament Hill in Ottawa. I am with my Parliamentary colleagues who contributed to passing the law establishing the event. From left to right: Judy Wasylycia-Leis, Jerry Grafstein, Scott Reid, Anita Neville and me.

Richard Marceau

With Palestinian President Mahmoud Abbas in May 2009. When visiting Ottawa, Abbas had asked to meet the leaders of the Canadian Jewish community. The exchanges were both honest and polite.

142

**Presenting Israeli President Shimon Peres with a copy of
my book in French.**

Let's Talk

15
Frankly Speaking

To say that Quebec is a more racist or anti-Semitic nation than, say, France, Great Britain,[91] or Sweden[92] is false and defamatory. While travelling and meeting people across Canada, I have been in a position to defend Quebec in general, and sovereignists in particular, against many such accusations. Defending Quebec has never been difficult as I know for a fact that Quebeckers are generous, tolerant, and welcoming.

The fact that Quebeckers want to defend and protect their small, seven-million strong French-speaking nation situated right beside the most powerful economic, political, military, and cultural empire in the history of the world, does not make them xenophobic.

Quebeckers do not have to apologize in any way, shape or form for their desire to continue to live, exist and prosper with their original and distinct personality. To the contrary, they should be proud.

That being said, it would amount to wilful blindness not to admit that, unfortunately like every other place in the world, there are some in Quebec who are close-minded, xenophobic, and even racist and anti-Semitic.

As a proud Quebecker and a proud Jew, I do not flinch from tackling this delicate and difficult issue. Certain portions in the following sections may be considered harsh. I want to make one thing clear: to make a society better, some things need to be said.

In fact, while writing the following chapters, I was reminded of what I was doing as the main English voice for the Bloc (besides Duceppe, of course) when trying to explain the sovereignty movement to Canadians outside of Quebec. Then, I had to fight misinformation, disinformation and, yes, some prejudice toward Quebec sovereignists. Now, I do the same thing with the non-Jewish world about Jews and Israel.

Jews are news. It is a well-known fact. Jews occupy a disproportionate amount of space in our media. There are probably a number of reasons. Allow me to attempt to give a few.

First, despite the disproportionate attention accorded to Jews and the Jewish state, people are not generally well informed about either. I have only to look at myself. I had always thought of myself as well informed, until I realized that I really knew next to nothing about the Middle East prior to travelling to the region multiple times.

Indeed, it is impossible to understand the Middle East by watching a 60-second segment on the nightly news or from reading a blurb in *The Globe and Mail*, *The National Post* or *The Toronto Star*.

Then there is the double standard regarding Israel. A double standard in terms of the attention given to what is after all a small state in a far away region, but also in terms of the severe criticism hurled at it constantly.

It is easy to note that over the past few years, criticism of Israel has become harsher and harsher without valid reasons. The lines between on the one hand criticism of Israel and on the other hand anti-Semitism have been crossed too often. This is inexcusable.

This latest development is particularly visible coming from a certain part of the Left. Mind you, I am not saying the Left as a whole, but part of the Left. The distinction is essential.

This certain Left is anti-American, anti-liberal, anti-capitalist and, I would venture to say, obscurantist. It sees Israel as an offshoot of the United States in the Middle East and/or the puppeteer, pulling the strings of the American superpower because of the all-powerful Jewish lobby. Of course, the U.S.-Israel alliance is for them, the root cause of every evil in the world.

Moreover, in past years this certain Left has allied itself with people whose values are the very opposite of theirs: the Islamists. This alliance against nature probably stems from the fact that they believe they have the same enemy: the liberal and capitalist Western world, led by the U.S. and whose incarnation in the Middle East is the State of Israel. Israel, with its rule of law, democracy, and respect for fundamental freedoms, sticks out like a sore thumb in a famously anti-democratic region.

The following chapters will, I hope, connect the dots on many issues, help the reader see things in a different light and, ultimately, bring about a better understanding of the Jewish situation in Canada and in Israel.

16
The Other Lobby

The Jewish lobby is a phantasm in many people's minds. Reports, articles, and discussions on the subject are too numerous to count. Often around this subject, one finds the odour of mystery, but the mystery of an occult and evil kind. Oftentimes, it is simply a reformulation of the old Jewish conspiracy canard, of Jewish control of banks, media, governments, etc.

Mainstream media outlets are not free from this phenomenon. For example, on April 9, 2010, in his weekly show on Radio-Canada (the French language CBC television), the pro-Palestinian host Jean-François Lépine broadcast a report filled with errors and approximations.[93] Even before the broadcast, Lépine was promoting his show[94] saying that the Jewish lobby was intolerant, insidious and dangerous - a lobby that was infiltrating the highest spheres of the Canadian government. The report itself went as far as to imply that Israel's friends in Canada were responsible for the unfortunate death of Rémy Beauregard, Chair of Rights & Democracy. The report accused Israel's supporters in Canada of McCarthyism when they disagree and state their disagreement with the pro-Palestinian view of the conflict. Moreover, it made important factual errors on the Canadian contribution to UNRWA, and implied that the pro-Israel lobby equates any criticism of Israel with anti-Semitism.

To the contrary, the pro-Israel community - which includes the Jewish community but is not limited to it - is transparent, at the very centre of Canada's political spectrum and shares the values of Canadian society of which it is an integral part.

The attention accorded to the pro-Israel community hides the very existence of the pro-Palestinian lobby,[95] a lobby which is incidentally more often anti-Israel than pro-Palestinian, and promotes values that are the polar opposite of Canada's.

Better knowledge of the pro-Palestinian lobby is a necessity to anyone wishing to better understand Canadian political dynamics.

The Canadian Arab Federation

The Canadian Arab Federation (CAF) is the cornerstone of the pro-Palestinian lobby in Canada. CAF is an umbrella for a group of smaller organizations purportedly representing various streams of Arab-Canadian society. The values espoused by CAF President Khaled Mouammar and CAF's overall leadership are not determined arbitrarily, but rather echo those of many of its member groups. CAF and its member organizations have repeatedly voiced their support for terrorist groups and radical Islamist ideology.

CAF and several of its member organizations promoted a number of protest rallies across the country where an effigy of the Prime Minister of Canada was destroyed, and public calls were made for intifada and death to Jews, as well as chants glorifying Hezbollah and jihad. CAF has repeatedly called for the removal of Hamas and Hezbollah from Canada's list of terrorist entities, asserting they are legitimate groups. Both factions have been classified as terrorist organizations by Canada since 2002.

CAF received a lot of attention when its January 16, 2009 *Daily Bulletin*, containing links to videos praising organizations such as Hamas and Palestinian Islamic Jihad, was forwarded to all MPs by Bloc Québécois MP Maria Mourani. She was subsequently forced by her leader to apologize to the House for her actions.

The Ahlul Bayt Center, a CAF member organization, until recently featured links on its website[96] to noted "scholars" such as Ayatollah Ali Khamenei, the Supreme Leader of Iran, and Sayed Mohammad Hussain Fadl-Allàh[97], the spiritual leader of Hezbollah and a known Holocaust denier.

CAF's record on this issue is as long as it is troubling. CAF Vice President Ali Mallah participated in a 2007 conference convened in Cairo by the Muslim Brotherhood and attended by Hamas and Hezbollah leaders. Following that, Mallah announced "solidarity with Iran, solidarity with the Iraqi resistance, and of course solidarity with the Palestinian resistance and with the Lebanese resistance."[97a]

In a speech he delivered on October 26, 2006, the same Ali Mallah bemoaned the fall of the Taliban regime and highlighted the imperative to support terrorist groups, declaring: "[had we supported groups like Hezbollah] we may never have lost Afghanistan. And God forbid, if we don't get our act together, we may lose more." [97b]

During the 2006 Liberal Party leadership race, CAF distributed a flyer denouncing Bob Rae's Liberal leadership campaign, citing his wife's involvement in the Jewish community. The flyer flagged Arlene Perly-Rae's position with the Canadian Jewish Congress and Bob Rae's affiliation with the Jewish National Fund as reasons to oppose his candidacy.

I was at that Liberal convention as an observer. I can say that as someone who has been to many political conventions held by various political parties, I had never before (nor since) seen something as repugnant as that. When I was given a copy of that flyer, I froze with disgust.

In a July 17, 2006 interview on CITY TV, CAF president

Khaled Mouammar said of Israel:

> *They're doing the same [as Nazi Germany]. They are attacking and invading neighbouring countries and occupying them. And when people resist they go in and bomb them and starve them. This is exactly what Nazi Germany did in Poland, Czechoslovakia and other countries in Europe.*

This Nazification of Israel is a good example of the toxic polemic political discourse with which this radical organization is trying to infect the Canadian debate. It crosses every red line (see chapter on anti-Semitism).

It is the same Khaled Mouammar who, following the horrific massacre by lone gunner Anders Breivik in Norway in July 2011 circulated an e-mail accusing Israel of being behind this tragedy, confirming his anti-Israel obsession.[98]

Palestine House

Palestine House is one of the most important member organizations of the Canadian Arab Federation. It recently made the news when it was implicated in an investigation of massive immigration fraud, and according to which more than 300 people allegedly used its address as their domicile address.[99]

Palestine House rejects efforts to reach a peaceful resolution to the Israeli-Arab conflict based on negotiation and compromise.

Palestine House supports the complete return of all Palestinian refugees to Israel, which is contrary to the idea of a two-state solution: two-states for two peoples – one Palestinian and the other Jewish. The naturalization of all Palestinian refugees in Israel would *de facto* dismantle the democratic Jewish State, resulting in the creation of two Palestinian states and the destruction of the world's only Jewish polity.

In addition to their advocacy against a two-state solution, Palestine House repeatedly demonizes Israel as an "apartheid" state, glorifying "martyrdom" and "resistance" – terms associated with acts of terrorism - in the struggle against the Jewish State.

On October 28, 2007, Palestine House signed on to the "Hamilton Declaration"[100], an open letter to Palestinian President Mahmoud Abbas denouncing the Annapolis peace negotiations, rejecting the two-state solution, and opposing the existence of Israel as a Jewish state:

It is our belief that the purpose of the Annapolis round of negotiations is to extract further critical concessions from the Palestinians while further delaying final status agreements. In particular, we believe that Israel will attempt to redefine the conflict with the Palestinians as being only about ending the occupation of Jerusalem, the West Bank and Gaza, or parts thereof. Such a redefinition leads the Palestinians into the trap of the "two-state" formula which subverts our legitimate rights under international law. We stress that the central issue in the Palestinian conflict with Israel has always been the dispossession of the Palestinian people from their land and property caused by the Zionist ethnic cleansing of 1948 and the Israeli denial to Palestinians of the basic human right to return and to live in peace and security as equal citizens on their land.

We further specifically caution you against any recognition of Israel as a 'Jewish' state. Such a recognition would give Israel the façade of moral and legal legitimacy while critically compromising the full implementation of the inalienable Palestinian right of return.

It is not only in foreign affairs that Palestine House is extreme. On March 30, 2009, Palestine House hosted Dr. Ekrema Sabri as the keynote for its 'Land Day' event. Sabri, the former Mufti of Jerusalem, delivered a lecture in 2005 criticizing the West for treating men who force their wives to have sex as rapists. He said:

> *[In the West] a woman who was rebellious against her husband sued him for sleeping with her against her will. He was treated as a rapist. The husband was considered a rapist and was severely punished. He was punished as a rapist merely because he slept with his wife against her will.*[101]

Sabri is also on record denouncing the right of Israel to exist and declaring his admiration for child martyrs, in an interview with Al-Ahram in 2000.

> *The land of Palestine is not only Jerusalem; this land stretches from the [Jordan] River to the [Mediterranean] Sea. Naturally, the [Palestinian] problem relates to all of this land. We cannot establish a homeland by only liberating Jerusalem. It is true that Salah Al-Din did not rest until Jerusalem was liberated, but this does not suggest that the rest of this blessed land is to be neglected or given up...*
> *There is no doubt that a child [martyr] suggests that the new generation will carry on the mission with determination. The younger the martyr - the greater and the more I respect him...*[102]

In February of 2008, Palestine House held an event[103] "In Memory of a National Leader" to "commemorate and honour the life and work of Dr. George Habash," founder of the Popular Front for the Liberation of Palestine. The organization in question, known as the PFLP, is a listed terrorist entity in Canada which pioneered the hijacking of airplanes as a Middle East terror tactic. Habash was the main leader of the "rejectionist" wing of the Palestinian nationalist movement, insisting that under no circumstances should any negotiations be held with the Israeli state for a peaceful resolution of the conflict. Palestine House posted the following notice on its website following Habash's death: "With deep sorrow we announce the passing of Dr. George Habash. Palestine House conveys our condolences to Dr. Habash's Family and his comrades in the PFLP and the PLO."[104]

On January 17, 2009, Palestine House organized a protest outside the constituency offices of Minister Peter Kent, promoted by the slogan "Shame on Stephen Harper!" At the event, Canadian Arab Federation president Khaled Mouammar, speaking explicitly on behalf of Palestine House, called Minister Peter Kent, Minister Jason Kenney, and Opposition Leader Michael Ignatieff "professional whores" for their support of Israel.[105]

There are also Quebec-based organizations that unfortunately share these radical values; Tadamon is one such group.

Tadamon

Tadamon's basis of unity describes it as "a Montreal-based collective which works in solidarity with struggles for self-determination, equality and justice in the 'Middle East' and in diaspora communities in Montreal and beyond... We strive for a world in which every human being is free to live and flourish in dignity and justice."[106]

This might sound harmless. However, Tadamon's mission statement refuses to acknowledge the legitimate right of the Jewish people to self-determination in their aboriginal homeland and completely denies the legitimacy of the State of Israel's existence. Tadamon asserts "that the colonization of Palestine has, from its inception, been connected to Western European aspirations to dominate the entire Middle East."[107]

They go on to condemn so-called "Israeli apartheid" and support "an international campaign of boycott, divestment and sanctions against Israel."

Furthermore, Tadamon consistently glorifies "resistance" – a term associated with acts of terrorism – in the struggle against the Jewish State. They explicitly advocate forms of resistance that maximize "the rights of the oppressed" and deride "the Western insistence on non-violence." Tadamon believes the word terrorism is misused "to delegitimize all resistance to imperialism in the Middle East."[108]

In reality, Tadamon (Arabic for "solidarity") is a militant coalition of Canadian and Lebanese activist groups involved in anti-Israel and pro-Hezbollah activities. They are dedicated to delegitimizing and demonizing Israel.

Tadamon supports the Lebanon-based radical Islamic terrorist organization Hezbollah. The aims of Hezbollah include removing all Western influences from Lebanon and the Middle East, as well as destroying the State of Israel and liberating all Palestinian territories and Jerusalem from what it sees as Israeli occupation. Hezbollah rejects the possibility of a negotiated peace. Hezbollah has been responsible for car bombings, hijackings, and kidnappings of Western, Israeli and Jewish targets in Israel, Western Europe, and South America. Tadamon advocates for its removal from Canada's list of terrorist entities.

On October 17, 2007, Tadamon and the Quebec Public Interest Research Group (QPIRG) co-hosted two presentations at McGill University both advocating "the importance of challenging Canada's categorization of Hezbollah as a 'terrorist' organization." Tadamon announced these were being presented "within the context of a campaign to challenge the listing of Hezbollah as a terrorist organization in Canada, within the context of providing a broader critique of Canada's list of terrorist organizations created after 9/11."[109]

In August of 2007, Tadamon organized a Montreal Community Commemoration of the Lebanon War with the Association des Jeunes Libanais Musulmans (AJLM) and the al-Hidaya

Association.[110] The AJLM featured a Hezbollah war anthem on its website and links to the website of Hezbollah spiritual guide Ayatollah Sayyed Muhammad Hussein Fadl-Allàh.[111]

The al-Hidaya Association holds annual remembrance events for the "Lebanese resistance martyrs."[112] Its Vice-President, Hussein Hoballah, is the editor of Sada al-Mashrek, a Montreal-based Arabic bi-weekly known for supporting Hezbollah.

This paper made the headlines when it published a poem on January 23, 2007, suggesting Quebec women are intoxicated and easy.

Tadamon leader Stefan Christoff was also a spokesperson for a brutal anarchist outfit called Anti-Capitalist Convergence, which violently disrupted economic fora and political conventions around the world, including in Montreal and Quebec City in the early 2000s, and the G8/G20 meeting in Toronto in 2010. He encouraged its militants, often masked and wielding sticks, with Molotov cocktails and other weapons, to attack police.[113]

When in 2003, hundreds of black-clad anarchists descended on Montreal's Ste-Catherine Street to protest a World Trade Organization forum, destroyed several storefronts and terrorized passersby, Christoff condoned the destruction of private property as legitimate.[114]

Christoff consistently affirms the use of violence as a legitimate means of protest and shows blatant disregard for others' security, freedom of expression, and freedom to gather in peace. Christoff was convicted of unlawful assembly in 2005 under Article 66 of the Criminal Code, found guilty of troubling the peace and public order (2008) and of violating several municipal and public transit by-laws (including hindering an inspector in the performance of inspection duties).

Finally, Tadamon has the assistance of Medical Aid for

Palestine (MAP), an organization lead by Edmond Omran.[115] MAP is recognized as a charity and can therefore provide tax deductible receipts to its donors. MAP served as an illegal front for two organizations in their fundraising activities, including Tadamon itself, which is not entitled to give tax credits.[116]

PAJU

Palestinians and Jews United (PAJU) is another such group. Its name might lead one to assume that it is a pro-peace organization. This could not be farther from the truth. PAJU is, in fact, a radical anti-Israel organization.

PAJU works against a peaceful resolution to the conflict by conjuring Zionist conspiracy theories, promoting Boycott, Divestment and Sanctions (BDS) initiatives and seeking to delegitimize and demonize the State of Israel with apartheid slander. PAJU also supports Palestinian "resistance" – that sticky term used by Tadamon and others.

PAJU's real agenda is – hopefully – becoming clearer. In a Radio-Canada review of the program *"Une Heure sur Terre"* broadcast on January 16, 2008, featuring PAJU leaders Bruce Katz and Rezeq Faraj, Radio Canada's Ombudsman conceded that "[I]t was inaccurate to present this group as being very important", stating the following: "It is at least highly debatable to present this group as pursuing solutions, given the anti-Israel nature of its slogans."[117]

The Ombudsman continued:

> We cannot say that the vocabulary used by PAJU is compatible with the pursuit of (peaceful) solutions (...) In one of its press releases, PAJU denounces the Gaza blockade and the 'genocide of the Gaza population'. It recommends the 'total boycott of the racist and apartheid Israel.

In his book *Palestine, Le refus de disparaître* (Palestine, The refusal to disappear), PAJU co-founder Rezeq Faraj proposes the disappearance of the State of Israel to be replaced by one state, from the Jordan River to the Mediterranean Sea. Indeed, according to Faraj, the creation of two states is not a viable solution. He proposes instead one democratic and secular state (in other words, the disappearance of the State of Israel) in which Israelis and Palestinians would cohabit, maybe under some kind of federalism yet to be defined.

I myself, when I was still an MP, had to deal with this lobby. One event I remember well, involved the Canadian Islamic Congress, a pro-Hamas and pro-Hezbollah[118] pressure group. Its founding president Mohamed Elmasry once condoned attacks against any Israeli adult,[119] and its current president, Wahida Valiante, has written that Judaism has "institutionalized racism."[120]

During election campaigns, many organizations grade candidates according to the positions they take on issues relevant to their organization. In 2004, the Canadian Islamic Congress did exactly that. At the time, I received an A, the highest mark.

For the 2006 election, not long after my coming out as a Jew, the Canadian Islamic Congress did not give me an A, nor a B, a C or a D, but an F, their lowest mark.

Between 2004 and 2006, I had not changed my positions one iota. The positions I had adopted, as evidenced in various speeches and articles, were in the same spirit as pre-2004. The only thing that changed was my religious affiliation, which turned me from a friend to one their worst enemies. The same thing was true, incidentally, of every Jewish MP. Coincidence?

I had never taken that kind of grading seriously, but this episode clarified things for me. For the Canadian Islamic Congress, a Muslim could not vote for a Jew, pure and simple. And to think that those groups pretend to fight against racial profiling, xenophobia, racism and intolerance...

The incident only highlighted the intellectual dishonesty of these organizations. Their extremism was denounced, in a surprising manner, by an important Palestinian personality a few years later.

During the summer of 2007, I received an invitation to have lunch with a few people including Yasser Abbas, son of the Palestinian President Mahmoud Abbas, who was passing through Ottawa. It was quite an interesting meeting.

He explained his father's difficult position at the time. Palestinian politics was described to us from the inside and the challenges facing the more moderate factious were clarified. But the most fascinating part of the discussion was on the so-called pro-Palestinian groups in Canada. On this topic, Yasser Abbas was biting.

He told us that those groups were controlled by extremists,[121] that they favoured the pro-terror Hamas over the more moderate Palestinian Authority and that they were trying to hurt his father. He further warned us that they did not want a peace of compromise (is there any other kind?) with Israel and that they were attempting to radicalize Canadian Muslims.

How I wished Canadian journalists had been there to hear all this!

The discussion raised many questions in my mind, questions for which I still do not have answers. Are these groups really representative of Muslim Canadians? If so, we're in trouble.

If not – and I hope this is the case – what are moderate Muslims waiting for to distance themselves from those groups and create more representative ones?

This kind of disturbing, polarizing attitude does not stop with those groups. During one of my elections, I was attacked by *La Presse*'s 'analyst' Jooned Khan[122] on my fundraising, attacks that were relayed by very influential Quebec City radio stations. In the attacks, I was accused of having been bought by the Jewish community simply because I had Jewish friends who were supporting me financially through election contributions.

For some, Jews=money=undue influence=Jewish lobby=disloyalty.

In an electoral campaign, one must react quickly. A fast but complete search revealed that between 1997 and 2005, my riding association raised $312,281.04. Of this amount, $9,975 (i.e. 3.16 percent) came from Jewish friends and supporters.

But, and more fundamentally, what is the problem with the fact that Jewish Canadians participate in the Canadian political process? Is it illegal? Unhealthy? Should I have refused their money because they are Jewish?

Maybe I should have refused money coming from homosexual friends and acquaintances, because they would be members of the 'pink lobby'. Oh! What about money I received from women who liked my egalitarian positions? Should I have turned that down too? This demonstrates not only how ridiculous their underlying position is, but also how low the anti-Israel lobby will go.

I believe that a real pro-Palestinian person is someone who wants what is best for the Palestinians, that is, someone who wants their legitimate national aspirations fulfilled. A real pro-Palestinian advocate does not treat Palestinians like children, he requires them to act responsibly and respect the fundamental values that we hold dear (basic freedoms, peaceful resolutions of conflicts, etc.). In other words, the world should apply the same standard equally to every nation – including Canada,

Israel, and the Palestinian Authority (and a future Palestinian state).

If, as I believe, independence means to assume all the rights and duties of a state, we must stop excusing the Palestinians from assuming responsibility. We must stop placing culpability for their numerous errors on the shoulders of the Israelis, the Americans, or anyone else.

It does the Palestinians no good when we are paternalistic towards them "as if they were minors whom we excuse for everything", to use Israeli author and peace activist A.B. Yehoshua's words.[123]

Yes, by all means, let us help the Palestinians, but let us not treat them like incapable people. That helps no one, least of all the Palestinians themselves.

Too often, the goal of self-proclaimed pro-Palestinian activists is not to help the Palestinians raise their standard of living and build their state. Rarely – if ever – have I seen these activists propose ideas and bring forth suggestions to concretely help the Palestinians. They offer no constructive ideas. All they do can be summarized as: criticism, demonization, and delegitimization of Israel.

For them, it is a zero-sum game. For them, being pro-Palestinian necessarily means being anti-Israel. To convince yourself of that, you only have to look at the rhetoric of their demonstrations here in Canada: Israel is racist, Israel is a Nazi state, Israel is an apartheid state, etc.

Where are their demonstrations for peace in the Middle East? Where is the idea that both Jews and Arabs have the right to a state? I have never seen such messages carried by the self-proclaimed pro-Palestinian movement, which would be better described as the anti-Israel lobby.

Unfortunately, the Israeli-Arab conflict seems to lead them to a rigid ideological reaction with one conclusion: every problem, every tragedy that the Palestinians experience, is because of Israel and its Western supporters.

One other thing on the subject of the pro-Palestinian/anti-Israel lobby: lying is an important tool in their arsenal. Let's take a look at two examples of this, one older (but which still makes the rounds) and one more recent.

In April 2002, in the middle of the second intifada, a ferocious battle took place in Jenin, in the West Bank, between armed Palestinians and the Israeli army.

Saeb Erakat, the lead Palestinian negotiator, whom I have met a few times, (the first time as noted above, lying straight to my face), said that there had been a terrible massacre in Jenin and that there had been 500 deaths.

Many international media outlets – CNN included – relayed those numbers. Anti-Israel groups circulated this number to the point that, still today, people talk about an Israeli massacre in Jenin.

The reality is very different.

It would have been much easier – and less costly in terms of Israeli lives – to use an air campaign to destroy the nest of armed terrorists situated in the Jenin refugee camp. But that is not what Israel did. It sent its own sons to engage in a door-to-door battle, the most dangerous, risky type of combat.

Israel lost 23 soldiers while 52 Palestinians (approximately half of whom were combatants) were killed. This is the result of a battle, not of a massacre.[124]

The other example, more recent, involves James Cameron, the well-known producer of hit movies like Avatar and Titanic.

A Toronto-based anti-Israel group circulated information according to which Cameron was a supporter of a boycott against Israel. As soon as he was made aware, Cameron not only denied it but also denounced any form of boycott against Israel.[125]

These examples do not include the commonly heard false accusation that Israel committed genocide against the Palestinians. The facts are that the Arab population of Jerusalem has multiplied 7.2 times between 1948 and 2009. Between 1967 and today, the Palestinian population in Jerusalem has grown from 25.5 percent to 35 percent. In addition, the number of Palestinians has grown from 600,000 in 1948 to 9,000,000 (according to some Palestinian numbers). These facts make it obvious that the accusation of genocide is ridiculous.

One last example of the activities and influence of this nefarious lobby. On June 2, 2010, a delegation from the Canadian Muslim Forum was on Parliament Hill. It was officially welcomed by Bloc MP Richard Nadeau with an official declaration[126] in the House of Commons.

What is the Canadian Muslim Forum?

It is an umbrella organization for a few others[127], including the Muslim Association of Canada (MAC-Quebec), a group that openly states that it gets its inspiration from the virulently anti-Western, Islamist, and fundamentalist Muslim Brotherhood.[128] In other words, a democratically elected Member of Canada's Parliament was promoting the anti-democratic Muslim Brotherhood at the very centre of Canadian democracy.

It was not the only gesture of this kind by Richard Nadeau. On September 4, 2010,[129] Nadeau was being honoured by the *Association islamique libanaise Al-Hidaya*, of the *Centre Communautaire Musulman de Montréal* during its annual day of 'commemoration of the martyrs of the Lebanese resistance', i.e. Hezbollah, an organization on Canada's list of terrorism organizations. This centre was named by Muslim Canadian author Tarek Fatah as being 'a hotbed of pro-Hezbollah activity in Montreal.'[130]

Even if one does not agree with the Bloc's agenda for Quebec sovereignty one can understand that its values are incompatible with those of the Muslim Brotherhood and Hezbollah.

The question still stands: how can an elected official promote a group in Parliament which espouses a fascist, backwards, extremist ideology like the Muslim Brotherhood and associate himself with another Islamist group close to Hezbollah?

17
Jewish Anti-Zionism

A quick word on Jewish opposition to the State of Israel.[131]

While a minuscule group in the Jewish world, as a result of being so exceptional, these Jews opposed to Israel attract a lot of media attention. As well, its adherents allow opponents to the existence of Israel – people who do not generally have Jewish interests at heart - to claim: You see? We're not anti-Semitic, we have Jews with us.

We can, *grosso modo*, divide Jewish anti-Zionism into two groups: religious and extreme Left.

Religious anti-Zionism is mainly the purview of a Hassidic movement called *Naturei Karta*, whose name means 'Guardians of the City' in Aramaic. These are people we see in Canada in many anti-Israel demonstrations. Theirs is often the image published in the media of anti-Israel demonstrations, as they are so visibly Jewish.

Basically, they believe that there can be no Jewish State before the coming of the Messiah and that any attempt to establish such a state beforehand contravenes God's will, and is therefore sacrilegious. They are a very controversial group, most exemplified by their links with Iranian president Mahmoud Ahmadinejad.

The video of the leaders of *Naturei Karta* meeting with and honouring Ahmadinejad[132] quickly went viral on the internet in every Jewish community in the world, and succeeded in marginalizing them even more than they already were.

Extreme left anti-Zionism, even if it is also marginal, attracts attention because of its willingness to ally itself with groups whose values are the polar opposite of the Left's own principles. They are willing to close their eyes to this fact as their hate – yes, hate – for Israel consumes them more than defending the values they claim to hold dear.

In Canada, the group representing this ideology is *Independent Jewish Voices (IJV)*. The main leader of IJV is an Ottawa woman by the name of Diana Ralph, whose political opinions are very peculiar.

I myself have met Diana Ralph a few times (the Ottawa/ Gatineau Jewish community is small) and I can indeed confirm her radical outlook.

In an article titled *"Islamophobia and the 'war on terror': The continuing pretext for imperial conquest"* for the book *The Hidden History of 9-11*, Ralph says that the September 11, 2001 attacks on New York and Washington were not carried out by al-Qaeda, but by American and Israeli conservatives in order to implement "a secret, strategic plan to position the U.S. as a permanent unilateral super-power poised to seize control of Eurasia, and thereby the entire world."

Of course, Israel is the one pulling the strings.

But that's not all. The Federal Court of Canada, not once but twice, commented unfavourably on Diana Ralph and her politics in the case of Almrei[133] when she volunteered to be a surety for the alleged terrorist. The Court noted her complete lack of objectivity, her judgment clouded by politics and her lack of respect for the court. Justice Lemieux stated notably:

[90]   As mentioned, Doctor Ralph testified before Justice

Layden-Stevenson who held "I am not satisfied that Doctor Ralph is an acceptable or appropriate surety in the circumstances of this matter. I am sure that Doctor Ralph means well and has Mr. Almrei's interests at heart. However, she is completely lacking in objectivity." (See paragraph 421).

[91] At paragraph 424, Justice Layden-Stevenson further held "I am not at all satisfied that Doctor Ralph possesses the requisite objectivity or necessary impartiality to stand as the primary supervising surety. She has had no experience with Mr. Almrei except when he was in a highly-regulated and controlled environment...I find Doctor Ralph's judgment to be clouded by her political beliefs. I am not convinced that she appreciates the onerous task that she has offered to assume. Moreover, Justice Layden-Stevenson held she was not confident that Doctor Ralph exhibited respect for the Court, as an institution, given her comments on the hearing of the application before her (June 28, 2005, transcript page 273).

[92] (…) He failed to convince me that I should come to a different view of Doctor Ralph than the one expressed by my colleague (…).

More recently, in a meeting of the left-wing, pro-peace movement Peace Now, held in 2009 at the Reform synagogue Temple Israel in Ottawa (in which I participated), Ralph tried to distribute a text extolling the virtues of Iran's president Mahmoud Ahmadinejad! This so angered the genuine peace activists present that they forbid the distribution of Ralph's text and clearly dissociated themselves from her outrageous and extreme views.

The ironic and sad thing is that if Ralph's allies were ever in power, she, as an openly lesbian woman, would be one of their first victims.

Another star of this movement is Judy Rebick, well known in extreme Left circles of English Canada. Rebick uses her Jewish origins to bash Israel. In fact, she even said in IJV's annual general assembly in Ottawa on June 12, 2009, that she had long ago broken with the Jewish community and that she self-identified as Jewish only when it served her political objectives: in other words, when she can use her Jewish origins to delegitimize, demonize, and attack Israel.

IJV is against the very existence of the only Jewish state in the world. IJV opposes the two-state solution. IJV supports *Israel Apartheid Week* on Canadian campuses. IJV supports the Boycott, Divestment and Sanctions (BDS) campaign against Israel (and only against Israel). IJV is aligned with extremist groups like the Canadian Arab Federation and Tadamon. IJV marched in demonstrations alongside activists yelling "Jews are our dogs".

Why do these Jewish supporters of minority, womens, and gay rights ally themselves with people who are totally opposed to these values, in order to demonize the Middle East's only democracy?

I have been considering this for some time now and I am not sure I know the answer.

Could it be because Israel is a liberal democracy, with a market economy, and an ally of the U.S., whereas this far Left is anti-globalization, anti-capitalist, and anti-American?

Not to be forgotten is that at the birth of Marxism, socialism, communism and other forms of radical left-wing political movements, far-left Jews were already of the view that Zionism (or other forms of Jewish particularism) contradicted the idea that Jews should form a sort of core group to lead the revolution to eliminate all forms of national or ethnic distinction. The same phenomenon exists today. Jewish proponents of this philosophy, who claim their form of Judaism is the purest, in fact ultimately negate their own Judaism. This is the subject of an excellent book "The Finkler Question" by Howard Jacobson.

But there is probably more at play here.

British (and non-Jewish) author Robin Sheppard came to the following explanation, which makes sense to me:

> *This also sheds different light on the status of that small but vocal group of secular Jews in the Diaspora who consider themselves anti-Zionist and who therefore oppose the existence of the Jewish State. Since their secularism blocks their route to a sustainable Jewish identity through immersion in the religion and their anti-Zionism blocks their route to a sustainable Jewish identity via a deep-seated identity with Israel, they are effectively positing for themselves a state of long-term conversion away from Judaism.*
>
> *Anti-Zionist Jews react to charges of this kind with a rejectionism bordering on bitterness. In a sense this is unsurprising. They are being presented with an edifice of argumentation to which there are no serious responses and which they are likely to take personally. They are therefore reduced to sophistry and denial centring on extremely vague and unconvincing definition of Judaism – Judaism as a set of 'non-essential' political-philosophical ideals, for example – whose weakness they themselves must be only too well aware of. (...)*
>
> *They may or may not be self-hating Jews but they are certainly self-negating Jews. They have adopted a maxim which, if adopted by all Jews, would negate absolutely the possibility of Jewish identity itself as a long-term constituent of the human race (with the exception, I repeat, of ultra-religious, closed communities). The secular, anti-Zionist Jew is a self-negating Jew because he and she lacks*

the ability to project a meaningful Jewish identity into the future.[134]

French intellectual Pierre-André Taguieff goes in the same direction:

Those 'alterjews', who systematically take the side of the Jews' enemies, can they still be considered Jewish? Beside the fluke of their birth, in what way are they Jewish? Can we apply to them the old Talmudic formula according to which 'the Jew who has sinned stays Jewish'? How can one tolerate the fact that they self-identify as Jews only to attack the Jews (the 'Jewish Jews'). Deutscher's 'non-Jewish Jew' was at once inside and outside (like Heine or Freud). The contemporary 'alterjew' is inside only to be against.[135]

All this to say that even if there are big differences of opinion in the Diaspora and in Israel regarding Israel's future, or Israel's relationship with its Palestinian neighbours, or what kind of society Israel should be, there is a vast, immense consensus about the right of the Jewish people to have an independent state in its ancestral land in the Middle East. Anybody who says that he is anti-Zionist, even if he professes to be Jewish, cannot be considered anything other than a representative of a very marginal group in the Jewish world.

It is ironic to note that, in anti-Israel environments, anti-Israel Jews are considered "courageous", like some kind of a hero. They run no risk whatsoever when they state their misguided opinion. One wonders: if there is no risk, how can they be considered courageous?

18
The Red-Green Alliance[136]

Truly courageous people are those who brave real danger - sometimes death - to denounce radical Islamists.

The question of the growing connections between radical Islamism and a certain element of the Left is an important one.[137] This is what I mean by the red (hard Left) - green (Islamism) alliance.

These connections have been denounced by Canadian Muslim moderates,[138] notably during a press conference in Montreal on October 2, 2008.[139] Three truly courageous Muslims (against whom *fatwas* have been pronounced), Dr. Salim Mansur, author Tarek Fatah, and intercultural specialist Raheel Raza, strongly denounced the Islamist threat in Canada and the wilful blindness of some politicians (mainly on the left side of the spectrum according to them) who try, consciously or unconsciously, to get closer to some of its spokespersons and leaders.

They called for vigilance against attempts at infiltration by these groups, whose values are the polar opposites of Canada's - whether on minority rights, gay rights, or the status of women.

How can we explain the growing relationship between this hard left and Islamists?

I think the main reason is that this Left subscribes to the old maxim 'the enemy of my enemy is my friend'. Indeed, these two movements are united by a certain hatred for the West and its two highest-profile standard-bearers, the U.S. and Israel.[140]

A good example of this phenomena is MNA Amir Khadir, the lone representative from Québec Solidaire in Quebec's National Assembly, who shows a remarkable lack of judgment in the positions he adopts. On August 15, 2006 (a few days after the notorious Montreal demonstration in which Hezbollah flags were flown), another demonstration took place in front of a Montreal hotel where a Jewish community activity was taking place. During this demonstration, once again Hezbollah flags were flown. Khadir who attended did not in any way dissociate himself from the display of terrorist symbols.

It is the same Khadir who, on June 7, 2006, in an interview with *La Presse* and in an open letter to this same paper[141] on December 14, 2001, gave the impression that the Americans might have been behind the September 11 attacks on New York and Washington. And who, on May 10, 2011, was the only member of the Quebec National Assembly to vote against a multipartisan (Liberal Party, Parti Québécois, Action Démocratique du Québec) motion[142] to mark Bin Laden's death.[143]

Khadir's radicalism is evident in other instances. On June 1st, 2010, following the Gaza flotilla incident, Khadir speaking in the House[144] implicitly accused the pro-Israel lobby of muzzling the Quebec government. He also held a press conference[145] during which he repeated his accusations but went further, accusing Israel's friends in Quebec of being directed by Israel's right-wing and Israel's army. Those are very grave, and patently false, charges.

It is one thing to express disagreement with the Israeli government or Israel's friends in Quebec. It is not only legitimate, it is healthy in a democracy. But that is not what Khadir did.

What Khadir effectively said is that some citizens of Quebec do not have the right to make representations to their elected officials as, when they do, he accuses them of muzzling the government, a very serious accusation. Moreover, he suggests that they do so on behalf of an army and political movement of a foreign state. This is Khadir's version of the age-old canard of the Jews' dual loyalty, and the dark Jewish conspiracy to control governments around the world.

With his grave and unfounded accusations, Khadir stigmatized the entire Quebec Jewish community in Quebec's very own parliament.

Khadir showed his sinister political philosophy and his bad faith in December 2010, after endorsing a boycott of the family-owned Montreal shoe store *Le Marcheur* simply because it sells shoes made in Israel. In a letter to well-known columnist and blogger Jean-François Lisée (published on Lisée's blog),[146] Khadir tried to get out of this controversy but succeeded only in digging himself in further.

It is worth analyzing.

Khadir argued that Québec Solidaire did not have a position on either Hamas or Hezbollah as the party "had not been called to comment" (since when does a party need to be asked to take a position in order to do so?). Going even further, Khadir stated, without any proof, that "Hezbollah is without doubt less fanatical than Hamas or the Ahmadinejad government in Iran". That argument fails to take into consideration that not only is Hezbollah an Islamist, radical, extremist and terror-exporting organization, it is also an Iranian puppet and not an autonomous Lebanese actor. It is absolutely ridiculous to attempt to distance Hezbollah from its Iranian masters.

Khadir then confirmed that his own problem with Iran is with its current president, and not with the Islamist Iranian regime. This ignores the fact that the repression of women, gays, and democratic forces did not start with Ahmadinejad's arrival to power in August 2005, but rather with the coming into existence of the Ayatollahs' regime in 1979.

Khadir then turned truth on its head, mentioning "Israeli threats of nuclear strikes" against Iran. Never, ever, ever has Israel threatened Iran with nuclear strikes. To the contrary, it is Iran that, on many occasions, has threatened to wipe Israel off the face of the earth.

Khadir continues by stating that Hezbollah and Hamas "have the right to resist oppression", which I suggest is a euphemism for supporting terror.

This is the real Amir Khadir, Quebec's most popular politician. *La Presse*'s Lysiane Gagnon was indeed right to call him fanatical.[147]

At the end of July 2006, a Québec Solidaire leader in Quebec City Ginette Lewis, declared her support for Hezbollah.[148] She cheered Hezbollah and defended its launching of missiles on Israeli civilian population centres. Finally, she saw some "signs of hope" in the intensification of the fighting.[149]

On Friday March 7, 2008, a coalition of left wing organizations,[150] including unions, held a press conference on the situation in Gaza. After the usual condemnations of Israel, the press release then published,[151] failed to mention either the rockets being fired from Gaza on Israeli cities and communities, or the horrible and deliberate attack against a Jerusalem school that killed eight young men (age 15 to 26) and injured a dozen more only the day prior!

As *La Presse* editorialist Mario Roy summarized: "We will then note the extent to which the cause of the Palestinians, who have succeeded the workers in the martyrdom of the standard Left, has attained control of everything that moves in Western societies."[152]

These are but a few examples of a certain part of the Left's recklessness, which is unfortunately found not only in Quebec but in every Western society.[153]

19
Anti-Semitism in Quebec

As French President Nicolas Sarkozy said about his own country,[154] one cannot say that Quebec is anti-Semitic even if, unfortunately, there is some anti-Semitism in Quebec. This is usually what I answer when I am asked about the issue.

Quebec is neither the racist hell that its detractors say it is, nor is it a paradise of brotherly love that some in Quebec might attempt to portray, in a vulgar attempt at propaganda.

From the "You, little Jew" ("*mon petit Juif!*") that my grandmother used when I was unruly, to the call to kill Jews heard in the streets of Montreal during a recent anti-Israel demonstration,[155] Quebec is not exempt from anti-Semitism.

I say it without any hesitation: the issue of anti-Semitism has been and still is a very delicate subject to tackle for any author. It certainly has been difficult for me. Professor Gérald Bouchard, an expert on the issue, says about this difficulty:

> *We believe there exists a reticence among French Canadians to recognize and analyze anti-Semitic expressions, the traces of which may be found in their history. We see it by the rarity of studies and historical publications on the subject. We see it also by the polemical and defensive quality of public interventions on the subject. (...) It is as if, for some, the French Canadian past is simply exempt from any anti-Semitism, which would make the French Canadians the only Western society to claim such privilege. What are the*

reasons for this reticence, for this resistance? What are the collective costs attached to this? The issues? What advantages would there be to surmounting this difficulty?

To which he partly answers:

One is permitted to see that the main (if not the only) reason for this reticence by French Canadians to study the history of their own anti-Semitism without after-thought is the (well-founded) fear that the results of their own self-criticism would be used against them, that they would be used mainly to portray them once again in an offensive and biased manner.[156]

I agree with Professor Bouchard. But I also believe that the issue of anti-Semitism in Quebec must be tackled head on.

Any form of anti-Semitism in Quebec hurts me doubly: as a Jew and as a Quebecker. I do not want to see fellow Quebec citizens infected by the virus of racism and anti-Semitism. Nor can I accept that this bile be hurled at my children, my wife, and myself.

Jack Jedwab, of the Association for Canadian Studies, tried to evaluate Quebeckers' perception of Jews. Some of the results he found are troubling. In Quebec, French Quebeckers form the group that is best perceived, followed by anglophones, then immigrants, then First Nations, and then Jews. Six and a half percent of Quebeckers answered that they detest Jews.[157] Not an insignificant number.

Another study,[158] published by the same organization in November 2010, found that only 34 percent of French-speaking Canadians were of the opinion that Jews have the same values as their own, compared to 73 percent of English-speaking Canadians.

Like that of every Western society, Quebec's history exhibits some anti-Semitism.

Broadly speaking, one can say that in Quebec, between the Patriots' Rebellion (1837-1838) and Vatican II, "the prevailing idea of the era was that Jews, as they had not been exposed to Christianity's light, should not be introduced into the heart of the institutions and social spheres reserved to French Canadians, for fear that they would threaten their ethnic coherence and ideological purity."[159]

This led Professor Gary Caldwell to say:

> *One can say without any doubt that Quebec society, in a moment of its history, adopted, nourished and expressed a clearly defined anti-Semitic ideology. Religious civil authorities subscribed to it and a part of the francophone intelligentsia embraced it with enthusiasm.*[160]

Following Vatican II, and Quebec's Quiet Revolution, which led to a withdrawal of the Catholic Church from sectors of Quebec society it used to occupy, "Jews (...) ceased to be considered potential converts or as marginal elements in an identity construct based on faith and took on more or less the same attributes of citizenship as the demographic majority."[161]

Unfortunately, anti-Semitism did not disappear from the Quebec scene in the 1960's. Let us consider a few recent illustrations of this unfortunate phenomenon.

Vigile: an electronic rag

When I was an MP, I used to regularly consult Vigile.net, a website whose goal is to serve as an electronic exchange place for sovereignists.[162] It is important to note that it does not have any institutional relationship with either the Parti Québécois or the Bloc Québécois. I even wrote for them while I was sitting in Parliament. It was a quick and easy way to see the latest ideas about independence and to read texts by both scholars and everyday sovereignists, to whom newspaper pages were rarely open.

The first time I was the subject of a Vigile column on an issue other than sovereignty, was when I was attacked by Bloc candidate (now MP) Maria Mourani. I was flabbergasted that an unknown candidate would attack a fellow candidate of the same party. Of course, the issue she attacked me on was the situation in the Middle East.

But given the views of those behind Vigile, Mourani's vicious charge was in good company. The website is run by Bernard Frappier, who has an anti-Israel obsession which frequently borders on anti-Semitism, not to mention a kind of primitive anti-Americanism - the kind held by a first-year Marxist philosophy college student who has not quite digested his material.

Neither would Frappier hesitate to quote shady characters like Alain Soral, a French ex-communist who is now at the extreme right of the French political spectrum with Le Pen's Front National. Frappier is so convinced of the Jewish conspiracy to control the world that he created two sections on his site: "Zionist colony - Canada"[163] and "Zionist colony - Quebec."[164]

Old anti-Semitic themes of conspiracy and money are constantly recycled. For example, on January 30, 2008, an editorial comment appeared:

> *We must boycott Israel, starting with the withdrawal of the Montreal public transit authority from a contract with an Israeli company, which we don't know whether it will protect us from terrorist attacks or if it will prepare them itself...* [165]

In other words, according to him, Israel may very well be behind terrorist attacks here, in Canada.

Still on January 30, 2008, another columnist Ivan Parent wrote: "I hope there will be a concert of nations to denounce Israel's exactions, unless it is part of another conspiracy."[166]

The conspiracy again! Parent then goes on, accusing Israelis of being Nazis: "Isn't it sad to see the Jews of Israel lower themselves to the level of their former torturers? I no longer want to hear even one of them complaining about the Shoah (Holocaust), they are doing the same thing."

It is so easy to delegitimize the State of Israel when one accuses it of acting like Nazi Germany! Indeed, for Parent, Israel is committing a genocide. At least Parent does not hide that he is racist against Jews (i.e. anti-Semitic): "I am not racist but when I see what is going on, even if I try to restrain myself, it is an attractive option for me."[167]

Parent regularly writes this kind of article. In a more recent anti-Semitic rant[168] worthy of Germany's 1930's press tendency to see Jewish conspiracies everywhere, Parent wrote: "Jews are allowed every exaction, every horror, every takeover in the societies in which they live and there is nothing we can say because, if we do, we are anti-Semites, Nazi ghosts (...) They are powerful, they control political parties and, above all, international banks."

In another piece, he wrote: "[b]y hypocritical detours, Jews shamelessly exploit, vampirize the country in which they live and it is not surprising that they are hated everywhere they have lived". In yet another entry, he wrote: "the very history of the Hebrews, the Jews' and later the Israelis' ancestors is one of massacres, of killings, of genocides under Yahweh's divine inspiration. The Bible is filled with these violent acts. They simply perpetuate their own history."[169]

On January 6, 2011, the same Parent wrote a piece which sounded eerily like the infamous treatise created by anti-Semitic Czarist authorities, The Protocols of the Elders of

Zion, to which he actually makes a reference without naming it:

> We all know that the Jewish lobbies are very powerful and that, in fact, through international banks, they control almost every country. They change interest rates as they want, and that is why the Euro zone is in so much trouble. These are corrupt practices cooked up by banks. We saw it very briefly in the case of Greece. The Jewish-American bank of Goldman-Sachs has been at the root of embezzlement of funds with the complicity of high-ranking Greek officials. We saw it in the newspapers but, strangely, it quickly disappeared. There will always be, everywhere, accomplices bought at a high price. Here in Quebec, Charest is an obvious example. One after another, States are strangled in order to manipulate them. We must also destroy the social benefits in order to, they say, pay the debt and, at the point we are at, it is next to impossible for anyone to pay those debts incurred mostly for military expenses. It is not very difficult to see why there are always wars on the planet. The principle was first outlined in a document (that I cannot name here as I would be censored), an anti-Semitic forgery they say, but one that daily becomes reality and was later adopted by Milton Friedman of the school of Chicago. In brief: cut the funds in order to destroy and to control.[170]

Obviously, the situation is often worse in moments of crisis. For example, during the conflict in Lebanon in the summer of 2006, the line was crossed and anti-Semitism manifested itself.

For example, on July 28, 2006, I was sick when I read the text of well-known author Victor-Lévy Beaulieu on Vigile.

Beaulieu is a very talented writer. This is despite the fact that he is not an example of intellectual coherence, as a sovereignist who supported the Parti Québécois, then the Action Démocratique du Québec before running as a candidate for the hard-line Parti Indépendantiste for a short time, and then running as an independent. Unfortunately, alongside his reputation as a folkloric political loose cannon, Beaulieu has put his skills as an author to writing a column that can only be described as hateful.

Entitled "Israel, the West and the Pig", Beaulieu harshly attacks the Jewish people:

> *The Jews, as God's sole chosen people, have always put the Law above everything else and considered justice as a weakening corruption of it. There has thus never been justice in the Kingdom of Judea and there is not now, two thousand years later, in the State of Israel.*
>
> *(…)*
>
> *Evoking their right to exist as God's sole chosen people, and as told in the Old Testament, Jews have always preferred warmongering to diplomacy, a state of war to a state of peace. The Ark of Alliance is related only to their sole god, which no doubt explains that during its entire existence, the Kingdom of Judea never had as a friend or as an ally any other nation but itself. Israel is simply acting like the Kingdom of Judea: what is not me is my enemy and I must destroy it completely. This is the law, this is my right. Thus the State of Israel acts based on this philosophy. It does not act out of love for itself but out of hatred of others. Having become a master in the art of playing the victim, this state only loves when it is a victim. And how good it is then! The Old Testament is full of preventive battles against the supposed enemies of Judea: from selective assassination to total war, from genocide to absolute extermination, the weapons of Jewish law do not know proportion; they even allow incest so that Jewish mothers can replace their missing soldiers with impunity for the quasi-eternal battlefields/mass graves.*

Rereading the Old Testament, we realize that the State of Israel is simply the continuation, in philosophy and in action, of the Kingdom of Judea. The only difference is that the West, because of a deep and absurd feeling of guilt, provided Israel with the murderous weapons with which Israel can now impose its own notion of law, the one symbolised by its Ark of Alliance with God alone, at the expense of the concept of justice. What are those wars against Palestine and Lebanon if not wars of extermination, if not odious genocides that should shame us, Westerners; remaining silent is to consent, is to accept that a totalitarian state, disguised as a democracy, distorts the law by taking possession of it, for itself alone?

(…)

Why don't we do anything with this warmongering, hateful and totalitarian, if not Hitlerian, Israel?

A disgusting text if ever I have read one.

But that's not all. On August 10, 2006, a man by the name of André Vincent published an article titled "Mister Jew"[171] which is essentially a call to murder.

After having related the story of a travelling salesman from his youth, Vincent explains: "It is my memory of Mister Jew and it is because of him, that it took me so long to come to detest him."

And then:

In Iraq, I vomited enormously but now… in Lebanon, it crosses all the lines. It does not stop: and it fucking hurts all the time. And the more it hurts, the more my hate for mister Jew and his buddy the cowboy grows, to the point I don't even recognize myself.

I never would have thought that this kind of thing could one day happen to me. I don't want this odour of death, I don't like this odour of mass grave; it is as if my heart had bad breath, there is even some temptation to kill mister Jew[172] and I am certain that if one of my grandsons had been killed in Lebanon or Palestine, I would spend the rest of my days trying to blow up mister Jews everywhere in the world, and even Mister Jew's children so that he hurts as I am hurting.

Vigile also published a text about Canadian fascist leader Adrien Arcand (also known as "the Canadian Fuehrer"), approving at least implicitly his anti-Semitism.[173]

Somebody writing under the pseudonym of Gébé Tremblay left a comment saying that Nazi Germany did not start World War II but the Jews did[174], while a regular contributor by the name of Robert Barberis-Gervais did not hesitate to say that the "Jewish lobby", through its control of the banks, controls Quebec.[175]

On December 28, 2010, a fascistic manifest[176] was published on Vigile by Jean-Roch Villemaire, on behalf of the 'Quebec Revolutionary Nationalist Movement.' The manifest proposed: "the closing of the borders to mass immigration", to suspend the right of landing, the right to citizenship based on immigration (or *jus soli*) and replace it with the right of descendancy (*jus sanguinis*), and access to citizenship based on bloodlines: "nationality is a heritage closely connected to the ethnic origin specific to every people". And, of course, the Movement is "anti-Zionist, it will break the backbone of the Zionist ideology and of its political avatars to give power back to the people of Quebec."

Unfortunately, there are many other examples that could be provided.

That being said, when the Montreal daily newspaper *La Presse* published an article in March 2011[177] detailing some of the unacceptable anti-Semitic articles found on Vigile, the Parti Québécois, as well as some of its high profile MNAs, including Louise Beaudoin[178], Bernard Drainville, and Agnès Maltais, immediately distanced themselves from the website.

One may not agree with the Parti Québécois and its goal of making Quebec an independent country, but there is no question that the party founded by René Lévesque (himself a well-known opponent of anti-Semitism) is an accepting and tolerant party.

Vigile certainly cannot claim to speak on behalf of the sovereignty movement.

Talkback

Media outlets have bloggers or use their journalists to blog. Readers are invited to comment in order to foster a more interactive relationship between writer and readers, as well as between the readers themselves. But as there is no requirement to identify oneself when commenting on-line, there are frequently extreme viewpoints expressed.

Let me be clear. I do not question the idea of talkback (or comment boards), nor do I blame the bloggers for the comments left on their sites by readers. I would however note, that many comments made online in the form of "feedback" cross the line into racism and anti-Semitism.

For example, Richard Martineau's views on reasonable accommodation are well known. I regularly consult his blog.

One may agree or disagree with Martineau, but despite his often provocative stance, he at least causes one to think in unconventional ways.

On February 11, 2010, he posted two entries on the topic of

illegal Jewish schools. A reader by the alias of "xxxxxxxxx yyyyyyyyyyyy" (such a courageous person...) wrote: "If you knew who fills the Liberal Party's coffers, you wouldn't wonder" and then, "[E]verything is allowed for the members of the Chosen People."

Then Martial Chehri wrote: "We should leave the Muslims alone – they ask openly for some accommodations – and pay more attention to the Jews who as usual work in secret – oh, yes, I forget, they are untouchable as they are God's chosen (...)."

This is followed by Michel Germain, who goes further: "The great Jewish theory... 'with money, we can buy everything, in particular the Liberal party'...it's unbelievable all the money they put out but what is amazing is that they get double their investment...".

I only used Martineau's blog as an example and because I am familiar with it. This type of comment is frequently found on *La Presse*'s Richard Hêtu's blog (Hêtu seems sometimes to be more interested in Middle East politics – which he obviously has not mastered – than in American politics and society, which he is supposed to cover) and on Radio-Canada's blog.

As more and more people, in particular young people, get their information from the web, it is important to realize that these kinds of comments, especially if they are repetitive, will necessarily have an impact on a lot of people.

The Bouchard-Taylor Commission[179]

The Bouchard-Taylor Commission, created to study the issue of reasonable accommodations for minority groups, held hearings all around Quebec which were broadcast live on Quebec TV. Wherever the Commission went, it drew a great deal of interest. Many intelligent comments were made. Many well-written briefs and studies were tabled. But many stupid things were also said.

Nonetheless, Quebec is the first high immigration Western society to collectively reflect on and study the important consequences of massive migration. This examination is obviously not over, but the discussions are now more open in Quebec than elsewhere. One objective should be to ensure that they are well directed and result in better ideas for the future.

The reason I want to address the Bouchard-Taylor Commission here is that more than once during its hearings, comments were made regarding the false report that the Jews want to impose a "kosher tax" on everyone.

On Friday May 11, 2007, the TVA TV network, in its flagship public affairs show JE (for which my sister was once the anchorwoman) broadcast a report[180] about the number of kosher products on the shelves of our grocery stores. According to this report, Quebec consumers were paying the cost of the kosher certification, without their knowledge and without wanting it. Of course these allegations feed the myth of a Jewish minority forcing the majority to conform to its religious rules.

The report failed entirely to state the business reasons that lead companies to obtain the kosher certification.

What is kosher food? Contrary to what was being said at the time, it has nothing to do with rabbis blessing the food. 'Kosher' in Hebrew means 'proper' or 'fit to be eaten'. Collectively, the rules regarding food are called *kashrut* and come from the Jewish Bible (generally called the 'Old Testament' by the Christian world) and the Talmud (a written transcription of the Jewish oral tradition).

To be considered kosher, the food product must be selected, combined and prepared according to well defined laws.

Jewish law defines very clearly the food that can be certified kosher. Broadly, the laws permit:

- Produce that is consumed in its natural state, like fruits and vegetables;
- Meat coming from cloven hoofed, cud-chewing mammals (like cows) and slaughtered according to specific rules that minimize pain suffered by the animal;
- Poultry raised and slaughtered according to the same rules;
- Fish with both fins and scales (hence shellfish are not kosher).

The mixing of milk products and meat is also forbidden (both in the preparation and the consumption of food), even if each is, in and of itself, kosher. As well, utensils and dishes can only serve for kosher food and then only either milk or meat.

To respect the rules of *kashrut* thus means to create an entire environment that is exclusively kosher. It also requires independent supervision of the space to ensure the rules are respected.

Therefore, for manufactured products to be kosher, they must be certified. For the consumers, the kosher certification is a guarantee of control of the produce and its manufacture.

Kosher meat that is consumed by observant Jews comes from kosher slaughterhouses and is sold exclusively in clearly identified kosher sections. The result is that kosher certification for meat is never applied to the public at large.

In the case of manufactured food, it will only be kosher if it has been produced under strict control, guaranteeing that all the rules have been followed. It is this oversight that may result in an extremely minor increase in cost for these kosher products.

The actual cost to the consumer is generally minuscule. In 1975 the cost per item for obtaining kosher certification was estimated by The New York Times as being 6.5 millionths (0.0000065) of a cent per item for a typical product.[181]

According to *La Presse*,

[t]he effect on the price is minimal as those products are mass produced. In the Métro grocery chain, 75% of the products are kosher. Métro's suppliers do not bill higher for this certification, said its spokeswoman Marie-Claude Bacon (yes, that really is her name!). To obtain the certification, companies must follow very strict rules and put aside certain ingredients. A minority of products are more expensive and those are not products usually bought by the mainstream public. Those are mainly kosher meats which are usually sold in specialized meat stores and in a few regular stores but then, it is always clearly marked.[182]

In Quebec, only 30,000 Jews (35% of the Jewish community), eat kosher food. It is a tiny market,[183] which does not, in and of itself, explain the number of kosher products in our grocery stores.

In the U.S., our main export market, the market for kosher food is estimated to be 10 billion dollars. Moreover, according to a study conducted by Kosherfest, the American kosher market has an annual growth rate of 10-15 percent.

Still in the U.S., only 14 percent of consumers who regularly buy kosher products do so for reasons of following Jewish law. The others buy kosher for other reasons: some are vegetarian, some are allergic to milk products or to seafood, some are Muslims who believe that a kosher product is automatically *hallal* (i.e. meets Muslim dietary laws), and some are simply people who believe that kosher products are cleaner or safer than non-kosher products.[184]

Numbers are different in Quebec. Here, only 30 percent of kosher product consumers are Jewish. The other 70 percent is divided between Muslims, environmentalists, and the general population. To demonstrate its potential as a growth market, 70 percent of those who purchase kosher products are between 18 and 35 years old. Only 21 percent of those who buy kosher, do so for religious reasons and they cite the main reason for their choice as the quality of the products and the way they are prepared.

In other words, a majority of kosher product consumers are not religious, but rather buy for the quality of the label. As absolutely nothing forces a company or an industry to adopt kosher certification, the explanation must be that it does so in order to develop its consumer base. Businesspeople simply show good business sense in anticipating or joining this trend in order to conquer market share, mainly in the U.S.

There is no Jewish conspiracy to impose a kosher tax on anybody.[185]

Anti-Zionism and Anti-Semitism[186]

We often hear anti-Zionists say that they are not anti-Semitic. But at the same time, they refuse to accord the Jewish people the same right to self-determination that they recognize for every other nation on the planet. Denying only one people their right to self-determination is racism. To deny the Jewish people their right to self-determination is anti-Semitism.[187] One can easily postulate that anti-Zionism is in fact, a form of racism.

The European Union also makes the connection between anti-Zionism and anti-Semitism. In 2004, the European Monitoring Centre for Racism and Xenophobia, an E.U. organization that was replaced in 2007 by the European Union Agency for Fundamental Rights, published a working definition of anti-Semitism and gave examples of anti-Semitic attitudes.[188]

Their working definition is as follows: "Anti-Semitism is a

certain perception of Jews, which may be expressed as hatred toward Jews. Rhetorical and physical manifestations of anti-Semitism are directed toward Jewish or non-Jewish individuals and/or their property, toward Jewish community institutions and religious facilities."

The Monitoring Centre goes on to say:

> *Examples of the ways in which anti-Semitism manifests itself with regard to the State of Israel taking into account the overall context could include:*
>
> *Denying the Jewish people their right to self-determination, e.g., by claiming that the existence of a State of Israel is a racist endeavour.*
>
> *Applying double standards by requiring of it a behaviour not expected or demanded of any other democratic nation.*
>
> *Using the symbols and images associated with classic anti-Semitism (e.g., claims of Jews killing Jesus or blood libel) to characterize Israel or Israelis.*
>
> *Drawing comparisons of contemporary Israeli policy to that of the Nazis.*
>
> *Holding Jews collectively responsible for actions of the State of Israel.*
>
> *However, criticism of Israel similar to that levelled against any other country cannot be regarded as anti-Semitic.*

Using this official European definition of anti-Semitism, it is easy to demonstrate that accusing Israel of being an apartheid state ("by claiming that the existence of a State of Israel is a racist endeavour") is anti-Semitic.

The connection between anti-Zionism and anti-Semitism

was described by Antoine Spire, a well-known professor and journalist in France who was then an important member of the French League of Human Rights (*Ligue des Droits de l'Homme*), as follows:

> *Today, anti-Zionism, even if it does not intend to be anti-Semitic, does not target only the oppressive Israeli policy against the Palestinians, but targets also Israel and its connection with its supporters in the Diaspora, who are accused without always checking first, of unconditional support (towards Israel); this anti-Zionism objects to the very existence of a Jewish State. This is where one can make the connection between anti-Zionism and anti-Semitism: from anti-Zionism to the wish of seeing the Jewish State disappear, there is just a small step, and from seeing the Jewish State disappear to hatred towards those who actively support Israel's right to exist, it's only one little step further.*[189]

I say this clearly and openly: anti-Zionism is a form of hatred, a hatred that leads to a desire to obliterate an entire country. Anti-Zionism means wanting the State of Israel to cease to exist - to disappear. And yet, incredibly, this hatred exists in Canada, and throughout the Western world (not to mention the Muslim world). I often wonder how a person promoting the disappearance of the U.K., Russia, or Canada would be treated.

Another connection between anti-Zionism and anti-Semitism? The Coalition for Justice and Peace in Palestine (*Coalition pour la Justice et la Paix en Palestine*), regrouping the unions CSQ and CSN, Alternatives, and Québec Solidaire, sat on the organizing committee of the BDS Conference[190] (i.e. boycott, divestment and sanctions against Israel[191]) which took place in Montreal, from October 22 - 24, 2010.[192]

Among the speakers invited to this conference was Bongani Masuku, who was found guilty of anti-Semitism by the South

African Human Rights Commission.

Indeed, on September 28, 2009, the South African Human Rights Commission held[193] that "the comments and statements made are of an extreme nature that advocate and imply that the Jewish and Israeli community are to be despised, scorned, and ridiculed and thus subjecting them to ill-treatment on the basis of their religious affiliation."

Moreover, the Commission held that Masaku "surely intended to incite violence and hatred" and his declarations are "intimidating and threatening". The Commission also held that Masuku's comments were "inciting violence based on religion" and that they were "offensive and unpalatable to society."

It is only when that very embarrassing information started to circulate on the internet,[194] some 11 days before the conference, that Masuku's name suddenly disappeared from the conference's website.

Try as I might, I cannot understand how important unions and a political party sitting in Quebec's National Assembly can participate in such events and associate themselves with such racist personalities.[195]

Ironically, while these elements of the Quebec Left were trying to organize a BDS campaign against Israel, Palestinian unions were ratifying a cooperation agreement with their Israeli equivalents on workers' rights in August 2008.[196]

The BDS movement has no credibility left. One illustration of this: in the fall of 2010, no less than 38 Nobel Prize laureates published a statement[197] condemning the attempts to impose BDS against Israeli academics, Israeli academic institutions, and institutes of research and training having affiliations in Israel. They state that BDS is "antithetical to principles of academic and scientific freedom, antithetical to principles of

---

freedom of expression and inquiry, and may well constitute discrimination by virtue of national origin."

Moreover, according to these prestigious Nobel prize winners, instead of favouring peace, BDS efforts are counter-productive and "serve as incubators for polemics, propaganda, incitement and further misunderstanding and mistrust."

On November 16, 2010, the director of the Gaza-based United Nations Relief and Works Agency for Palestine Refugees in the Near East (UNRWA) since 2006, John Ging, also came out as opposing BDS.[198]

On January 18, 2011, in a letter to Quebec Jewish Congress president Adam Atlas, Parti Québécois Leader Pauline Marois clearly stated her opposition to any form of boycott against Israel. She went even further by stating that: "to the contrary, we are proud to remind people that it is a Parti Québécois government that initiated, in 1997, the ratification of the first Agreement of cooperation in the matters of culture, science and technology with the State of Israel."

On January 20, 2011, Bloc Québécois leader Gilles Duceppe, also in a letter to Atlas, declared his own opposition to the boycott.[199]

And on February 9, 2011, every member of Quebec's National Assembly (except of course Amir Khadir), supported a motion in favour of the Le Marcheur store in Montreal and reiterated their support for the 1997 Quebec-Israel agreement.[200]

French socialist leader Martine Aubry similarly stated in November 2010: "I believe that those who advocate boycott are fighting the wrong fight: instead of bringing peace, they bring intolerance, they bring hate. When one wants a road to peace, one does not begin in that way."[201]

I deeply wish Québec Solidaire co-leaders Françoise David

and Amir Khadir would listen to those eminent personalities, instead of wasting their time and talent trying to radicalize Quebec society on issues relating to the Middle East. Khadir, who seems to lose all perspective whenever the Middle East is discussed, should in particular constrain himself, as one of his close associates suggested.[202]

There is an easy way to distinguish between legitimate criticism of Israel and anti-Semitism. It is called the 3-D test[203] and it comes from former Soviet refusenik (and later Israeli minister) Natan Sharansky.

The first "D" is the test of demonization. Such is the case when Israel is criticized out of all proportion, for example when it is compared to Nazi Germany. This is what *Journal de Montréal* columnist Stéphane Gendron did in his June 1, 2010 column,[204] when he wrote: "What is the difference between the Warsaw Ghetto and the Gaza concentration camp?"[205]

The second "D" is the test of double standards. When, for example, Israel is condemned for doing things for which other states are not so condemned. In the column mentioned above, Stéphane Gendron virulently attacks Israel following the Gaza flotilla incident. While I agree that each innocent death is a tragedy, I have never read Gendron condemning Iran's atrocious human rights record against its own population. I have never read Gendron attack China for its treatment of its citizens or its occupation (and cultural genocide) of Tibet. To the contrary, in July 2007, Gendron - who is also the mayor of the Montreal-area city of Huntington - was trying to attract Chinese investment to his city.[206]

The third "D" is the test of delegitimization. This is very clearly at play when someone says that the State of Israel should not exist. And this is what Gendron said when he wrote: "Nobody in the international community dares to call to order this small illegitimate country."[207]

According to this simple 3-D test, the demagogic populist Gendron wrote an anti-Semitic column.

On June 10, 2010, *La Presse* columnist Pierre Foglia published a column[208] flashily titled "We are not anti-Semitic".

In the column, Foglia basically wrote that criticizing Israel is not anti-Semitic. He is absolutely right.

Is criticizing the Gaza blockade, as Foglia does in this column, anti-Semitic? In and of itself, absolutely not, even though Foglia's analysis fails to consider Israel's very real security interests.

Is stating his inability to understand American support for Israel, as Foglia does, anti-Semitic? Very clearly not.

Is questioning the Jewish settlement project in Judea-Samaria/ West Bank, as Foglia does in his column, anti-Semitic? Absolutely not. I myself do the very same thing, including in this book.

But I return to what Thomas Friedman wrote:

> *Criticizing Israel is not anti-Semitic, and saying so is vile. But singling out Israel for opprobrium and international sanction – out of all proportion to any other party in the Middle East – is anti-Semitic, and not saying so is dishonest.*

Is this test always passed by our pundits, columnists and analysts?

In an August 12, 2010 column, Foglia again addresses a Jewish-related subject: French and Jewish-born intellectual Edgar Morin. Foglia essentially writes that Morin deserves to be considered great because he broke with the Jewish people.

Foglia writes: "I read again Morin's writings on complex thought, but for me, Morin is also - I dare not say above all else - the Jew who broke away from the chosen people: 'I break with the Jewish people but stay with the damned people.' (Mes démons, 1994)"[209]

In other words, Foglia writes that a good Jew is a dejudaized Jew, a deZionized Jew, a non-Jewish Jew as Morin described himself.[210]

I wonder how Quebeckers would react if they read, for example, that a good Quebecker is one who decided to stop speaking French, to cut himself off from his Quebec roots and systematically criticizes anything the Quebec government does.

I leave the last word to Booker Prize winner Howard Jacobson:

> *Let's get something out of the way. I don't think that being critical of Israel makes anyone an anti-Semite. Only a fool would think it does. But only a fool would think it follows that criticism of Israel can never be anti-Semitic, or that anti-Zionism isn't a haven in which anti-Semitism is sometimes given leave to flourish.*[211]

The accusation of the invention of the Jewish people

In certain circles, a theory is making the rounds according to which the Jewish people were 'invented' by the Zionists. The objective of this theory is obviously to delegitimize Israel as the nation-state of the Jewish people.

The new guru of this theory is an anti-Zionist Israeli professor by the name of Shlomo Sand. Sand wrote a book called *The Invention of the Jewish People*, which was quite well received in France. I would note that Jewish history is not Sand's specialty. Recently hired by a Montreal university, he is a professor of contemporary history, specializing in the writings of Georges Sorel and the history of cinema.

The Quebec union CSN invited this pseudo-expert to Montreal for a conference. The underlying message is clear: if the Jews do not constitute a people, the Jewish State of Israel is illegitimate.

However, to the contrary, recent scientific and genetic studies[212] demonstrate that Jews around the world (but for the small Indian and Ethiopian communities) are in fact descendants of Hebrews from the Middle East.[213] Historical research also contradicts Sand's thesis.

As *The New York Times* writes, these studies "refute the suggestion made last year by the historian Shlomo Sand in his book *The Invention of the Jewish People* that Jews have no common origin but are a miscellany of people in Europe and Central Asia who converted to Judaism at various times."[214]

I wonder if the CSN will also invite the genetic specialists who conducted these scientific studies to speak about the proof of their findings: that Jewish peoplehood is very real and far from a mere invention of the Zionists.

20
Reasonable Accomodations

The issue of identity has always played a central role in Quebec's political debate and I suspect it always will. Entire books have been written on the subject. Allow me nonetheless, to share a few thoughts on the subject.

These are my starting points, my non-negotiable principles:

a) Quebec is a democracy. It may sound like an obvious thing to say, but it is an important principle to reiterate as important consequences flow from it.

b) There must be separation between religion and state.

c) Women are men's absolute equals and gender equality must be reflected in our institutions.

d) French is the language of the nation of Quebec, with its corollary: the continuation of the historic respect for minority rights that Quebec has always shown. On this subject, it is interesting to note that "since René Lévesque's time, the Canadian Jewish Congress has not put into question either the importance of the integration of new arrivals within a French-speaking framework or the legitimacy of the linguistic demands of the demographic majority, as long as the fundamental principles of law have been preserved in Quebec's territory."[215]

Having clarified those points, let us consider the application of those principles.

The current debate over reasonable accommodations

The debate over reasonable accommodations in Quebec started after the Supreme Court of Canada ruled in favour of allowing a young Sikh man to carry his kirpan, a ceremonial dagger, in school, if the said kirpan was worn under his clothes and fully sewn into a cloth sheath and inaccessible.

This was followed by the decision of a Montreal YMCA to frost its glass windows, upon the request of a nearby ultra-Orthodox boys school. This decision, agreed on between neighbours, created a media storm and an intense debate across Quebec society. One can disagree with the YMCA's decision to respond favourably to the Hassidic school's request (as I do), without creating such controversy.

Next came the debates over the Muslim veil, the niqab and the burka. Then the media started to look for any incident related to any minority and to amplify them.

Of course, all high immigration societies have debates over issues like minority rights and immigration. It is normal, even healthy. But it must be done right.

Quebec openly debates tough identity issues

It is remarkable that Quebec decided to openly debate these tough issues. I believe that it is a sign of democratic health. Too often, immigration and identity issues are swept under the carpet so that when they come forward, it is in public debate within the frame of reference of the hard right and populist movements.

All is not perfect with immigration. And if a society refuses to openly and honestly tackle the issues, due to political correctness or out of fear of being accused of being xenophobic or racist, it will eventually be forced to do so under the pressure of groups that will not only question the modalities of immigration (selection, number, provenance, etc.), but will also want to question the very desirability of immigration.

In Quebec, the first attempt to publicly structure the debate came under the guise of the Bouchard-Taylor Commission.

The Commission held public hearings across Quebec that were broadcast live and were closely watched by a large number of Quebeckers. As with any such exercise, some comments and submissions were very well considered and insightful, others much less so.

In my view, one of the troubling messages heard time and time again from "old-stock Quebeckers" (for lack of a better expression) toward minority groups and immigrants was: "We are small. We are weak. We might disappear. Join us!"

I am not sure that this is the best signal to send to people that we want to join our society.

As I have said over and over again: the francophones' situation in North America is precarious. They represent only some two percent of the North American population. They live beside the most powerful linguistic, cultural, political, economic and military empire in world's history. Given this reality, some fears are normal and even healthy.

In fact, to the best of my knowledge, Quebec is the only society which is both a minority and a high immigration society. In relation to the size of its population, "since the end of the 1940's, Quebec has always been one of the ten industrialised societies which welcomed the most immigrants per person."[216]

I believe that Quebec is stronger than how it was represented by some people who intervened before the commission. This small, original society has survived for more than 400 years in difficult circumstances. It has prospered culturally, economically and politically, even more so after the Quiet Revolution of the 1960's.

Identity: an existential issue for Quebec, in particular for sovereignists

Quebec sovereignists, who seek to build an independent state, give special attention to the issue of identity.

The Bloc Québécois was the first political party, at the turn of the millennia, to focus on this issue.[217] It started its reflection prior to the beginning of the debate on reasonable accommodations.

Former Bloc leader Gilles Duceppe has said that "French Canadians, English Canadians, new arrivals, those who came here a long time ago, all became, over time, Quebeckers. We are not what we once were nor are we what we want to become. This is why I call on all of us to become the founding people of a sovereign and modern Quebec."[218]

The debate has become more intense since then. Many have contributed and we have not yet heard from the last one.

The sovereignist movement continues its quest to have the idea of an independent Quebec progress, despite the population's current apathy to the idea. Some even make the connection between the fact that support for sovereignty has levelled out and the debate on identity.

In his recent book, Joseph Facal writes:

> [o]ne can perceive the swinging between cultural nationalism and political nationalism. It is not a coincidence that at the time the sovereignist movement seems to have topped out and the possibility of a constitutional reform is more remote than ever, the concerns about the French language

and Quebec's demographic situation come back with a vengeance. When the political route is blocked, nationalism retakes a cultural tone.[219]

Le Devoir columnist Michel David is of a similar mind when he writes about the Parti Québécois' programme, divulged in June 2010: "In the absence of a referendum, the issue of identity has become a PQ trademark issue, Quebec citizenship, a secularism charter, teaching of national history and more importantly, a strengthening of Bill 101."[220]

To go back on these fundamental issues is not per se a problem. I do not condemn the PQ for tackling these issues. But I do hope that it will not become a return to the past and an inward focus that takes us back to an identity that no longer exists and which results in the exclusion of many Quebeckers whose families may not be traced back to New France, but who are nonetheless as much a Quebecker as I am, someone whose ancestors arrived in 1635.

There seems to be the following phenomena: many French-speaking Quebeckers, realizing that their dream of an independent Quebec might not be realized in the short term (or ever), have decided to return to their roots, which are essentially French Canadian. They have decided to focus on the protection of what they consider the heart of their identity.

But in a globalized world, with the many challenges facing Quebec, a society that needs immigrants, we must avoid dividing Quebeckers against themselves, avoid the "us" and the "them" of Quebeckers of French Canadian origin and those Quebeckers of other origins.

The Quebec identity that has been built since the 1960's, and especially after Bill 101, is open. It is inclusive. It is modern. This is not to say that it is perfect. Some dangers – notably radical political Islam – lurk, and that is the subject of other parts of this book.

One cannot become French Canadian. One is born French Canadian. But one can become a Quebecker. One must not necessarily have grown up eating *tourtière* or poutine to be a Quebecker. One could have easily grown up eating paella, couscous or *gefilte* fish and be a Quebecker. People from many places, origins and cultural backgrounds can be, and are, Quebeckers. They are part of this very unique experience that is the building of a majority French society in North America.

In other words, the goal must be integration, a bringing together of peoples, and not assimilation, the attempt to cause the disappearance of all differences.

Multiculturalism: a dangerous ideology for Quebec

This does not mean that everything goes.[221] I am not a fan of multiculturalism. Not only was this ideology imposed on Quebec by Pierre Trudeau (without Quebec's assent) in order to weaken if not destroy Quebec's national identity, it has also been the source of many problems of integration, extremism and anti-liberalism in many countries.[222] While today's Quebec is multiethnic, which is a good thing, it does not follow that it must adopt the ideology of multiculturalism.

I agree with *La Presse* editorial writer Mario Roy when he writes:

> The 'new' immigration, the one coming from societies – Muslim societies in particular – whose values are very different from those of the welcoming societies, are on a collision course with the latter.
> (…)
>
> Why do the immigrants come? Essentially, for prosperity, security, and liberty that they do not have, or have very little of, in their country of origin. However, we have not yet sufficiently understood that these attractions owe their existence to the shared values of Western nations,

including ours. Gender equality, freedom of expression or the secularism of the public sphere, for example, are not little figurines that one puts on a cake of prosperity, security and liberty when it come out of the oven. They are the very ingredients needed to cook!

No values inspired by the Enlightenment, no cake!

So why is it that there are always minorities that attack these values? And that there are majorities willing to tolerate this suicidal enterprise? This is the practical and not the theoretical consequence of multiculturalism: to saw off the branch upon which we, whether old stock or new, are all sitting![223]

The main criteria to which we always return, is the question of reasonableness.

Secularism

State and religion must be separate. But secularism, what is referred to in French as *laïcité*, does not mean the absence of religion in a given society. It means that the state is and must stay neutral. In other words, secularism is a state duty, not a constraint imposed by a state on its citizens.

Of course, Quebec is a society with a Catholic majority.[224] But it does not necessarily follow that it must be institutionally Catholic.

Many defend the principle of strict secularism (*laïcité stricte*). Total secularism has as a consequence a state that is absolutely neutral religiously. Taken to its extreme, it would result in the abolition of religiously based holidays like Christmas and Easter. Logically, in a secular state, there can be no recognized religiously based holidays.

Nobody in his/her right mind is asking for this. There is

general consensus that there can and must be exceptions to the principle of secularism, notably to take into account a nation's history and its majority. It is, one could say, a reasonable accommodation to the principle of secularism.

Some make the argument that Christmas is no longer a religious holiday. This is obviously erroneous. Christmas' very nature is religious. Indeed, its very name comes from the words 'Christ' and 'Mass'. The fact that Quebeckers are not as religiously observant as they once were, does not change the nature of the day. In this situation, we accept an exception to the principle of secularism, because it is reasonable.

Neither does secularism mean that people have no beliefs or religious customs. It is an error to put the neutrality of the school system on the same footing as the appearance of religious manifestations (veil, turban, etc) by individuals in schools.

Secularism does not require a state's citizen to stop believing in whatever religious doctrine he or she follows. Secularism places the rights of citizens of every faith – and of no faith – on the same footing.

When we hear "the crucifixes are coming out of the schools while veils and turbans are going in", it is comparing apples to oranges. Personal manifestations of religious beliefs do run contrary to state secularism. That remains true as long as the basic rules and fundamental values of the society in question are respected.

This brings us back to the burka and the niqab.

Contrary to the position adopted by a group of Orthodox Jews who went to Quebec's National Assembly to oppose the Charest government's Bill 94 banning the niqab and the burka in government offices,[224a] I was in favour of the bill. While I have no issue with religious symbols, I clearly and firmly draw the line at face covering.

To cover one's face is a sign of social separatism, a self-exclusion from society that goes against the necessity of a certain desire to live together, essential for a pluralistic society to function.

As for the school system, all Quebec schools (including Jewish Hassidic schools) must respect the Ministry of Education's curriculum. No derogation to this principle should be accepted. None.

That being said, if a school wants to open its doors and have classes on a Saturday or a Sunday in order to teach additional subjects (including religious), why not? Again, that is based on the express condition that the mandatory Quebec curriculum be fully respected.

A short conclusion on this very complex and highly emotional subject of reasonable accommodation: I am confident that there is ample collective intelligence and intellectual openness in Quebec in order to find reasonable solutions to the challenges posed by the integration of Quebeckers from different traditions, while continuing to build an open, original, pluralistic and French-speaking society in North America.

21
Conventional Wisdom or Ignorance?

Canadians have a tendency to quasi-deify some organizations, rendering them above criticism. It is as though given the important goals they pursue, the organizations themselves are perfect. I for one do not believe that any organization, be it civil, religious, political, national or international, is above criticism.

The United Nations (U.N.) is part of Canadians' DNA. We have huge respect for the U.N., a reverence that sometimes borders on wilful blindness.

Let me be clear. I am not saying that the U.N. has done nothing worthwhile. What I am saying however, is that the U.N. is far from perfect, notably in relation to the protection of minority rights, women's rights, and the Israeli-Arab conflict.[225]

I will illustrate my point with two shocking examples.

On April 10, 2010[226], Iran, one of the most repressive and misogynistic regimes in the world, was elected to the U.N. Commission on the Status of Women.

The Commission's goal is to advance the status of women around the world and to achieve complete gender equality in every sphere.[227] This is even more ironic, when one considers the fact that Iran has yet to ratify the Convention on the Elimination of All Forms of Discrimination Against Women.

In any event, who really denies the existence of an inferior status for women in Iran, of – dare I say the word? – an apartheid status for women, under the regime of the ayatollahs?

Speaking of ayatollahs, one of the most important of them said, "[M]any women are improperly dressed (i.e. they do not respect the Islamic way of dressing), corrupt the youth, and the increase in illicit sexual relations augments the number of earthquakes."[228] In other words, women who are dressed provocatively are the cause of earthquakes! Let us not forget that there is no separation of state and religion in Iran, as Iran is officially an Islamic Republic.

Can we really give credibility to an organisation like the U.N. when, without any hesitation, they allow the Islamic Republic of Iran to sit on their organization in charge of the status of women?

Second example: the Human Rights Council. Since its establishment in 2006, the Human Rights Council has issued condemnations fifty times against member states, including thirty-five against the State of Israel, i.e. 70 percent.

Of the ten emergency sessions held by the Human Rights Council, six were against Israel. Massacres in Iran, China, Nigeria, Pakistan, Kenya, and Zimbabwe were swept under the carpet.

Reality is sometimes stranger than fiction. On May 13, 2010, Gaddafi-led Libya was elected to the U.N. Human Rights Council[229] after receiving 155 votes out of 192 voting member states. Libya was elected at the same time as other stellar examples of human rights, such as Qatar and Angola. These countries would thus join fellow stalwarts of freedom and human rights protection like China, Russia, and Cuba. This despite the fact that everybody on the planet knew about the dictatorial nature of the Gaddafi regime, whose bloody rule came to an end in the fall of 2011.

On March 26, 2008, the Human Rights Council appointed Richard Falk as Special *Rapporteur* on the Situation of Human Rights in the Palestinian Territories Occupied Since 1967.[230] His report[231] dated June 7, 2010 makes no mention of the numerous human rights violations of which Hamas is guilty, Hamas political executions and the radical Islamist ideology that its Charter[232] openly promotes. Falk's bias is so obvious that, according to Falk himself, the Palestinian Authority asked him to step down for being a Hamas supporter.[233]

This is the same Richard Falk who signed the foreword of a book titled *The New Pearl Harbour*[234] by David Ray Griffin, the thesis of which is that September 11 was orchestrated by the U.S. government. The foreword was neither the first nor the last time Falk put this idea forward.[235]

In January 2011, U.N. Secretary General Ban Ki-moon himself condemned Falk for similar statements he had published on his blog.[236]

With this kind of character, who in his right mind would ever think the U.N. is credible?

The Human Rights Council has only one issue that is permanently on its agenda. Guess which state it is? Of course, it is Israel.[237] How can anyone think that the U.N. is neutral and credible on anything related to Israel?

Some very important personalities also believe that the U.N. is not impartial regarding Israel. In his last speech as U.N. Secretary General on December 12, 2006, Kofi Annan (not known for his pro-Israel sympathies) said the following that is, unfortunately, still relevant:

> *Some may feel satisfaction at repeatedly passing General Assembly resolutions or holding conferences that condemn Israel's behaviour. But one should also ask whether such steps bring any tangible relief or benefit to the Palestinians.*

There have been decades of resolutions. There has been a proliferation of special committees, sessions and Secretariat divisions and units. Has any of this had an effect on Israel's policies, other than to strengthen the belief in Israel, and among many of its supporters, that this great Organization is too one-sided to be allowed a significant role in the Middle East peace process?

Even worse, some of the rhetoric used in connection with the issue implies a refusal to concede the very legitimacy of Israel's existence, let alone the validity of its security concerns. We must never forget that Jews have very good historical reasons for taking seriously any threat to Israel's existence. What was done to Jews and others by the Nazis remains an undeniable tragedy, unique in human history. Today, Israelis are often confronted with words and actions that seem to confirm their fear that the goal of their adversaries is to extinguish their existence as a State, and as a people.[238]

Closer to home, ex-PQ minister and current HEC professor and political commentator Joseph Facal wrote about the U.N., calling it the "hate factory" (*La fabrique de la haine*).[239]

In this outstanding piece, Facal classifies the U.N. as "a monument to incompetence, to hypocrisy and to bad faith." The numbers he uses speak for themselves:

The war in Congo between 1998 and 2003 left about 4 millions victims. It led to 56 motions in different U.N. bodies.

The civil war raging in Sudan since 1983 killed about 1.3 million people. But only 14 motions were brought forward at the U.N. Africans can kill one another with the world's complete indifference.

The Israeli-Palestinian conflict apparently killed about

7,000 people between 2000 and today. But Israel was the subject of... 249 motions of condemnation at the U.N. Isn't this somewhat disproportionate?

Facal then draws the conclusion that the U.N. "suffers from some kind of anti-Israel obsession" and as such, every time Israel is being discussed, the "diplomatic and moral criteria change." Thus, "every time Israel is the issue, the U.N. looks like a mental institution under the control of its own patients."

How I wish I had penned that line!

I insist on reviewing the U.N.'s approach to the Middle East, as what happens in this forum is closely followed by Canadians. Unfortunately, its inherent anti-Israel bias feeds every attempt to delegitimize and demonize Israel.

The latest example is the infamous Goldstone Report following the December 2008 - January 2009 Gaza conflict. Gallons of ink were spilled in order to analyze and criticize this report.[240] Here is not the place to examine it in depth. However, allow me to highlight a few of its elements.

The report does mention that Palestinian armed groups committed war crimes and, possibly, crimes against humanity in bombing the south of Israel. However, it is obvious from reading the report that this attempt to be even-handed is a poor one. The report really focuses on Israel, practically ignoring Hamas' crimes that led to the Israeli military operation.

Moreover, the Report's sponsor was none other than the same U.N. Human Rights Council that, as we have previously established, is well-known to be biased against Israel. It is well worth repeating that the Human Rights Council condemned the State of Israel more than all the other member states put together!

Even before the Goldstone committee had started its work,

the Human Rights Council had already decided that Israel was guilty of "grave violations of the human rights." Indeed, the mandate of the Goldstone Committee started with a statement that the Human Rights Council "[s]trongly condemns the ongoing Israeli military operation carried out in the Occupied Palestinian Territory, particularly in the occupied Gaza Strip, which has resulted in massive violations of the human rights of the Palestinian people and systematic destruction of Palestinian infrastructure."

In other words, Israel's culpability was determined before the committee started its work.

The Goldstone committee's mandate was so biased that: a) it ignored Hamas' well-known and poor record on human rights; and b) many prestigious candidates refused to chair the committee, including Irish ex-president Mary Robinson (who is usually quite critical of Israel), as in her view, the Human Rights Council resolutions are "guided not by human rights but by politics."[241]

Among the members of the Goldstone committee was Professor Christine Chinkin. During the Gaza conflict (thus before her appointment to the Goldstone Committee), Chinkin had signed a letter titled "Israel's bombardment of Gaza is not self-defence – it's a war crime."[242]

This of course clearly goes against the well-known common law principle that not only must there be justice, but there must also be the appearance of justice. Chinkin's letter proves that she had prejudged the conclusions. Her letter had also, incidentally, led more than 500 British and Canadian jurists to ask her to excuse herself from the Goldstone committee.

Referring to that letter in an August 2009 interview, Goldstone said, "If it had been a judicial inquiry, that letter she'd signed would have been a ground for disqualification."[243] Still, by pretending to judge Israel according to international law, the

Goldstone committee acted as if it were indeed a tribunal.

Judge Goldstone became a judge under the South African apartheid regime. As the Israeli newspaper *Yedioth Ahronoth* reported, not only did he serve the racist regime condemning 28 black defendants to the gallows and having other defendants whipped, he clearly defended the death penalty in his judgments.[244] His defence of "I was only following the law", resembles Nazi criminals' defence after the Second World War.

The supposed military expert of the Goldstone committee, Irish colonel Desmond Travers, later showed his anti-Israel bias when he said that Hamas had only fired two rockets on Israel before the Gaza conflict.[245] This is obviously not true as not only did Hamas itself glorify and publicize the thousands of rockets it launched on Israel, I myself saw and held in my hands hundreds of those spent missiles when I was in the Israeli city of Sderot, on the Gaza border.

Moreover, the democratic members of the Human Rights Council – including all the E.U. members then sitting on it (France, Germany, Italy, the U.K.), Japan, Canada and Switzerland – refused to back the mandate of the Goldstone mission as they considered it biased.

As French intellectual Pierre-André Taguieff wrote:

> *The objective of the Jewish state's enemies is to confer an international legitimacy to the criminalizing accusations against Israel, and then to forbid it in the future to respond to the attacks of Islamist groups. Which is a death sentence against Israel (...) For those who support the Goldstone Report, the goal is to, at the same time, delegitimize the Jewish state by accusing it of war crimes, if not of crimes against humanity, and to take away its right to respond militarily.*[246]

The last shreds of credibility left to the Goldstone report were destroyed by…Judge Goldstone himself. On April 1, 2011, in *The Washington Post*[247], Goldstone basically retracted his report. In his op-ed, he wrote: "If I had known then what I know now, the Goldstone Report would have been a different document." Goldstone stated unequivocally that "[Palestinian] civilians were not intentionally targeted [by Israel] as a matter of policy." As well, Goldstone confirmed the number of civilian deaths cited by the Israeli army all along.

Goldstone also added "[T]hat the crimes allegedly committed by Hamas were intentional goes without saying — its rockets were purposefully and indiscriminately aimed at civilian targets."

Thus, the accusations of war crimes and crimes against humanity hurled at Israel on the basis of this report are worth less than ever. I am now waiting for the apologies of all those who attacked Israel in such a defamatory way. I know, I know. I should not hold my breath.

I know how prestigious the U.N. is for Canadians. I also know that the U.N. is the main building block of Canadian diplomatic thought. And I am aware of how politically incorrect it is to so harshly criticize the U.N.

Nonetheless, the U.N., which should be part of the solution to the Israeli-Arab conflict, is part of the problem. It has neither the credibility nor the neutrality, to play a constructive role in this troubled region, at least at this point.

Another point of conventional wisdom must be refuted, namely that major international NGOs have no political agendas, are neutral, and are largely above criticism. I disagree.

One example: Human Rights Watch (HRW). While this organization may do good work on some files, it fails to do so on all files.

HRW is often quoted by critics of Israel, as if all its reports were God-given. Too few know, or too many pretend not to know, that HRW is biased against Israel.

In July 2009, the Wall Street Journal revealed that HRW solicited money in…Saudi Arabia, boasting (in order to garner funds) that it stands up to criticism from pro-Israel groups.[248]

In other words, HRW was using its anti-Israel positions to raise cash in countries like Saudi Arabia. Of course, Saudi Arabia's record on human rights, women's rights, and minority rights is well known and far from exemplary.

Another example. From 2000 on, HRW published more reports on supposed abuses by Israel than any other country in the region but two.[249] As of spring 2011 there are more reports on Israel than on Iran, Saudi Arabia, Syria, or Algeria. Or, put another way, there are about as many reports on Israel (a Western-style liberal democracy) than on Iran, Libya, and Syria combined!

HRW's anti-Israel bias has become so strong that its founder and ex-president, Robert Bernstein, openly took a position against his own creation. In an op-ed in *The New York Times*[250], Bernstein denounced the loss of credibility of the organization.

All of this is to say that the Israeli-Arab conflict has become so toxic, so charged with symbolism, that even otherwise credible organizations have lost their way.

In the Congo, civil war has left more than 7 million dead. Murders, massacres, rapes, and forced self-cannibalism have been documented. The situation is absolutely horrific.[251]

The NGO superpowers that are HRW and Amnesty International (AI) gave the Congo minute attention compared to Israel. For example, in 2009, AI issued 62 releases criticizing Israel and only one on the Congo.[252]

It seems that for HRW and AI, the lives of people in the Third World are not as important as those in other parts of the world. I believe it speaks to both a form of racism and moral blindness.[253]

This is why I tell people I meet, teach and debate with, not to limit themselves to media reports. Don't accept U.N. resolutions or NGO reports at face value. Go to Israel. Go to the West Bank-Judea/Samaria.

And if you are equitable and honest, you will have an opinion that is radically different from the one all too common in Canada and in many regions of the world.

22
The Middle East... in Quebec

As mentioned, while serving in Parliament, I was the unofficial English voice for the Bloc Québécois. Within the sovereignist movement (and with the exception of Duceppe), I more than anyone else dialogued with English Canada, participated in English television and radio programs and delivered speeches outside Quebec.

Of course, the main reasons for this were my years spent in Ontario, my personal connections and my comfort with English. I have always appreciated Canada and as an MP I was careful to engage Canadians from outside Quebec with the greatest respect.

Even when I addressed the subject of Quebec's independence from Canada head on, the tone was generally respectful, even during open line radio shows in parts of Canada where there is hostility to the idea of Quebec sovereignty.

In fact, ironically, I have found that it is easier to talk about Quebec's independence with Canadians than to have a respectful discussion on the situation in the Middle East with them. This becomes even more evident of course, during periods of tension.

I would even argue that prevalent among Israel's adversaries is a tendency to import the Middle East conflict to Canada, leading to an unsupportable level of toxicity in our civic discourse - and poisoned rhetoric in our society.

Prologue to the Second Lebanon War

Only a few short months after I began working at the CIC, the Second Lebanon War started. To understand this conflict a very brief recall of history is necessary.

On May 24, 2000, Israel withdrew entirely from Lebanon, in total fulfilment of its obligations under United Nations Security Council Resolution 425. Israel repositioned its troops on the Israeli side of the internationally recognized border. Not a single Israeli soldier remained in Lebanese territory.

Israeli Prime Minister Ehud Barak had taken the initiative in the context of trying to reach a broader regional peace accord. In other words, Barak wanted a peace deal with Syria. The main territorial stumbling block for peace between Israel and Syria is the Golan Heights, conquered by Israel in 1967 during the Six Day War.

A deal with Syria, which in 2000 was occupying Lebanon, did not materialize, and Israel decided to unilaterally withdraw from every inch of Lebanon's territory.

Since then, Hezbollah, a Shiite Islamist militia supported, armed, trained, and ultimately commanded by Iran, has been claiming a small patch of territory called the Shebaa Farms (known as Har Dov by the Israelis).

The U.N. has always considered this territory part of the Golan Heights and, as such, part of the negotiations between Syria and Israel. However, in order to preserve its *raison d'être* and demonstrate its legitimacy as a Lebanese national movement, Hezbollah has continued to use Shebaa Farms as a pretext for launching attacks on Israel.

The Lebanese government, afraid of destabilizing the country's delicate political balance, has never really intervened to disarm Hezbollah and impose its authority in the area bordering Israel.

Many times over the years, Israel has asked the international community to pressure Lebanon into controlling and disarming Hezbollah and exercising its sovereignty on its own national territory, in accordance with its responsibilities as a state.

Unfortunately, the Lebanese people have suffered the consequences of their own government's inaction. Lebanon's unwillingness to fulfill its obligations under any understanding of the legal concept of sovereignty, as well as those flowing from U.N. Security Council resolutions 425 and 1799, has encouraged Hezbollah (and its sponsors Syria and Iran) to continue using South Lebanon as a base for its multipronged campaign aimed at destroying Israel.

On top of the sporadic firing of missiles, in October 2000, Hezbollah terrorists entered into Israeli territory and kidnapped three Israeli soldiers.[254]

Hezbollah: An armed militia diametrically opposed to Canadian values

Hezbollah is a movement originating from the Shiite community in Lebanon. It started to grow in the 1980's and received popular support following its harassment of Israeli troops, until Israel left Lebanon.

Hezbollah opposes Israel and the West and wants to establish a fundamentalist Muslim government in Lebanon. Canada, the U.S. and Israel consider Hezbollah to be a terrorist organization.

Hezbollah (meaning Party of God in Arabic) won the support of part of the Lebanese population by developing schools, hospitals and other social services. It is also a political party, with 14 of the 128 members of the Lebanese Parliament. In fact, today, Hezbollah has *de facto* control over the Lebanese government.

Hezbollah has been implicated – or strongly suspected – in many terrorist attacks against Israel, the U.S., and other Western targets, including the suicide attacks in Beirut in 1983, which killed 241 American Marines and 58 French soldiers. As well, according to an in-depth report by the CBC's Neil MacDonald, broadcast in November 2010, Hezbollah was almost certainly behind the assassination of former Lebanese Prime Minister Rafik Hariri.[255] Indeed, in the summer of 2011, arrest warrants were issued by the Special Tribunal for Lebanon created to investigate this ignoble act.[256]

The suicide attacks against the Khobar Towers in Saudi Arabia in 1996 (which left 19 people dead) were attributed to Hezbollah militants. In 1994, an explosion at a Jewish community centre in Argentina, which caused the deaths of 85 people, was also attributed to Hezbollah.

I have been shocked to hear some people here in Canada say that Hezbollah is a resistance movement. Resistance to what? At the time of the Hezbollah attack which led to the Second Lebanon War, Israel had been out of Lebanon for more than 6 years!

Even though many Canadians do not want to see it, what is at issue here is an ideological struggle between the Western world and Islamist movements who want to impose their fanatical and extremist ideology on the entire planet.

These radical Islamist movements appear willing to do anything in the pursuit of their goal, including the murder of innocent victims. Some examples: Hamas in Israel, Hezbollah in Lebanon, Al-Qaeda in Iraq, the Taliban in Afghanistan (159 Canadian deaths), Madrid on March 11, 2004 (190 deaths), London on July 7, 2005 (52 deaths), Beslan, Russia in September of 2004 (323 deaths), and Mumbai on July 11, 2006 (180 deaths). Those are in addition to the 2,819 deaths in New York and 125 dead in Washington, at the hands of Al-Qaeda on September 11, 2001.

One can easily see that militant, extremist Islamism is a danger not only to Israel, which is in a geographically precarious position, but also for all Western democracies that value human rights and freedoms. Hezbollah is a central player in this threat.

Lebanon: A different country than we think it is

I doubt that Canadians really know Lebanon. What they think it is - a small state, always the victim of its more powerful neighbours, powerless to forge its own destiny - is far from reality.

I thought it ironic to hear the pro-Palestinian/anti-Israel crowd promote the notion of a virtuous Lebanon fighting against a racist State of Israel. This became particularly clear after my conversation with a taxi driver, a Palestinian born in Lebanon and now living in Canada. He told me that in his view, there is no more anti-Palestinian society than Lebanon. Somewhat surprised, it was only after checking the facts myself that I realized he was right.

Today, there are more than 400,000 Palestinian refugees in Lebanon. Their refugee camps are among the worst of all Palestinian refugee camps in the world.

The Lebanese government has refused to grant Lebanese citizenship to the refugees for decades, including those born in Lebanon and even those born of Lebanese mothers and Palestinian fathers. In other words, they have the status of foreigners, even if they were born, raised and remained in Lebanon!

Palestinians do not have access to public schools, are not permitted access to a majority of professions[257] including law and medicine,[258] have no access to the Lebanese health care system and have no access to land ownership. To work, Palestinians must obtain a permit from the Lebanese government, something which is rarely delivered. Between 1982 and 1992, for example, none was given to Palestinians. None!

It is easy to understand the vicious circle in which the Palestinians in Lebanon find themselves. They have no access to the Lebanese public school system, and those who study in U.N. schools have no incentive to pursue their studies as most professions are closed to them. Unemployment is very high and poverty widespread.[259]

Health issues are numerous and yet it is not uncommon for Lebanese hospitals to refuse to treat Palestinian patients.

As for property, the rare Palestinian who somehow succeeds in becoming a landowner will see his asset pass into the hands of the Lebanese government when he dies.

This state of affairs is the result of an active policy of discrimination by the Lebanese against what the propaganda machine ironically refers to as their Palestinian brothers. If Lebanon is ignoble towards Palestinian refugees on its territory, it is also far from pure and innocent in its relationship (or lack thereof) with Israel.

And what can one discern from the triumphal welcome given to Iranian president Mahmoud Ahmadinejad in October 2010 during his visit to Lebanon? The entire world knows Ahmadinejad's role in the bloody crackdown against his own people in 2009. He continues to lead an illegal effort to acquire nuclear weapons, despite the international community's repeated condemnations. He is a Holocaust denier and his regime exports a hateful extremist ideology throughout the region. On the home front in Iran, women are discriminated against and homosexuals are executed. But in Lebanon, Ahmadinejad received a hero's welcome.[260]

Hezbollah starts a war

On July 12, 2006, Hezbollah crossed the Israel-Lebanon border and entered onto Israeli soil where they killed eight Israeli soldiers and kidnapped two others. In international law, this constitutes an act of war and a state has an absolute right to defend itself in such a situation. That was the cause of the summer 2006 conflict.

Supported by international law, Israel could no longer tolerate having its citizens under the constant threat of Hezbollah attacks and the firing of Hezbollah's missiles. As is true for every sovereign state, Israel has the legal right to take necessary measures to bring back its citizens and ensure the protection of its civilians. This remains the case whether Hezbollah acts by itself, or as a pawn on behalf of Syria or Iran.

Indeed, like Canadians, Israelis have the right to live in peace, without a constant threat of violence. It can easily be argued that a state's first duty is to protect its citizens' lives and security.

As a result, Israel decided to try to free its kidnapped soldiers and to eliminate the threat posed by Hezbollah on its northern border.

There can be no doubt that Hezbollah would not have been able to amass its military arsenal if the Lebanese government had really wanted to stop armaments entering the country. The threat posed by Hezbollah on Israel's northern border is due to the incapacity or unwillingness of the Lebanese government to really control its southern territory.

According to its leaders' own words, Hezbollah works with and supports Hamas and is in a very tight relationship with its masters in Tehran. There can be no doubt that Israel – and all Western democracies – face a network of Islamist extremists determined to create instability and conflict.

Ironically, whereas the Arab world understood the stakes of the conflict (notably the risks that Islamist extremists pose to the stability of the entire region and Iran's role in all of this), a large part of Canadian society pointed the finger at Israel as being the aggressor.

Moreover, as Christian Rioux wrote in *Le Devoir* on July 21, 2006: "what Hezbollah and Hamas' radical faction contest is not the 1967 border but the 1948 one" – in other words, the very existence of Israel.

Hezbollah leader Hasan Nasrallah demonstrated his intransigence, extremism and complete refusal to reach peace in the Middle East when he said that there would never be peace as long as the State of Israel existed.[261]

Many in Canada seem not to have noticed that Hezbollah's actions only serve the extremist regimes in the region: Syria and Iran. That is why Hezbollah was strongly criticized by the moderate Arab states, including Jordan, the Gulf states, and the two main Arab states (Egypt and Saudi Arabia) during the Arab League Summit at the time of the conflict.[262] In fact, at the beginning of the conflict, even members of Lebanese Prime Minister Siniora's inner circle wanted, and stated their hope, that Israel annihilate Hezbollah.[263]

As for the world's leading powers of the G8, during their July 16, 2008 meeting, they squarely put the responsibility of the crisis on the shoulders of Hezbollah and Hamas. Their official communiqué stated:

> *The immediate crisis results from efforts by extremist forces to destabilize the region and to frustrate the aspirations of the Palestinian, Israeli and Lebanese people for democracy and peace. In Gaza, elements of Hamas launched rocket attacks against Israeli territory and abducted an Israeli soldier. In Lebanon, Hezbollah, in violation of the Blue Line, attacked Israel from Lebanese territory and killed and*

captured Israeli soldiers, reversing the positive trends that began with the Syrian withdrawal in 2005, and undermining the democratically elected government of Prime Minister Fuad Siniora.[264]

During that time, some horrible things were being said in Canada, no doubt due in part to the media that, while very sympathetic toward the Lebanese and astonishingly easy on Hezbollah, were quite harsh towards the Israelis.

Whereas images of devastation in Lebanon were shown constantly on 24-hour news channels, the Israeli civilians' situation was, in the main, obscured and ignored. While the north of Israel was being emptied of its inhabitants, with a third of Israel's population requiring relocation, Quebec's media was almost entirely silent on that fact. Why?

Comments made on open line shows tested Quebec Jews. The line between criticism of Israel and hostility, if not hate towards Jews, was crossed more than once.

An ignoble demonstration in Montreal

Then came the now-famous demonstration in the streets of Montreal.

Many things have been said about this demonstration. Were the vast majority of participants demonstrating in good faith? Yes. Did they march simply to ask for the conflict to be stopped? Assuredly. But they were misled by the organizers who, from the beginning, had deformed the meaning of the protest.

The call for the demonstration[265] was published on August 3. It was titled: 'Quebec mobilizes for justice and peace in Lebanon now!' (*Le Québec se mobilise pour la justice et la paix au Liban maintenant!*) And peace for Israel? Wasn't Israel attacked daily with missiles? Wasn't its civilian population explicitly targeted? Let us remember, Hezbollah was not targeting Israeli military centres but cities and villages in Israel.

Why the silence?

Israel's military campaign was called an act of aggression. This despite the clear and well known fact that it was Hezbollah who had started the conflict by crossing an international border and killing and kidnapping Israeli soldiers on Israeli soil, a clear act of aggression. No mention of this was to be found in the call to demonstrate.

One of the explicitly stated goals of the demonstration was to "[D]emonstrate our solidarity toward the Lebanese and Palestinian peoples". What about the Israeli people? Weren't they bombed by Hezbollah and Hamas? Didn't they too deserve our solidarity?

The call for this demonstration, endorsed notably by Quebec's biggest unions, was not *for* peace but *against* Israel.

Then what was bound to happen did happen. Hezbollah flags were flown in the streets of Montreal. Those images were seen the world over. Not the image Quebeckers would want to portray of themselves.

Let me be clear: I am not saying that all the demonstrators were Hezbollah supporters. I am not saying either that a majority of them were or even a substantial minority. I would say however that the strongly anti-Israel – if not occasional anti-Jewish – views that had been aired for weeks, served to exacerbate the xenophobes.

To deny that a certain anti-Israel atmosphere had blinded people to the real nature of Hezbollah would also be dishonest. In the minds of some, Hezbollah was simply a small resistance group to the big bad Israel.

Obscured were the facts that Hezbollah's values are antithetical to Canada's, that Hezbollah is a terrorist and Islamist group, that Hezbollah opposes minority rights and women's rights, and that it pursues a greater Iranian influence in the region.

This is the same Iran that killed Canadian photojournalist Zahra Kazemi. The same Iran that hangs homosexuals and stones adulterous women. That is what Hezbollah stands for. And that is without mentioning its ugly anti-Semitism. I am not talking only about its opposition to the State of Israel. Hezbollah yearns for the Jews' disappearance, pure and simple.

Its previous leader Hussein Massawi clearly said so when, addressing Israelis, he said: "We are not fighting so that you will offer us something. We are fighting to eliminate you."[266]

Its current leader Hassan Nasrallah said: "If we searched the entire world for a person, more cowardly, despicable, weak and feeble in psyche, mind, ideology and religion, we would not find anyone like the Jew. Notice, I do not say the Israeli."[267]

Nasrallah also said: "If they [the Jews] all gather in Israel, it will save us the trouble of going after them worldwide."[268]

His meaning could not be any clearer.

I am not sure Canadians realize what is at stake here. To fly a Hezbollah flag is not banal. It is a message sent to me. When I see someone in Montreal flying a Hezbollah flag, what I understand is that this person supports an organization that wants me, my wife, and my two children dead.

It is now, I hope, easier to understand my strong reaction - and that of the Canadian Jewish community.

That being said, during his speech at the demonstration, Duceppe was much more nuanced than the call to demonstrate, which his party had unfortunately endorsed. While critical of Israel's action (which is, in itself, a defensible position to take), he also clearly and forcefully condemned Hezbollah's terrorist acts. For his denunciation of Hezbollah, Duceppe was booed by some at the demonstration.

What does *that* mean?

The myth of influential neutrality

Public opinion in Canada, and more so in Quebec, was quite critical of Israel. Many were of the opinion that Canada should have been neutral in this conflict, not like the courageous position adopted by Stephen Harper.

It is, to paraphrase Winston Churchill, as if one could be neutral between the fire and the firefighters. As if one could be neutral between a liberal democracy, where minority rights (religious, sexual, ethnic, etc.) are respected, protected, and valued, and a fundamentalist Islamist group.

It has been said that Canada's "tradition" is neutrality. That the most important foreign policy legacy is the blue-helmeted peacekeeper, and that that should make us stay neutral.

One's knowledge of history must be very poor to take this position. Canada is not Switzerland. Nor is it Sweden. Canada is a member of NATO, the Western military alliance.

In 1956, when France, Great-Britain, and Israel attacked Egypt, they were severely condemned. By the U.S., by the Soviet Union and by Canada.

Through Lester B. Pearson's voice, Canada was not afraid to announce what it thought was right and just. The world listened to Canada because it had an opinion, because it had taken a position. Not because it was neutral. It is at that moment that Canada suggested the idea of peacekeepers to the U.N., an idea that it adopted.

Liberal leader Michael Ignatieff was right to say: "But let us also be very clear – a democratic state like Canada cannot be neutral as between a democratic state and terrorist organizations. There is no honest broker between those two."[269]

The unfortunate victims of the conflict

The relatively high number of Lebanese civilian deaths resulting from the 2006 war is tragic. There is no other word. It is, however, the result of an unnecessary war imposed on Israel by Hezbollah and its sponsors.

Most of the civilian victims were the result of a very cynical Hezbollah practice, started in the 1980's, consisting of placing its fighters in civilian clothes and its bases and missile launch sites in densely populated areas. Thus, Lebanese citizens were turned into human shields by Hezbollah in its manoeuvre to attack Israel with impunity. Moreover, from the October 2010 Wikileaks documents, we discovered that Iran used Red Crescent ambulances to bring weapons and agents to Lebanon during the conflict.[270]

It is generally unknown in the world that Israeli armed forces were warning Lebanese civilians - by radio, with tracts from planes, and even by phone - before launching attacks. This led to obvious dangers for Israel's soldiers.

Of course, any innocent death is a tragedy. Clearly. Still, there is a fundamental difference between groups like Hezbollah and Hamas who deliberately target civilians and a democratic state that exercises its right to self-defence by targeting terrorist infrastructures and, collaterally but not deliberately, hits civilians. The failure to differentiate between these is morally and intellectually dishonest.

Afterword on the Second Lebanon War

The Second Lebanon War finished on August 14, 2006, with

U.N. Security Council Resolution 1701. This resolution called for a ceasefire, for the Lebanese army to return to the south of Lebanon (from which it was practically non-existent), for Israel's army to withdraw completely from Lebanon's territory and for Hezbollah's disarmament and the unconditional freeing of the kidnapped Israeli soldiers.

Today, hostilities have ceased. Israel's army has completely withdrawn from Lebanon. A multinational force is in place in South Lebanon, in conjunction with the Lebanese army. But Hezbollah has rearmed.[271] According to French intelligence sources, Hezbollah now has 40,000 rockets, more than 10,000 fighters, and has built a vast and autonomous communications system.[272] All this has been achieved with the active help of both Iran and Syria.

On July 16, 2008, in exchange for the bodies of two of its kidnapped soldiers, Israel freed four members of Hezbollah, handed over about 200 corpses and a man by the name of Samir Kuntar - alive and well.

Kuntar is a terrorist and a killer. He was found guilty by an impartial court of justice for the 1979 terrorist attack during which he entered the home of an Israeli family and abducted the father Danny Haran and his four-year old daughter Einat. After taking them to a nearby beach, Kuntar shot Haran in front of his four-year-old daughter, before killing her by bashing her skull with the butt of his gun. While this was taking place, the mother, trying to hide from the terrorists she had heard in the home, accidentally killed her two-year-old daughter while trying to muffle the toddler's cries. Kuntar also killed a policeman that night.

It is the freedom of this butcher (is there any other word for him?) that Hezbollah demanded in exchange for the bodies of the two Israeli soldiers.

Some might say: "You know, it's only a terrorist group asking for the liberation of one of its own."

But that is not the worst of it. Upon Kuntar's liberation, the Lebanese government decreed a national day of celebration. When he arrived in Beirut, Kuntar got a hero's welcome, not only from thousands of joyful Lebanese, but also by Lebanese President Michel Suleiman, Lebanese Prime minister Fuad Siniora, Lebanese Parliament's speaker Nabih Berri, and many members of parliament as well as Christian and Muslim leaders.[273]

The presence of these high officials to welcome this murderer shows a side of Lebanon that Canadians do not know: that of a nation that has developed a kind of death cult.

The contrast between the culture of life in Israel and the culture of death in important segments of Lebanon could not have been starker.

When the President, the Prime Minister, and other Lebanese national leaders go out of their way to triumphantly welcome a child killer at the airport, we cannot talk about a nation of victims. The Lebanese people shouted out to the entire world about the kind of "heroes" it wanted to celebrate.

Finally, it is important to note the departure from the prime ministership, under Hezbollah's pressure, of the pro-western Saad Hariri (Rafik's son) in January 2011 and his replacement by Najib Mikati, supported by Hezbollah. In other words, Hezbollah's (and consequently Iran's) hold on Lebanon is growing. Nothing good can come of this.

And yet, at the risk of being accused of naïveté, I am still hoping for peace between Israel and Lebanon.

Gaza and the right to self-defence

Before the latest conflict in Gaza in December 2008 - January

2009 began, the south of Israel had been hit with more than 6,000 Palestinian rockets and mortars in less than eight years.

In the first two months of 2008, more than 1,000 rockets or mortars were fired on Israel, with terrible costs.

The relatively small number of Israeli victims is not because of Hamas' tender heart, but rather because its weapons are more primitive, although in constant improvement due to help from Iran.

Another reason is Israel's bomb shelters. However they come at a cost, both financial and societal. Israel has spent many millions of dollars building them for the one million Israelis who live in the vicinity. Thanks to Israel's alarm system, residents are typically given warning, albeit mere seconds, prior to missile strikes. While they can then take shelter, which makes all the difference between life and death, is living in a state of constant bomb alert any way for one million people, including children, to experience daily life?

The number of Israelis suffering from post-traumatic stress disorder in towns and villages under fire from Gaza is ten times that of the national average. Moreover, with the introduction of more powerful missiles (provided by Iran and smuggled through Egypt), the number of Israelis living within reach of Hamas missiles has grown exponentially.

What country would allow its civilians to be under attack without reacting?

For more than seven years, the international community ignored rocket attacks against Israel.

It is more than time for the international community to reject a false moral equivalency, and finally distinguish between the pyromaniacs and the firefighters.

Richard Marceau

Hamas is an armed militia dedicated to the destruction of Israel. It holds genocidal positions[274] and rejects any form of compromise based on the two-state solution. It is entirely opposed to the Western liberal principles that are the foundation of Canada's value system.

Hamas, like Hezbollah, identifies itself as a resistance movement. But Israel had completely evacuated Gaza. Not one Israeli house, not one Israeli soldier, not one Israeli citizen remained in Gaza. Zero.

Proportionality

During the Gaza conflict, many called for proportionality, notably some in Canadian political circles.

I have to make a confession. The proportionality argument leaves me baffled.

Logically, if the Israeli response was to be proportional to the attack Israel suffered, for each Palestinian rocket launched blindly on an Israeli civilian town, Israel would have to launch a rocket on Gaza City, on Palestinian civilians.

That would be proportional. That would also be nonsensical.

In all my discussions with critics of Israel, they agree with me on this point. I then ask what *would be* proportional. Not what is *not* proportional, but what would be proportional. In other words, I place the onus on them to tell me what Israel should do that would be proportional, and thus acceptable in their view, to respond to the rocket attacks.

I have never had an answer. They are incapable of providing one.

Does Israel have the right to target the leaders of Hamas, who sponsor and organize those attacks against Israel? No, they

236

say, as that would constitute targeted assassination and thus be illegal under (their interpretation of) international law.

Can Israel impose punitive economic measures against the territory controlled by Hamas? No, they say, as that would be collective punishment.

Does Israel have the right to dismantle Palestinian rockets through limited military incursions? No, they say, as even when limited, a military incursion always leads to too many civilian deaths and injuries and is thus disproportionate.

In other words, Israel has the right of self-defence *in theory* but not *in practice*. That of course, makes no sense – and is a framework applied to no other country in the world.

According to the proportionality theory, the proper response from Israel should have been 6,000 rockets and mortars on Palestinian civilian targets in response to the 6,000 fired on Israel between 2001 and the Gaza War.

But we are told that proportionality is the appropriate response, without any detail or realistic meaning given to such proportionality. However, the true concept of legitimate self-defence allows a military force to kill innocent civilians *as long as the target is a military target and not civilians.*

This is the principle followed by Western militaries whenever they are in action. For example, the U.S. military in Mogadishu in 1993, or the NATO aerial campaign against Serbia in 1999 - a campaign during which no NATO pilot was killed whereas Serbian civilian deaths have been estimated at approximately 500.

Western societies are very sensitive to the deaths of their soldiers - and they have every right to be. We saw it in Canada whenever a Canadian soldier lost his or her life in Afghanistan. Thus, in order to minimize the number of soldiers killed,

Western armies are willing to accept a certain number of unfortunate civilian deaths, not as targets but as an unavoidable product of war.

We must not avoid the question of responsibility, that is who created the situation that placed innocent civilians at risk.

Consequently, the common sense principle "what is good for the goose is good for the gander" must be applied. In other words, if this principle applies to Western armies (including Canada's), it must also apply to that other Western military called the Israel Defense Forces.

The issue of proportionality also raises the following question: have proportional responses won wars in the past or helped solve conflicts?

During the Second World War, the Luftwaffe (German Air Force) killed about 50,000 people in Britain. The Allied response killed 600,000 Germans, 12 times the number of British victims.

One could obviously not qualify the Allied response as being proportionate. But the ferocious aerial raids over Germany helped the Allies in their victory.

Who are we, Canadians, Americans and British, to lecture Israelis as to the proportionality of their response?

The rules of the laws of war must be updated. By definition, terrorist groups like Hamas and Hezbollah do not play by established norms. They target, and hide behind, civilians. What can a state do in this situation to defend itself, to exercise its right to self-defence?

On November 1, 2010, Hamas admitted that 700 fighters were killed during the conflict in Gaza[275], out of a total of 1,166 Palestinians killed. If a figure proves that Israel did all it could to avoid civilian deaths, it is this one.

It is always difficult to avoid civilian victims in a modern conflict. Nonetheless, Palestinian civilians represent about 40 percent of the total deaths during the Gaza conflict - much lower than the 90 percent norm in any modern war.

Indeed, according to a 2001 report by the International Red Cross, civilians are the main victims of modern warfare, with 10 civilian deaths for each soldier killed since the middle of the 20th century. This is to be compared with nine soldiers killed for each civilian death during the First World War.[276]

To be clear: each and every innocent civilian death is to be deplored and is, in itself, tragic. That being said, despite very difficult circumstances, Israel has shown a great deal of restraint in order to avoid as many civilian deaths as possible. Numbers do not lie.

I am not a pacifist. Unfortunately, in our world, war is sometimes necessary. But war is always tragic. And we must never, ever glorify it.

Consequences of the reaction of the international community

The reaction of the international community to the Gaza conflict can only push peace further away.

The international community had long been asking Israel to withdraw from the territories it captured in 1967. This is exactly what Israel did in evacuating from Gaza in 2005.

The *quid pro quo* was, obviously, that in withdrawing from Gaza, Israel would be at peace with the territory and, if attacked, could exercise its right to self-defence.
But what happened?

Israel withdrew from Gaza. Hamas took control of Gaza. And missiles were launched from Gaza at Israel.

When Israel had had enough and responded to the missile attacks, the international community did not say "we understand" but, to the contrary, effectively negated Israel's right to self-defence. It was a flurry of condemnations, culminating with the Goldstone Report.

What can Israelis think now of international guarantees, according to which if Israel withdraws from the West Bank/Judea-Samaria and is then attacked, it will have the right, like every nation, to respond in self-defence?

Hate in our streets

During the conflict with Gaza, anti-Israel demonstrations took place in Toronto and in Montreal. Having learned from the 2006 fiasco, the vast majority of the political sector stayed away.[277]

Some of what occurred during those demonstrations went way too far. "Jews are our dogs" and calls for the murder of Jews were heard.[278] Hezbollah flags were flown. Despite what one may have thought, they were not the streets of Nablus, Baghdad or Tehran, but our own streets here in Canada. It was astonishingly toxic and un-Canadian.

Following those very ugly demonstrations and the Jewish community's reaction, *La Presse* columnist Rima Elkouri minimized what had happened.[279] I have always wondered if she would have written the same thing if what we had heard had been: "Death to homosexuals" or "Women are our bitches". I would tend to think that she would have harshly denounced – and with reason – any demonstration during which those comments had been heard. A clear case of a double standard.

She was however, taken to task by *Le Journal de Montréal*

columnist Richard Martineau, who did not hesitate to renounce this form of racism. Martineau also took on the clear bias on the part of the journalistic class on the issue.[280]

While virulent anti-Israel demonstrations were taking place in our streets, pro-Israel meetings were held inside and all of them began with a minute of silence for innocent Israeli *and* Palestinian victims.

That is the Canadian way to show one's support for a cause or a nation during a period of conflict.

The Gaza Flotilla[281]

In the night between the 30 and 31 of May 2010, the Israeli Navy stopped a flotilla of boats en route to Gaza, despite the Israeli-Egyptian blockade on the territory after Hamas' takeover. Unfortunately, this incident led to nine deaths.

It is well known that the organizers were looking for a confrontation with Israel. This was not the claimed humanitarian convoy of goods. It was a PR operation, aimed at attacking Israel in the court of world public opinion.

Israel made numerous offers to land the material in the Israeli port of Ashdod (30 minutes from Gaza) and to securely transfer it to Gaza. The organizers responded that the mission was not of a humanitarian nature but was aimed at breaching the (arms) blockade of Gaza. This is, in any event, what organizer Greta Berlin told AFP on May 27, 2010.

In fact, many of the flotilla's participants were armed and well-trained extremists with links to the Muslim Brotherhood and other jihadi groups, notably as members of the Turkish IHH.[282]

The day before the confrontation, Arab TV *Al-Jazeera*, not known for its pro-Israel tendencies, broadcast a report.[283] In it, one can hear the people on board the ship chanting a well-known Islamist saying, referencing the murder and defeat of Jews. "Khaybar, Khaybar o Jews, the army of Muhammad will return."

Khaybar is the name of the last Jewish village defeated by Mohamad in 628 where many Jews were killed. That battle marked the end of the Jewish presence in the Arabian peninsula. The battle is seen by Islamists as a precursor to the Jews' fate in Israel and in the world. In other words, it is a threat of extermination made against Jews. This alone should prove that the boat in question was not filled with "peace activists".

Some still said that the flotilla was lead by people looking for peace in the Middle East. Some pointed to the presence of Swedish author Henning Mankell on one of the boats, as proof of the activists' desire for peace. What they fail to mention is that Mankell has openly stated his desire that Israel disappear.[284]

Israeli sailors who tried to board the Mavi Marmara (one of six ships in the flotilla) were attacked by dozens of fighters, armed with knives, iron bars and pistols.[285] Israeli soldiers, afraid for their lives, defended themselves. At least four Israeli soldiers were injured, including being shot.

In an interview on Israeli television on September 24, 2010, Turkish journalist Sefik Dinç, who was on the Mavi Marmara and wrote a book on the incident, clearly said that no gunfire came from Israeli helicopters and that Israeli soldiers fired only when their lives were at risk.[286] Dinç corroborates the Israeli soldiers' version.

There is no humanitarian blockade of Gaza

The entire cargo of the flotilla to Gaza[287] was delivered by Israel on June 1, 2010, after inspection a day after it was unloaded in the port of Ashdod. Unfortunately, the following day, Hamas refused entry of the cargo into Gaza.[288]

At the time, the Canada-Israel Committee analyzed the amount of humanitarian aid Israel had been delivering to the people of Gaza before the flotilla incident. As the CIC noted:

Over one million tons of humanitarian supplies were delivered by Israel to the people of Gaza in the 18 months preceding the incident – that's equal to nearly one ton of aid for every man, woman and child in Gaza.

In the first quarter of 2010 alone (January-March), Israel delivered 94,500 tons of supplies to Gaza. It's very easy to miss what that actually means for the people of Gaza – the breakdown includes:

- 40,000 tons of wheat – which is equal to 53 million loaves of bread;
- 2,760 tons of rice – which equals 69 million servings;
- 1,987 tons of clothes and footwear – the equivalent weight of 3.6 million pairs of jeans; and
- 553 tons of milk powder and baby food – equivalent to over 3.1 million days of formula for an average six-month-old baby.

This reflects a long-term effort on the part of Israel to ensure delivery of a massive and comprehensive supply of aid to Gaza's civilians, while restricting Hamas' ability to import missiles that are then launched at the cities of southern Israel.

In 2009 alone:

- During the Muslim holy days of Ramadan and Eid al-Adha, Israel shipped some 11,000 head of cattle into Gaza – enough to provide 8.8 million meals of beef;
- More than 3,000 tons of hypochlorite were delivered by Israel to Gaza for water purification purposes – that's 60

billion gallons of purified water; and
- Israel brought some 4,883 tons of medical equipment and
medicine into Gaza – a weight equivalent to over 360,000
260-piece mobile trauma first aid kits.[289]

Finally, on June 8, 2010, Israel lifted the embargo on all goods destined for civilian use into Gaza.[290]

On that same day, the Canada-Israel Committee published statistics[291] that give a very different perspective than what we may think about Gaza. Just to consider one example:

Infant mortality rate: Countries facing humanitarian crises have very high infant mortality rate. In Niger, the rate is 114 deaths for 1,000 births. In Somalia, it is 107 for 1,000 births.

In Gaza, the infant mortality rate is 17.71 for 1,000 births. It is better than Mexico, Brazil and Vietnam. In fact, it is better than most countries in the world, the world average being 44 deaths for 1,000 births.

Unfortunately, even humanitarian deliveries had been used in the past to support Hamas' terror. For example, in 2007, a European Union aid delivery purporting to transport sugar, in fact contained an essential component for missile and explosives production.[292] It is thus easy to understand why Israel wants to inspect any cargo going into Gaza, even "humanitarian aid" shipments.

The goal of the Israeli arms blockade on Gaza (which, at the risk of repeating myself, does not stop humanitarian aid), is to prevent dangerous individuals and materials from getting to Hamas.

Hamas smuggles huge quantities of arms and weapons into Gaza in order to fortify its positions and continue its attacks on Israel. According to international law, Israel has the right to stop any vessel, if it is believed on reasonable grounds to be carrying contraband or breaching a blockade, and after prior warning they intentionally and clearly refuse to stop, or intentionally and clearly resist visit, search, or capture.[293]

As for Canadian critics of the interception of the flotilla in international waters, I am still waiting for them to similarly condemn the Canadian Navy's participation in NATO's Apollo Operation in 2001 and 2003,[294] as well as in operations off the coasts of Somalia and Yemen in 2009-2010.[295]

It is also to be noted that the so-called peace activists refused a request to deliver a letter from the family of Gilad Shalit to their son who had been held hostage for more than four years by Hamas at that time without contact with his family or even the Red Cross, contrary to international law. Strange peace activists...

Finally, it is to be noted that Turkey's secular opposition harshly criticised[296] the Islamist Turkish government's role in this sad episode, as it is well aware of the Erdogan government's real agenda.

Palmer Report or basically, Israel is in the right

This incident, which in the scheme of things is actually minor, is probably one of the most studied and analyzed event in recent years.

Firstly, Israel - which has a solid reputation of examining itself by independent bodies - set up its own independent public commission, chaired by former Israeli Supreme Court Justice Jacob Turkel. It included two international observers, one being Canadian Brigadier General (Ret.) Kenneth Watkin and reported in January 2011.[297] It found that Israel's blockade of Gaza was lawful, as was the capture of the flotilla. The report also found that the Israeli commandos who boarded the Mavi Marmara "acted professionally and in a measured manner in the face of extensive and unanticipated violence". They were met with force from Turkish Islamist IHH activists that was "planned and extremely violent". It is important to note that the two international observers on the Turkel commission are signatories to the report and described it as independent and rigorous.

Nonetheless, after the incident, in August 2010, U.N. Secretary General Ban Ki-Moon asked former New Zealand Prime Minister Geoffrey Palmer to chair a committee to study what happened.

The main conclusions of the U.N. committee, published in the summer of 2011, shatter much of what was said following the event.[298]

Contrary to what many pro-Palestinian activists have been saying – which was repeated by some sloppy analysts - the Palmer Report acknowledged the legality of the Israeli blockade and the legal and practical necessity of its enforcement. It found that it "was imposed as a legitimate security measure in order to prevent weapons from entering Gaza by sea," that its implementation "complied with the requirements of international law," that Israel had a "right to visit and search the vessel and to capture it if found in breach of a blockade," including in international waters, that the flotilla organizers planned "in advance to violently resist any boarding attempt" and that "Israeli Defense Forces personnel faced significant, organized and violent resistance from a group of passengers when they boarded the Mavi Marmara" and responded in self-defence.

The Palmer Report also confirmed that, even though the living conditions were difficult in Gaza, there was no humanitarian crisis in the territory. In so doing, it dispelled false myths about Gaza and certainly contradicted what had become conventional wisdom. It also stated that anyone interested in sending humanitarian aid to the Gaza Strip must do so in coordination with Israel and the Palestinian Authority and must transfer the aid via the land crossings.

Furthermore, the commissioners noted that they had serious questions about "the conduct, true nature and objectives of the flotilla organizers, particularly [the Turkish NGO] IHH," and described the decision to breach the blockade as a "dangerous and reckless act," which "needlessly carried the potential for escalation." The report harshly criticized the flotilla organizers, stating "they acted recklessly in attempting to breach the naval blockade".

The report also said that while the Turkish government made efforts to persuade the IHH organizers to avoid an encounter with Israeli forces, "more could have been done" by the Turkish government.

That being said, the Palmer committee criticized the execution of the flotilla interception, noting that Israel should have anticipated, but did not, that there would be significant violent opposition to an attempt to board the ships, which was a failure of Israeli intelligence. I believe that this is the hardest part for the commissioner to comment on, as operational issues are hard to evaluate after the fact. This is thus, not coincidentally, the weakest part of the report. I found the Turkel commission report on this issue more credible.

The committee suggested that Israel make an appropriate statement of regret and offer a payment for the benefit of the deceased and injured, not because of any legal obligation or liability but symbolically "to advance the interests of stability in the Middle East". Israel did the first and would probably be willing to follow the second suggestion.

Unfortunately, Turkey, instead of accepting the Palmer report as a basis to close the incident, decided to put gas on the fire, leading many Western governments – including its many friends in the European Union - to doubt the current Turkish government's maturity and judgment. The current Turkish leadership is turning away from the West, as it seeks to lead the Muslim world.

Double standards applied to Israel: a form of racism against... Muslims

Obviously, the Arab-Muslim community rose in anger after the Gaza flotilla incident. The Arab street was inflamed. The U.N. was seized by the issue.

Let us compare the situation with, for example, that of Ahmadi Muslims.[299] A week before the Gaza flotilla incident, about 100 Ahmadi Muslims were massacred in Pakistan[300] while they were praying in a mosque. Why? Because the Taliban, who are Sunni Muslims, consider Ahmadi Muslims to be heretic, and thus deserving of death. Where was the international condemnation?

At the end of January 2010, in Iraq, a suicide attack (another one) was carried out.[301] A woman, a Sunni Muslim, detonated herself in the middle of a crowd of Shiite Muslims. She left behind 41 dead and 106 injured.

And where were the demonstrators when a kamikaze detonated himself in Tal Afar, in the north of Iraq, during a soccer game on May 14, 2010, killing 25 spectators and injuring approximately one hundred?[302]

All this passed almost unnoticed. The Muslim world remained silent.

But when cartoons of the Prophet Mohammad were published in Denmark, violence erupted around the world: an intense and deadly violence.

When a Palestinian civilian dies during battles between Israel and its enemies, the Muslim-Arab world rises up in outrage. Anti-Israel activists in the West organize protests. The U.N.

meets for emergency sessions. NGOs issue scathing press releases and reports.

If an Israeli Jew kills a Muslim, streets are filled with protesters, newspapers are filled with indignant letters denouncing Israeli barbarism. But when Muslims kill Muslims, it barely makes the news in our media. There are no protests in the streets of the Arab world, nor here in Canada.

When Muslims kill one another – which happens often – nobody reacts. Not so-called peace activists, not Western governments, and not Muslim leaders. Could there be a better example of a double standard?

French Muslim analyst of Algerian origins Mohamed Sifaoui underlined this fact when he wrote about the anti-Israel demonstrations during the Gaza conflict of 2009:

> *Where were all those Muslims with all the compassion towards Gaza children and towards the terrorists who lead them to war, where were they when Grozny was being razed by the Russian army, while Chechen women were openly raped by Putin's soldiers and while deaths were daily in the hundreds? (…)*

> *Or where were all those Saturday protesters when Algerians were being diced in small bits by the monsters of the GIA and when their throats were being slit by the disciples of Ali Belhadj?*

> *Why did all those Muslims who protest today, eyes out of their sockets, spit on their chins, all teeth showing never protest after a terrorist attack? Why did they not protest while Islamists were killing fellow Muslims? Why did they not walk after September 11th, Madrid, or London? Where were they when the Taliban was executing women in stadiums? Why, every time I hear them, are they moaning, saying that they belong to an 'oppressed religion'? Why*

do they never denounce, in similar protests, those who oppress in the name of that same religion? Why are they more virulent, more heinous and, sometimes, more violent than the Palestinians and Jordanians that I know? Why is there so little dignity in the expression of their emotion, be it sincere or feigned? What does this selective compassion hide? What does it hide? Let us be clear and impolitic. Isn't the Israel-Palestinian conflict simply a fixation, fed, including by the Muslim states, to fan hatred? Could the issue really be the religion of the enemy, Israel? Could it be anti-Semitism?

Here is what I really think. I think that many of those Saturday protesters protest more against Israel than for Palestine. Many protest not because they love Palestinians but because they ideologically detest all that is Jewish and all that is related to Israel. I even think that most of them – excuse me for the expression – don't give a shit about the Palestinians. Because, in the end, if those protesters were so humanist, I would have met them in demonstrations for Darfur or for the Chechens, and in demonstrations in solidarity with the Algerian victims of Islamism and in demonstrations denouncing terror and fundamentalist fascism. Maybe they would have protested against Hamas violence not towards Israelis, but against their Fatah brothers.[303]

This is indeed a form of racism. However, racism directed not so much against Jews (which it is, nonetheless, with Israel being held to a unique standard) but primarily against Muslims. It seems that when Muslims kill one another, people think it normal. They are in effect, judging Muslims to be uncivilized people, from whom one cannot expect more.

With Israel, Jews have built a democratic state based on the rule of law, and so the bar is placed higher for them. It highlights the strength of anti-Muslim prejudice: rather than holding them to a similar standard, the world expects the worst from them. This is, I believe, a kind of insidious racism. They deserve better from us. They deserve better, period.

I'll leave the last word to columnist Burak Bekdil, from the Turkish English-language newspaper Daily News (from the same group as the very influential Hürriyet). Bekdil does not mince his words:

> *But why do the Turks have the "Palestine fetish" even though most of them can't point the Palestinian territories out on a map? Why did they not raise a finger when, for instance, the mullahs killed dissident Iranian Muslims? Why did the Turks not raise a finger when non-Muslim occupying forces killed a million Iraqi Muslims? Why did we not hear one single Turkish voice protesting the deaths of 300,000 Muslims in Darfur?*
>
> *(...)*
>
> *How many Turks protested when there was civil war in Algeria? How many volunteered for humanitarian aid missions for Sudan? Why were the protests too thin during the Serbian atrocities against Muslim Bosnians? What makes nine Gaza martyrs more sacred than all the other martyrs?*

And he concludes:

> *Subconsciously (and sadly) the Muslim-Turkish thinking tolerates it if Muslims kill Muslims; (...) but is programmed to turn the world upside down when Jews kill Muslims.*[304]

Land for Peace. Is it that simple?

We often hear so-called experts say, simplistically, that if only Israel were to leave the territories it captured in 1967, all would be solved in the region. This is wrong. It would not solve Arab rejection of a Jewish state in the Middle East, a rejection that existed long before Israel conquered the Golan, the West Bank, and the Sinai.

I want to be clear. I am not saying that Israel should not withdraw from the disputed territories. Neither am I saying that Palestinians should not have their own independent, viable and peaceful state. I have made that clear.

What I am saying, however, is that if history provides lessons for the future, the land for peace solution is, in itself, not enough.

Israel left south Lebanon in 2000 and Hezbollah not only took control of the area, but used it to attack Israel.

Israel left Gaza in 2005 and Hamas took over, using the territory as a base from which to attack Israel with hundreds of missiles and mortars.

It is not really difficult to understand Israel's scepticism, is it?[305]

23
Apartheid, You Say?

I was never really involved in student politics, either at CEGEP or at University.

At the time, I thought that the people in and around student associations were wanna-be revolutionaries, simply repeating Marxist slogans from books they had read but obviously not understood. They were completely disconnected from the realities of the students they were supposedly representing.

So, when I was first approached by Jewish students telling me what was going on on campuses across Canada, I cannot say that I was particularly troubled. My initial view was that they were likely the usual ideological battles common to all campuses.

I only realized the gravity of the situation when I was fully informed of the intimidation and bullying to which they were being subjected. This intimidating environment now crystallizes around a yearly event called *Israel Apartheid Week*.

As unbelievable as it may sound to any informed individual, Israel is accused by Arab and pro-Palestinian groups of being an apartheid state. This accusation is the centrepiece of an organized campaign, culminating in a week-long festival of slander. And every year, Israel's friends and Jewish students are the victims of this calumnious campaign. This includes scores of non-Jewish students who support Israel on campus, and are deemed guilty by association – and subjected to vicious hostility.

It is ironic when one considers the source of the accusation. A few facts are sufficient to show how ridiculous this accusation is.

First, it is not because Israel defines itself as a Jewish[306] and democratic state that Israel is therefore an exclusionary state.[307] The word "Jewish", should not be understood here as relating to religion. In fact, the word "religion" is not found in the Torah. The biblical terms for the Jews are *Am Yisrael* (the nation of Israel) and *B'nai Yisrael* (the children of Israel). In other words, for Jews, the identity is national before being religious. That is why for example, there is such a thing as a Jewish atheist whereas one cannot be a Christian atheist.

Furthermore, to qualify as an apartheid state, Israel would need to practice systemic discrimination against non-Jews or any other minority.

a) Israel is a democracy

Israel is the sole liberal Western-style democracy in the Middle East. The only state with the rule of law. The only country with an independent judiciary.

Israel's Arab citizens have the same rights as Israeli Jews. They have the right to vote. They are represented in the Knesset (the Israeli Parliament), in which they hold 14 of 120 seats.[308] Arab Israelis sit on the Supreme Court of Israel.

In Israel, Arabic is an official language. All the statutes are also published in Arabic. Road signs are in Hebrew, English and Arabic. I don't recall seeing many bilingual road signs in Canada, a country with two official languages.

While Israel is a vibrant democracy, it is not perfect. The pure proportional system gives too much power to small parties, resulting in parliamentary instability. Since the birth of Israel, not one party has obtained a majority of seats in its parliament. This is the best example I know of why we should not adopt the system here in Canada

b) Religious apartheid

Israel's religious system gives the same status to the religious laws of different communities: Muslim *sharia*, Christian canonical law, Druze law, and Jewish *halacha*, in issues like marriage, divorce, and adoption.

Another interesting fact: Israel is the only country in the Middle East with a growing Christian community. In fact, Israel's Christian population has grown by 345 percent since the establishment of the Jewish state.[309] Between 1995 and 2009, the Israeli Christian community grew by 26 percent from 120,300 to 151,700. By contrast, when Israel ceded Bethlehem to the Palestinian Authority in 1995, 60 percent of its inhabitants were Christians. Now, Bethlehem is a Muslim town, with a Christian population of only 20 percent. In fact, it is now "difficult for a Christian to acquire a house or land as 'one does not cede Islamic land to a crusader,'"[310] i.e. a Christian.

According to Reverend Canon Andrew White, Vicar of St. George's Church in Baghdad and president of the Foundation for Relief and Reconciliation in the Middle East, "[t]he fact is that the only place in the Middle East that Christians are really safe is Israel."[311]

The Centre for Christian-Jewish Understanding agrees when it says that "[i]n the last 50 years, the Christian populations in the region have dropped significantly in every country except Israel. This trend has accelerated in the last 10 years."[312]

At a time when Christians are being bombed, shot, and intimidated in places like Iraq and Egypt, Israel's Christians enjoy security, freedom, and equality with their Jewish peers.

c) Ethnic apartheid

Israeli Arabs have complete and free access to Israeli universities. For example, 20 percent of the students at Haifa University are Arabs.

As Canadian Muslim author Irshad Manji wrote in an Australian paper:

> In a state practising apartheid, would Arab Muslim legislators wield veto power over anything? At only 20 percent of the population, would Arabs even be eligible for election if they squirmed under the thumb of apartheid? Would an apartheid state extend voting rights to women and the poor in local elections, which Israel did for the first time in the history of Palestinian Arabs?

> Would the vast majority of Arab Israeli citizens turn out to vote in national elections, as they've usually done? Would an apartheid state have several Arab political parties, as Israel does? In recent Israeli elections, two Arab parties found themselves disqualified for expressly supporting terrorism against the Jewish state. However, Israel's Supreme Court, exercising its independence, overturned both disqualifications. Under any system of apartheid, would the judiciary be free of political interference?

> Would an apartheid state award its top literary prize to an Arab? Israel honoured Emile Habibi in 1986, before the intifada might have made such a choice politically shrewd. Would an apartheid state encourage Hebrew-speaking schoolchildren to learn Arabic? Would road signs throughout the land appear in both languages? Even my country, the proudly bilingual Canada, doesn't meet that standard.

Would an apartheid state be home to universities where Arabs and Jews mingle at will, or apartment blocks where they live side by side? Would an apartheid state bestow benefits and legal protections on Palestinians who live outside of Israel but work inside its borders? Would human rights organisations operate openly in an apartheid state? They do in Israel.[313]

Even the hero of Palestinian nationalism, the preeminent intellectual Edward Said, wrote that Israel was not South Africa.[314]

Arab Israelis have their own school system. More than 300,000 Israeli children are studying in Israel's Arab high schools today, whereas in 1948, the year of Israel's birth, there was only one Arab high school.

According to the Abraham Fund Initiative, since Israel's birth, the number of schools in the Arab Israeli school system grew fifteen fold, while the number of Hebrew schools only grew fivefold. Moreover, "[t]he number of classes offered in the Arab Israeli system increased more than seventeen fold, and since 1961 the literacy rate of Arab Israelis jumped from 49.6 percent to 90 percent."[315]

It is undeniable that, globally, the level of education of the Arabs has gotten much better in the last fifty years, leading to the creation of a dynamic and active intelligentsia. It is also true that the rate of schooling of the Arabs living in Israel is much better than that of their "brothers" living in Jordan or in Egypt. Thus, many are of the opinion that the Arabs have largely benefitted from the socio-economic modernisation that accompanied their insertion into Israeli society compared to those who were living in the neighbouring Arab states.[316]

Seventy-seven percent of Arab Israeli citizens prefer living in Israel to living in any other country in the world.[317] If Israel was an apartheid state, would the number be that high?

Recently, when the Arab newspaper *Kul Al-Arab* surveyed Israeli Arabs of the city of Umm al-Fahm, asking if their town should join a Palestinian State, 11 percent agreed, and 83 percent disagreed, preferring to remain Israeli.[318]

A more current study[319] conducted in November 2010 among Arab residents of the eastern part of Jerusalem shows a higher preference for citizenship in the State of Israel than in an independent Palestinian state. When asked to choose, 35 percent prefer being Israeli, 30 percent chose Palestinian citizenship, and 35 percent either refused to answer or do not know. Forty percent went so far as to say that they would rather move to a new house within Israel's borders than to live under Palestinian rule.

This should not be surprising. Ironically, it is in Israel among all the nations of the Middle East that Arabs enjoy the most rights.

In a more anecdotal – but as important – perspective, Canadian Muslim author Tarek Fatah writes in his latest book that, when asked whether Israel was an apartheid state, every Israeli Arab he met answered categorically 'no'.[320]

Israeli democracy has all the tools necessary to fight racism. A recent example: in December 2010, a group of extremist rabbis declared that it is forbidden (in their interpretation of Jewish theology) for Jews living in Israel to sell or rent apartments to non-Jews (which, in Israel, means Arabs).[321] The reaction? President Shimon Peres,[322] Prime Minister Benjamin Netanyahu,[323] Knesset speaker Reuven Rivlin, every national newspaper, *Yad Vashem* (the Holocaust Martyrs' and Heroes' Remembrance Authority) all firmly condemned those rabbis. Hundreds of Diaspora rabbis also condemned this ridiculous statement, strongly denouncing any discrimination on the basis of religion.[324] Many individuals, including the top leaders of Reform Judaism,[325] requested a judicial inquiry into the matter.

In Canada, the Canada-Israel Committee also strongly condemned the rabbis,[326] as did the editorial of the *Canadian Jewish News*, Canada's main Jewish newspaper.[327]

Quebec media also talked about this scandal. Anti-Israel groups made a fuss as well. I agree with them on this point: those rabbis had indeed taken a racist position.

Recall, however, that this reaction was over a mere statement made by a fringe group of Israeli rabbis and not a law.

My question therefore is the following: why is nothing being said by the Palestinian leaders, pro-Palestinian groups, or the Quebec (and other) media about the fact that the sale of Palestinian land to an Israeli is punishable by death under Palestinian Authority law?[328]

In 1984 and in 1990, in two distinct operations (Operation Moses and Operation Solomon), Israel used extensive resources to find, transport, and settle 25,000 Black Ethiopian Jews in Israel. It was the first and only time in history that Black men, women, and children were taken out of Africa *en masse* not for slavery, but to freedom. Still today, there is ongoing Ethiopian immigration to Israel. The community now numbers approximately 120,000 proud Israelis.

Indeed, they represent just one of the many inspirational stories resulting from Israel's absorption of immigrants from more than 140 countries, who have built a truly diverse nation.

d) Sexual apartheid

In Israel, women are not obligated by the government to cover their hair or face. From the very moment of its establishment, women in Israel have had complete equality with men.[329]

When she became the Israeli Prime Minister in 1969, Golda Meir was only the second woman in the world to reach that level of power.

e) Apartheid against gays and lesbians[330]

Gays and lesbians, persecuted in the Arab world and executed in Iran, are protected under Israeli law. A homosexual person in Israel is not under the threat of being fired, of imprisonment or death, and can generally count on the Supreme Court legally protecting his or her rights.

Mario Roy, an editorial writer at Montreal's *La Presse* newspaper, wrote in reference to Israel that it is: "the only nation in this region of the world where homosexuals are not persecuted, imprisoned, executed or... non-existent, like in Iran!"[331]

I myself have met Israeli gays and lesbians, participated in their events around Israel's Gay Pride celebrations, and shared drinks with them in gay bars. Tel Aviv's gay community is particularly dynamic and impressive.

I have written above, that I am not a fan of Jewish settlements in the middle of the West Bank – which puts me in good company, as the vast majority of the Israeli public agrees with me on this issue. But to equate the Israeli occupation of the West Bank (which continues, let us not forget, because of the repeated Palestinian refusals of the two-state solution) with apartheid, requires more than twisting the meaning of the word.

Yes, indeed, Israel has a *Law of Return*, allowing Jews from around the world to enter and become citizens. But other countries have similar statutes on their books, including Bulgaria,[332] Hungary, Ireland,[333] Italy, Spain, Japan, Germany,[334] and Greece[335] - which all have statutes facilitating the immigration of individuals with historical connections to those countries.[336]

Israel is far from what could possibly be called an apartheid state. To the contrary, when one looks closely at the rights and freedoms in Israel, it is clear that the besieged Jewish state has standards on par with that of Western liberal democracies. That it is, in fact, part of the Western world.

To compare, Islam is the only official religion of the Palestinian Authority, Arabic is its only official language, and sharia law the cornerstone of its legal system. Homosexuals live under danger of persecution and women are not equal to men.[337] And it is Israel that stands accused of practicing apartheid?

Taking all of this into account, it is ironic to note that Omar Barghouti, the very founder of the Palestinian campaign for the academic and cultural boycott of Israel, is... a doctoral student in an Israeli university.

For a demonstration of the functioning, democratic character of the State of Israel, one needs to look no further than the recent trial of ex-Israeli President Moshe Katsav, well summarized by Jeffrey Goldberg:

1) *An ex-president of the nation was brought to account for his alleged crimes. Doesn't happen too often in Israel's neighbourhood.*

2) *The crimes in question were crimes against women. Happens only rarely in the non-democratic East.*

3) *Two of the three judges in the Katsav case were women -- doesn't happen.*

4) *Here's the stunner -- the head judge of the three-judge panel was an Arab Israeli named George Karra.*

5) *Maybe this is the real stunner -- No one in Israel seemed to think it abnormal for an Arab citizen of the Jewish state to sit in judgment of a Jewish ex-president.*

6) *And, by the way, the president was convicted.* [338]

Let us now compare Israel with its neighbours.

Richard Marceau

a) Democracy

As I am writing these lines, the Arab world is undergoing profound upheaval. I passionately hope (but am nonetheless doubtful) that from this, democratic, liberal, and peaceful governments will be born, based on the rule of law.

But, as of now, one cannot say that democracy is alive and well in the Arab-Muslim world.

Of the 171 non-Arab States in the world, there are 123 democracies, or 72 percent. Of the 22 Arab States, there are no democracies. None.

Of the 47 States with a Muslim majority, only 9, or 19 percent, are democracies. On the other hand, of the 146 non-Muslim States, 114 or 78 percent are democracies.

Those numbers, by the way, help explain why Israel will never accept the one-state solution, or a Jewish-Arab bi-national state. With the high Arab birthrate, Jews would quickly become a minority in an Arab state that would be, from what we know about the existing Arab world, a non-democratic state.

Rami G. Khouri, an influential columnist with both Lebanon's *The Daily Star* and Canada's *The Globe and Mail*, wrote an overview of the situation of the member states of the Arab League.[339]

In this group, according to Khouri:

> *[W]e find Arab states that can be described as authoritarian, weak, strong or fragile. We also have broken states (Somalia), states that disappeared and/or returned (Kuwait, South Yemen), security-dominated states (Tunisia, Syria, formerly Baathist Iraq), erratic states (Libya), pirate states (Somalia), vulnerable states (Lebanon, Palestine[340]), privatized states in the hands of small ruling elites (most*

Arab states), family states that carry a family's name (Saudi Arabia, Jordan), tribal states (Yemen, Oman), mini-states (Kuwait, Qatar, Bahrain), occupied states (Palestine, Iraq to an extent) and various degrees of client and proxy states, rogue states, gangster states and others that defy description.[341]

Khouri also writes that "[n]ot a single Arab country can say with any certainty that the configuration of the state, the policies and values of the government, or the perpetuation of the incumbent ruling elite have been validated by the citizenry through any kind of credible, transparent and accountable political process."[342]

In Ottawa on December 16, 2010, Jordan's former Foreign Affairs Minister and Vice-Prime Minister Marwan Muasher was of a similar opinion, stating that no Arab state had put into place a democratic system with checks and balances, transparency and accountability.[343]

b) Religious apartheid?

As writer Jean Mohsen Fahmy wrote in the Montreal daily *Le Devoir* on March 16, 2010, the Christians' situation in the entire Middle East is tenuous. In his text, he provided many troubling examples of the persecution of Christians in Muslim lands.

In August 2009, seven members of a Pakistani Christian family - including two young children - were locked into their home and burned alive.

On January 6, 2010, Egyptian Coptic Christians were gunned down coming out of Christmas Midnight Mass by Islamists driving by in a car, leaving six dead.

On February 23, 2010, in the city of Mosul, in northern Iraq, an Islamist commando invaded a Christian family's home, killing a father and his two sons in front of his wife and their daughter. This massacre crowned a week during which eight Christians from the same city had been assassinated.[344]

In Saudi Arabia, only Muslims can be citizens, judges, or members of the government. A Jew cannot step foot in the country. Christians are arrested by Saudi police for the "crime" of holding a religious service in a private house. People were praying in a private house because, in Saudi Arabia, it is forbidden to build churches, not to mention synagogues. It is strictly forbidden to practice any religion other than Islam in that country.[345] This is even more ironic considering that Saudi Arabia finances the building of mosques around the world.

As well, non-Muslims are strictly forbidden from entering the holy cities of Mecca and Medina. Can you imagine the cries we would hear if, for example, Israel prohibited non-Jews from going to the holy city of Jerusalem or if Vatican City was off-limits for Muslims?

In Yemen, non-Muslims cannot run for political office and Jews have restrictions as to where they can live.

The Baha'is,[346] are members of a small, monotheistic and peaceful religion that are harshly persecuted in Iran.[347] Of course, as Iran is governed according to *sharia* law, conversion to any religion but Islam is punishable by death.

Things might change in Egypt – I hope – but, in the meantime, what *Le Devoir*'s Serge Truffault wrote still stands: "Coptic Christians are prohibited from joining security forces, the army and even obtaining university positions."[348] This is true despite the fact that Copts make up 10 percent of Egypt's population. As Coptic Christians are very prominent in the tourism industry, I had the occasion to talk with a number of them when I traveled to Egypt during the summer of 2008. When they open up, what they report of their persecution and fears makes one's hair stand up on end.

Fahmy goes as far as saying that "a rejection of Christians, sometimes subtle, sometimes violent, is happening now in the Muslim world."[349]

As previously said, one cannot convert out of Islam in Iran, the penalty being death. The same is true in Saudi Arabia. Converting out of Islam is also forbidden in Egypt, Jordan, Oman, and in North Sudan. In Algeria, active Christians are brought before tribunals.[350] In Algeria, one cannot transport Bibles, and the celebration of non-Muslim religious ceremonies is strictly regulated.[351]

Saudi Arabia,[352] Egypt,[353] and Iran have all put into place systematic discriminatory regulations (legal, social and/or economic) against non-Muslims or minority Islamic movements.

For example, article 2 of the Egyptian constitution[354] states: "Islam is the religion of the state, and the Arabic language is its official language. The principles of Islamic law are the chief source of legislation."[355] The practical result has been that Coptic Christians cannot obtain high positions in the army, the police, the universities, the embassies, or the ministries.[356]

The Egyptian state itself has contributed to the persecution of Coptic Christians. For example, churches must receive a presidential permit to renovate existing churches or build new ones. In November 2010, government security forces killed a Christian and injured dozens of others as they were protesting the government's decision to stop the building of a church.

Still in Egypt, more than 30 massacres of Christians were reported between 1981 and 2000.[357] On New Year's Eve 2011, an Islamist attack against a Coptic church left 21 dead and dozens injured.[358] At the beginning of May 2011, attacks against Coptic churches led to 13 deaths and more than 230 injured.[359]

Jacques Julliard, an important columnist in the French left-wing newsweekly *Le Nouvel Observateur*, displayed his understanding of what was happening in the Middle East with respect to the Christians when he wrote in October 2010:

Christianity has become, by far, the most persecuted religion. But the West buries its head in the sand.

(…)

Only the Christians are being killed. Religious communities are being persecuted. Where? Here and there. (…) Where they are in a minority situation. And mainly in Muslim countries. Not only in Saudi Arabia where Christian practice makes one liable to the death penalty. But also in Egypt, in Turkey, in Algeria. In today's world, Christianity is the most persecuted religion.

But it is in the Middle East, where Christianity was born, that the situation is the gravest. In Turkey, Christian communities, older than Islam itself, are on the verge of disappearing. In Egypt (Copts), in Lebanon (in particular, the Maronites), they are either turning inwards or leaving for the West. In Iraq, the war had a devastating impact. Close to 2,000 dead, populations transferred by hundreds of thousands, notably to the more welcoming Turkish Kurdistan. Throughout the Middle East, we cannot keep track of the communities attacked, the religious leaders assassinated, the churches burnt down, professional interdictions against Christians, in fact or in law. It is a slow religious genocide.

(…)

For centuries, later-coming but now in the majority Muslims and Christians lived well together. But what has been happening in the last 50 years? Firstly, Islam's awakening, in a form that is aggressive and asserting its identity, as if the Middle East belonged exclusively to the Muslims. It is the

Muslim Brotherhood leading the attacks against Egyptian Copts: in Nag Hammadi, 60 kilometres from Luxor, in Upper Egypt, a car gunned down the faithful coming out of Christmas Mass (January 6, 2010). The result: seven dead. In an imaginary paradox, democratisation reinforces Muslim intolerance and exclusivism: Iraq's Christians were less threatened under Saddam Hussein's dictatorship than they are today. Despots were in the main the heirs of traditional pluralism. In nearly all of those countries, Islam is now the state religion. And anti-Western jihad as well as the American aggression on Iraq turned Christians into representatives of the cursed Western world.

(…)

In the meantime, the West buries its head in the sand. As for me, who has spent the majority of my life defending Muslim populations (Tunisia, Algeria, Bosnia, Darfur), I noticed that when the same thing needed to be done for Christians (Lebanon, South Sudan), professional human rights activists (with the exception of Bernard-Henri Lévy or Bernard Kouchner) would simply cop out. A new kind of cultural Yalta is being created: in the East, the monopoly of a single, more and more intolerant Islam. In the West, pluralism, tolerance, secularism. This Yalta leads, like the previous one, to a Cold War, if not more. Thus, we must, without any ulterior motives, nor complacency, defend the Christians' right to exist in the East.[360]

In Jordan, it is even forbidden for Israelis to enter if they are in possession of *tefillin* (religious phylacteries)[361] or if they wear a *kippa* (head covering).[362]

As an aside, on October 31, 2010, a massacre of 58 Christians by Islamists took place in Baghdad. What was the reaction in the Muslim world? Silence. Nothing. As important, and inexcusable, what was the reaction of Arab groups in Canada, groups that are so quick to condemn Israel? The same silence.

No denunciation. No condemnation. No demonstration. What a bunch of hypocrites.[363]

In sum, if apartheid exists in the Middle East, it is to be found in the "religious cleansing" of Christians and other religious minorities in the Muslim world. As the French daily *Le Monde* rightly put it: "for those Christians communities, more than radical Islam, it is now the daily confrontation with political Islam that endangers the very survival of Christian culture and traditions."[364]

This, in combination with the quasi-total absence of Jews in the Arab-Muslim world, is what led well-known French philosopher Bernard-Henri Lévy to say that Christianity was the most persecuted religion in the world.[365]

c) Ethnic apartheid

In Syria, Jews and Kurds[366] cannot participate in the political system. Jews cannot be employees of the government and are the only group whose religious identity is put on passports and identity cards. As for the Kurds, even though they are 10 percent of the Syrian population, they are the victims of a policy of forced Arabization; the majority either are not considered citizens or have an inferior citizenship status compared to that of Syrian Arabs. As well, Kurds do not enjoy the same education and health services as Arab Syrians.

Jordan, considered a moderate state, has a statute banning Jews from becoming citizens[367] and another forbidding Jordanians from selling land to a Jew.

Discrimination against Jews is so entrenched in the Palestinian territories that, as previously alluded to, a Palestinian selling land to an Israeli is liable to be put to death by the Palestinian Authority.[368]

Moreover in September 2011, the PLO Ambassador to the

U.S. Maen Areikat, said that a future Palestinian state should be free of Jews. Sixty years ago, we would have called this *Judenrein*.[369]

Jews are victims of persecution, discrimination, and incitement in the Palestinian territories,[370] in Egypt, Jordan, Syria, Iran, Saudi Arabia, Lebanon, Libya, Sudan, in the United Arab Emirates, and in the Gulf States.[371]

As I mentioned earlier, in Lebanon,[372] Palestinians are excluded from dozens of professions. They cannot work as accountants, pharmacists, electricians, cooks, and in other trades. Neither can they be owners of a money exchange business, a gold business, a publishing business, a car mechanic business, an engineering business, or a health care business. Palestinians were excluded from 72 professions by Lebanese law (which, as described earlier, marginally changed in 2010).

As recently as June 2011, the mufti of Lebanon, Sheikh Mohammed Rashid Qabbani, was quoted as saying that Palestinians are no longer welcome in his country, calling them "trash".[373]

During a meeting I had organized in Jerusalem on July 14, 2010, between a group of Canadians and Mr. Xavier Abueid, an official PLO representative, Abueid clearly told the group that the place where Palestinians were treated the worst in the world was Lebanon.

This discrimination is not however limited to Lebanon.[374]

In Jordan,

> *[a]lthough Palestinians constitute around half of the population, they remain vastly under-represented in Jordanian government. Nine of the 55 Senators appointed by the king are Palestinian, and in the 110-seat Chamber of Deputies, Palestinians have only 18 seats. Of Jordan's 12*

governates, none are led by Palestinians.

Discrimination against Palestinians in private and state-sector employment remains common and a quota system limits the number of university admissions for Palestinian youth. Government security operations disproportionately target Palestinians, especially operations conducted in the name of fighting terror.[375]

For two generations or more, Palestinians have been refused citizenship in Kuwait, Syria, Saudi Arabia, Egypt, and Iraq.

d) Sexual Apartheid

It is an open secret that women in the Muslim world

suffer from unequal citizenship and legal entitlements, often evident in voting rights and legal codes. The utilization of Arab women's capabilities through political and economic participation remains the lowest in the world in quantitative terms, as evidenced by the very low share of women in parliaments, cabinets, and the work force and in the trend towards the feminization of unemployment. Qualitatively, women suffer from inequality of opportunity, evident in employment status, wages and gender-based occupational segregation. Society as a whole suffers when a huge proportion of its productive potential is stifled, resulting in lower family incomes and standards of living.[376]

According to the World Economic Forum's *Global Gender Gap Index 2010*, which studied 134 states, among the worst in this domain may be found: Lebanon (116th), Jordan (120th), Iran (123rd), Syria (124th), Egypt (125th), Turkey (126th), Morocco (127th), Saudi Arabia (129th), and Yemen (134th).

Of course, it is not only a question of numbers.

For example, Saudi Arabia practices a form of gender separation unacceptable in societies like Canada. Women cannot drive a car in Saudi Arabia. All this, by the way, did not hinder Saudi Arabia's accession, on November 10, 2010, to an important position in the new U.N. agency dedicated to the status of women.[377]

Recently, a Saudi imam issued a *fatwa* to the effect that anyone who promotes women and men working together, or otherwise compromises gender separation in the kingdom, should be subject to execution.[378]

In October of 2010, the United Arab Emirates' Supreme Court ruled that a man could beat his wife and children as long as no visible physical trace remained.[379]

In Syria, it is legal for a man to stop his wife from traveling abroad. In many countries (Egypt, Iraq, Jordan, Libya, Oman, Yemen) married women require written permission from their husbands to travel abroad.[380]

In Saudi Arabia, permission is required from the closest male relative, not only to leave the country - as in the case of Canadian Nathalie Morin[381] - but also to use public transportation.[382] Women cannot marry a foreigner, drive a car or a bike, sit in the front of buses, enter a public place without being accompanied,[383] or sue for domestic violence or rape.[384]

There also exists the phenomenon of "honour killings"[385] or, in other words, the murder of women and girls to preserve the honour (!) of the family due to "unacceptable" behaviour by the female. For example, Rofayda Qaoud, from the Palestinian village of Abu Qash, was raped by her brothers and became pregnant as a result. Because she refused to kill herself to save the family's honour, her mother strangled, stabbed, and beat her to death the night of February 23, 2003.[386] The mother received a light sentence as honour killing is a mitigating circumstance in sentencing in the Palestinian legal system.

In Saudi Arabia, gender-based apartheid is so pervasive that it leads to absurd deaths. In 2002, fifteen young girls were burned alive when Saudi police refused to let them out of their flaming school, because the clothes they were wearing violated the modesty rules of the kingdom. A witness testified that he saw three police officers beat the young girls to stop them from exiting the school, as they were not wearing their *abaya*.[387]

e) Apartheid against gays and lesbians

Despite Iranian President Mahmoud Ahmadinejad's statement to the effect that there are no homosexuals in Iran,[388] of course there are. They are however, very discreet. It is easy to understand why, given that homosexuals in Iran are liable to be criminally convicted and sentenced to the death penalty. Those found guilty of this crime are executed in a most public and grotesque way – usually by hanging. Between 1979 and 1999, 4,000 homosexuals were reported to have been hanged in Iran.[389]

In Morocco, s. 489 of the Penal Code states that the penalty for consensual homosexual acts is prison.

In Egypt, homosexuals are persecuted, condemned, and imprisoned.[390]

While in Israel, I personally witnessed the birth of one of the most touching and interesting projects on this subject.

I was leading a group comprised of Canadian gays and lesbians visiting Israel. The group included author Irshad Manji, Michelle Douglas (who was responsible for having the ban on gays in the Canadian military overturned), now-Ontario provincial minister Glen Murray, and others.

Understandably, they were all very sensitive to the persecution of homosexuals in many countries, notably in the Muslim world.

Every group I bring to Israel, I bring to *Yad Vashem*, Israel's Holocaust National Memorial and Museum. It is truly a must-see museum that never fails to move those who visit. One comes out of *Yad Vashem* with a greater understanding of this dark period of history.

This group came out of the museum deeply moved, deeply touched. Let us not forget that gays were also targeted for extermination by the Nazis. The group considered that Jews were massacred for racial/religious reasons and the world did nothing. Today in many countries, homosexuals are imprisoned, persecuted, tortured and killed simply because they are gay. And they decided they must do something.

They created an informal group, that they named the Rainbow Railway (inspired of course by the network, called the Underground Railway, that brought Black American slaves to freedom in Canada). This group helps homosexuals leave the countries in which they are persecuted, notably Iran. It assists in completing the legal applications necessary for recognition of these individuals as refugees by the U.N.

Many are now safely in Canada, thanks to the Rainbow Railway. I am very proud that the visit to Israel's *Yad Vashem* prompted this amazing group of women and men to establish this project - one that changes and saves lives.

Where is the real apartheid?

Let us compare. According to the Palestinian Authority's Basic Law, Islam is the official religion, Arabic is the only official language and the principles of Islamic *sharia* shall be a principal source of legislation.[391]

The Palestinian Authority has a law that authorizes the execution of Palestinians selling lands to Jews. Moreover, as theoretically this law applies to Israeli territory as well, an Israeli Arab who sells his property to a fellow Jewish citizen would be subject to this penalty.

As to what the future holds for the future Palestinian state, one needs to look no further than their draft Constitution.[392] It states: "[T]his constitution is based on the will of the **Arab** Palestinian people" (s. 1), that "the Palestinian people are a part of the **Arab and Islamic** nations" (s. 3), that "Sovereignty belongs to the Palestinian **Arab** people" (s. 10), and that "[T]he legal character of the **Arab** Palestinian people shall be embodied in the state" (s. 13). Further to this, "Islam shall be **the** official religion of the state" (s. 6), "**Arabic** shall be the official language" (s. 5), and "The principles of the *Islamic sharia* are a primary source for legislation" (s. 7). (The emphasis above is my own).

And it is Israel that is accused of apartheid? It is Israel that is attacked by the pro-Palestinian groups?

It is disturbing – and sad – to note that an Arab member of the Knesset, Masud Ganaim, as recently as May of 2010, called for the establishment of an Islamic caliphate,[393] going as far as to say that it would be in the Jews' interest.

Knowing the treatment reserved for Jews under *sharia* law, one has to have a lot of *chutzpah* to both accuse Israel of apartheid and call for an Islamic caliphate.

Let us be clear: to accuse Israel of practicing apartheid is, as seen above, anti-Semitic, pure and simple.

Indeed, according to the official European Union definition of anti-Semitism, to accuse Israel of being an apartheid state (i.e. to pretend that the existence of the State of Israel is a racist endeavour) is anti-Semitism.

This war against Israel is now being waged on campus. In 2005, a Toronto university launched Israel Apartheid Week. And this initiative has been exported to 40 campuses around the world (including 13 in Canada).

The goal of this campaign is very simple: to demonize Israel, to delegitimize the Jewish state. It is an existential threat because if Israel is an apartheid state, the solution is not to encourage the Israelis to negotiate with the Palestinians, but to dismantle their very country. Apartheid being a crime against humanity, a state practicing it must be eradicated.

The genesis of this strategy comes from the realization that Israel cannot be defeated on the battlefield. This being the case, according to its enemies, the way to destroy Israel is in the same way white-supremacist South Africa was dismantled - to attack its very legitimacy, its very right to exist.

The objective of the "Israel = apartheid" accusation, is to convince the world that Israel is evil incarnate. Indeed, is there anything worse than a country that institutionalizes discrimination and racism? Of course, such a country must be destroyed and certainly it is not to be negotiated with. Such is the logical conclusion of this argument.

To compare Israel to apartheid-era South Africa is vicious as it necessarily leads to two conclusions, neither of which would lead to real peace.

First, if Israel is based on segregation, Israel must be isolated by the international community.

Second, if we were to apply a South Africa-style solution to the Israeli-Palestinian context, i.e. one person, one vote in a single unitary state, based on population, it would lead to the end of the two-state solution. In other words, it would ensure the disappearance of Israel, the planet's only Jewish state.

Those at the forefront of the campaign to slander Israel as an apartheid state are part of the problem, not part of the solution. By fanning the flames of passion, by using falsehoods and outright lies, by rejecting Israel's right to exist, by denying Israel's right to self-defence without suggesting a credible alternative, by closing their eyes to much more serious discrimination elsewhere and, finally, by impeding the progress of those Israelis and Palestinians seeking a negotiated peace, they are exacerbating the conflict rather than resolving it.

Moreover, as mentioned above, apartheid is a crime against humanity. Accusing Israel of apartheid means as a consequence accusing millions of supporters of Israel whether Canadian, American, British, French or other, of being accomplices to the worst crime possible and of supporting systemic human rights violations and institutionalized racism.

In other words, charging Israel with the crime of apartheid means effectively turning regular Canadian citizens into criminals.

Israel's supporters and Jewish students on campus are being accused of supporting war crimes. They are insulted, intimidated and threatened to the point that many of them refuse to go on campus during Israel Apartheid Week.

This is not an issue of freedom of expression. As then Canada-Israel Committee Chair Moshe Ronen said: "Israel Apartheid Week stifles dialogue, does not constitute legitimate criticism and is simply hateful."[394] Noah Kochman, a student at McGill University and member of the executive of the Canadian Federation of Jewish Students, has reported that he was the victim of anti-Semitic insults, like "criminal" and "dirty Jew."[395] This on 21st century Canadian campuses!

Many Canadian political leaders have taken a stand against this festival of hate. Conservative MP Tim Uppal - of Sikh confession – showed leadership when he tabled, in the House of Commons, a motion condemning Israel Apartheid Week (IAW). He was supported by the Liberals.

Liberal leader Michael Ignatieff also published an eloquent press release on the subject[396] and reiterated his condemnations against IAW in a speech on November 8, 2010.[397] The Bloc Québécois also tabled a motion condemning the use of the word apartheid to describe Israel.

Ontario's legislature unanimously condemned IAW. It showed more maturity than its federal counterpart, where the political parties could not agree. For this, responsibility must be borne by NDP House Leader Libby Davies.

Not only did Davies, a Member of Parliament on the fringe of the Canadian political spectrum, do everything in her power to stop any attempt to condemn IAW, she bragged about it on Canadian ultra-Leftist blogs. It is important to note that this was to the marked displeasure of more responsible caucus colleagues, like Thomas Mulcair, Pat Martin, Judy Wasylycia-Leis, Peter Stoffer and many others.

The bottom line is clear. Canadian students must be able to study and live on our campuses in a spirit of dialogue and respect, not one of intimidation and fear.

Many anti-Israel activists regularly quote South African bishop Desmond Tutu and former U.S. President Jimmy Carter to support their allegation that Israel is an apartheid state. This is certainly what Québec solidaire MNA Amir Khadir did while trying to defend his support of the boycott of the Montreal shoe store *Le Marcheur*, simply because it sells some shoes made in Israel. What Khadir and his friends forget to mention is that Tutu has a very elastic definition of the concept of apartheid as he accused Canada of practicing it,[398] and that Carter has apologized for drawing similarities between Israel and South Africa.[399]

Finally, in all countries, including the most advanced, there is unfortunate and inevitable discrimination. There is, in Israel, some discrimination against Arab Israelis. This is recognized by Israeli society itself. However, Israel possesses the legal mechanisms necessary to deal with it.

In Australia, Aboriginals numbering 455,000 (2 percent of Australia) have a life expectancy 17 years lower than other Australians.[400]

We also know of the damning poverty and prison rates of Black Americans.

Closer to home, according to Quebec immigration minister Yolande James, the rate of unemployment for Quebeckers of North African origin is 27 percent as of May 2010.[401] The infant mortality rate in Inuit communities is four times that of the Canadian average, not to mention that seven out of ten Inuit children do not have enough to eat.[402]

On June 26, 2010, the Montreal daily *La Presse* reported[403] that, according to the Canadian Council of Provincial Child and Youth Advocates, the suicide rate of young Inuit is eleven times higher than the Canadian average. Even if they are only 5 percent of Canadian children, First Nations children represent approximately 25 percent of children under the care of the government for one reason or another. The percentage of First Nations' people between the ages of 25 and 64 who do not have a university degree is 19 points higher than the same age group in the non-First Nations population. In 2006, 49 percent of First Nations children living off-reserve were living in low-income families.

According to Dorothy Williams, an historian and author of a number of books on Montreal's Black community, a Black person with a university degree will earn less than a White person who has not finished high school. Gaétan Cousineau, president of Quebec's *Commission des droits de la personne et de la protection de la jeunesse* (Human Rights and Child Protection Commission) confirms that with the same diploma, a black Quebecker has more likelihood of being unemployed than a white Quebecker.[404] I am fairly certain that the situation is similar in the rest of Canada.

I know that all this does not excuse the discrimination facing Israeli Arabs. I do not for a minute pretend otherwise. What I do say, however, is that many of Israel's detractors, in Canada and around the world, apply a standard that they do not apply to any other country, including their own.

Which country is perfect? Which society is perfect?

To accuse Israel of apartheid for not being perfect is to accuse every country on the planet of being an apartheid state. It is as absurd as it is offensive.

24
Conclusion

Questions of identity are never easy.

This is true for individuals and nations alike. Twice, Quebeckers said no to independence. But they are still unhappy with the current situation, which led them to vote *en masse* for the Bloc Québécois federal election after federal election until 2011. Quebeckers still feel attached to Canada, or at least to a certain idea of Canada. This reflects Quebeckers' proverbial ambivalence about who they are - or about who they think they are. Debates on secularism, reasonable accommodation and what it means to be a Quebecker in the 21st century are all symptoms of this question of identity.

Jews of the Diaspora, the vast majority living in liberal and democratic countries, are torn between on the one hand loyalty to their roots and distinct personality, and on the other hand, the call for universalism inherent in Western civilization. The high rate of assimilation plaguing the Jewish people outside of Israel, raises questions on the very continuity of the Jewish experience outside the Jewish state.

As for Israelis, they are also facing serious questions. Tensions between the ultra-Orthodox, still a minority but growing in terms of both numbers and influence, and the secular majority are but one illustration of the challenges Israel faces, to say nothing of the place and role that the Israeli Arabs play in the future of the country.

Questions of identity are complex for individuals as well.

By converting to Judaism, I did not become less of a Quebecker. I remain a Quebecker, with a difference. I did not subtract from my Quebec identity. I added to it.

Born a Quebecker, I remain a Quebecker.

To be a Quebec Jew, or a Jewish Quebecker, is not always easy. As Daniel Amar of the Quebec Jewish Congress wrote:

> *To be a Quebec Jew is to assume a twice-minority identity, is to be a minority within a minority. It is also to be doubly fragile, not in one's existence but in one's essence and identity.*[405]

But my story, albeit unusual, is a Quebec story.

In fact, this Quebec story is both ordinary and extraordinary.

It is ordinary as I am a French-speaking Quebecker like millions of others. It is extraordinary because, through my conversion, I am one of a handful of Jews coming from the Quebec majority. I belong to two peoples.

Jewish tradition is crystal clear: there is no contradiction between a strong bond to the Jewish people and an unwavering loyalty to the country in which a Jew lives.

This very principle can be found in the Bible itself when the Prophet Jeremiah, speaking at the time of the Exile in Babylon 2,600 years ago, said:

> *Build houses and live in them; plant gardens and eat their produce. Take wives and have sons and daughters; take wives for your sons, and give your daughters in marriage, that they may bear sons and daughters; multiply there, and do not decrease. But seek the welfare of the city where I have sent you into exile, and pray to the LORD on its behalf, for in its welfare you will find your welfare.*[406]

Jewish law teaches us that the law of the state is the law we must respect and uphold.

It is therefore an obligation for Jews living in Canada to obey the applicable provincial and federal laws.

But it is more than an obligation. Quebec Jews are justifiably proud of their contribution to Quebec and to Canada. They are happy to live here. And so am I. This, despite the occasional anti-Semitic and anti-Israel comment.

My work in the Jewish community is not always easy. To defend the State of Israel's right to exist does not mean always being in agreement with whatever government is at the helm at any given time. The Israeli government, like any democratically elected government on the planet, can and does make mistakes.

This has led me to realize however, how easily intellectual shortcuts are taken when talking about Jews and Israel. As a result, fundamental differences are obscured between a democracy – imperfect maybe, but still a democracy – and the dictatorships, theocracies, and terrorist groups of the Middle East.

We see a dangerous drift when human rights and progressive groups join with militant Islamic organizations whose very objective is to take us back to the Middle Ages. How can feminist groups ally themselves with those religious extremists who want to lower the status of women to that of a subservient role to the men? It is the hatred of Israel, an irrational hatred akin to anti-Semitism, that cements this nauseating alliance.

There is a difference between democracy and tyranny. There is a difference between the right to self-defence and terrorism. There is a difference between anti-Semitism and vigorous – but respectful - debates.

I want Jews in Quebec and Canada to be comfortable here.

I want Israel to live in peace and security. I want Quebeckers and Canadians to support that noble goal.

And I want Quebeckers and Canadians to recognize that Israel is a reflection of us; that Israel is a fellow democracy that shares our values.

Picture taken at the Kotel, unbeknownst to me, in 2011

Thank You

This book is an adaptation of my French book titled *Juif, Une histoire québécoise*, which was published in October 2011.

My goal was to write a book in French for Quebeckers, using Quebec cultural references. It took me more than four years.

While I was writing it, many English-speaking friends expressed their desire to read the book, something they were unable to do in its original language.

As a result, I decided to write an English version. This turned out to be much more complex and difficult than I had thought it would be. Translating is an art in itself, and not one in which I am particularly gifted.

As well, for the English book I wanted to ensure the balance between the necessarily Quebec-centered *spirit* of the book and making it understandable for people who do not live in Quebec and may not have the same cultural references. I hope I have achieved the right balance.

I was inspired to write the original book by the writings of two outstanding writers and analysts of Israeli and Jewish life: Rabbi Daniel Gordis and Yossi Klein Halevi. Both of them are able to weave personal stories together with deep geopolitical analysis, turning their texts, articles and books into fascinating reading.

I want to also thank a few people who played an important role in this book.

For some parts, I based myself on the solid research work of Noah Shack, formerly with the Canada-Israel Committee, and of David Ouellette, formerly with the Quebec-Israel Committee, both now with the Centre for Israel and Jewish Affairs.

Steve McDonald from the long lost Jewish tribe of the McDonalds, a *ger tzeddek* like me, is a rising star in the Canadian Jewish community. Not only do we constantly exchange ideas, reading suggestions and arguments, Steve spent untold hours working on the manuscript, making great improvements to it. I am privileged to count him as a friend.

My *shul* mate, Jack Shapiro, a retired English professor, also went through the manuscript with a fine tooth comb, catching many grammatical and syntax errors.

My sister-in-law Deidre Beckerman also took time from her very busy schedule to proof read this text.

My publisher, Natania Étienne, showed a great deal of patience for both the French and English versions. Many times, as I was about to simply throw the manuscript out the window, she helped me persevere.

My fantastic wife Lori helped me through the process, despite the difficult period she was going through health wise. Not only did she encourage, inspire, prod and push me, she is the overseer of the English-language text. This book is almost as much hers as it is mine.

I say almost as, despite all this help, some mistakes may have been included in the book. Any errors are my responsibility alone.

Glossary

Hanukah: Traditionally a minor Jewish holiday commemorating the rededication of the Temple in Jerusalem after Jewish warriors defeated the occupying Greek armies. Due to the fact that this holiday usually occurs in December, it has taken on greater importance in North America as it coincides with the Christian celebration of Christmas.

Hassidism: Religious Jewish movement founded in 18th century Eastern Europe by the Rabbi Israel ben Eliezer, known as the Baal Shem Tov, it emphasizes not only study but also celebration. Its followers are easily recognizable by their clothing, inspired by the time and place of the movement's origin.

Havdallah: Ceremony marking the conclusion of the Sabbath.

Israel: Signifying "he who wrestles with God" in the sense of "beside" and "against". New name given by God to Jacob after he fought with a celestial creature (Genesis 32:28). Used in many expressions:

"Am Yisrael" - meaning the nation of Israel

"B'nei Yisrael" - literally the children of Israel, the Israelites.

"Eretz Yisrael" - the land of Israel.

"Medinat Yisrael" - the State of Israel.

"Kingdom of Israel" - Kingdom founded in 932 B.C. It includes part of the north of the Kingdom of David and Salomon. Its destruction in 721 B.C. gave birth to the 10 lost tribes of Israel.

Minyan: Quorum of 10 men of at least 13 years of age (for Orthodox Judaism) or 10 people (for the liberal forms of Judaism), necessary for the collective prayers.

Pesach: Jewish holiday of Passover marking the liberation and exodus of the Jews from Egypt led by Moses. The exodus lasted eight days. The first two dinners of the holiday are called "seders" and are conducted in a precise order.

Rabbi: Specialist in Jewish law. In Western civilization, the influence of Christianity has resulted in the Rabbi also often becoming the community religious leader.

Rosh Hashanah: Jewish New Year, generally occurring in early autumn.

Shabbat: The Jewish Sabbath occurring on the last day of the week (from sundown on Friday to sundown on Saturday). Traditional Jews refrain from all types of work and do not drive cars or turn electrical appliances on or off.

Synagogue: Jewish place of worship. Sometimes called a "Temple" in the Reform or Liberal movements.

Yom Kippur: The day of Atonement. The most solemn day of the Jewish calendar taking place ten days after Rosh Hashanah. It is marked by a 25 hour fast.

[1] Every Jew has a Hebrew name for ritual purposes.

[2] http://www.unhcr.org/refworld/country,CHRON,CAN,,469f3877c,0.html : South African Archbishop Desmond Tutu visits Osnaburgh Ojibway Reserve in northwestern Ontario. He says that Canada's treatment of its Native people is similar in many ways to South Africa's treatment of blacks under the system of apartheid.

[3] See: Lorne Gunter, "The Separatist and I", March 8, 1999 editions of the *The National Post* and the *Edmonton Journal*.

[4] Radio-France international: http://www.rfi.fr/actufr/articles/067/article_37680.asp .

[5] In his book *Mariage gai, Les coulisses d'une révolution sociale*, on the battle around same-sex marriage, published in 2005 at Éditions Flammarion, journalist Sylvain Laroque called me *"one of the most effective defenders of gay marriage"* (p.200).

[6] See SRC Télévision - Le Téléjournal / Le Point - Le Téléjournal / Le Point, June 5, 2005 - 22:00 and Jean-Denis Bellavance, "Les partis fédéraux se frottent les mains", *La Presse*, Monday, June 6, 2005, p. A6.

[7] "Lonely Planet's top 10 cities for 2011 ", October 31, 2010 http://www.lonelyplanet.com/usa/new-york-city/travel-tips-and-articles/76165 and *"Tel-Aviv is in top three cities in the world, says Lonely Planet"*, *Haaretz,* November 1, 2010 http://www.haaretz.com/news/national/tel-aviv-is-in-top-three-cities-in-the-world-says-lonely-planet-1.322274.

[8] In July 2010, *National Geographic Magazine* wrote that Tel Aviv was among the ten best beach cities in the world: http://travel.nationalgeographic.com/top-10/beach-cities-photos/#beaches-tel-aviv-cities_22323_600x450.jpg .

[9] Referenced by Pierre Anctil, "René Lévesque et les communautés culturelles," *René Lévesque, Mythes et réalités*, edited by Alexandre Stefanescu, VLB Éditeur, Montréal, 2008, p.164 which quotes from an article titled *"Get Close to French Canadians, Levesque Urges Quebec Jewry,"* *The Gazette*, June 11, 1963.

[10] Gilles Duceppe understood this well. See: Gilles Duceppe, *Entretiens avec Gilles Toupin*, Montréal, Richard Vézina Éditeur, 2010, p.140.

[11] Referenced by Pierre Anctil, "René Lévesque et les communautés culturelles," *René Lévesque, Mythes et réalités*, edited by Alexandre Stefanescu, VLB Éditeur, Montréal, 2008, p.167 which quotes from *The Gazette*, in *Inter-Office Information*, Canadian Jewish Congress, no. 2733, June11, 1963.

[12] To read more, see Dave Senor et Paul Singer, *Start Up Nation, The Story of Israel's Economic Miracle*, McClelland & Stewart, Toronto, 2009

[13] Philippe Mercure, "Israël: les leçons pour le Québec", *La Presse*, October 4, 2010 http://lapresseaffaires.cyberpresse.ca/economie/international/201010/04/01-4329218-israel-les-lecons-pour-le-quebec.php?utm_categorieinterne=trafficdrivers&utm_contenuinterne=cyberpresse_BO4_la_2343_accueil_POS2

[14] Pierre Fortin, Jean Boivin and Andrée Corriveau, *L'investissement au Québec: on est pour*, rapport du Groupe de travail sur l'investissement des entreprises au Québec, Gouvernement du Québec, 2008, p.19 (d'après FMI et Statistique Canada) http://www.gtie.gouv.qc.ca/fr/documents/Rapport_InvestissementENT.pdf

[15] "Israeli export grew 11,250 times since 1948 ", *Ynetnews*, April 20, 2010 http://www.ynetnews.com/articles/0,7340,L-3878340,00.html?utm_source=CIC+Mailing+List&utm_campaign=386894bc18-DYK_100421&utm_medium=email

[16] Adhésion: l'OCDE accueille le Chili, l'Estonie, Israël et la Slovénie, May 27, 2010 http://www.oecd.org/document/6/0,3343,fr_21571361_44315115_45344390_1_1_1_1,00.html.

[17] Ari Rabinovitch, "Arid Israel recycles waste water on grand scale," *Reuters*, November 14, 2010 http://www.reuters.com/article/idUSTRE6AD1CG20101114?pageNumber=1

[18] Referenced by Pierre Anctil, "René Lévesque et les communautés culturelles" in *René Lévesque, Mythes et réalités*, edited by Alexandre Stefanescu, VLB Éditeur, Montréal, 2008, p.167 quoting *Inter-Office Information*, Canadian Jewish Congress, no. 3856, June 2, 1975, quoting *The Montreal Star*.

[19] Referenced by Pierre Anctil, "René Lévesque et les communautés culturelles," *René Lévesque, Mythes et réalités*, edited by Alexandre Stefanescu, VLB Éditeur, Montréal, 2008,

p. 167, quoting Richard Cléroux, "Levesque Tells Jewish Delegates Some of the Things They Want to Hear but not Others" *The Globe and Mail*, May 14, 1977.

[20] Referenced by Pierre Anctil, "René Lévesque et les communautés culturelles," *René Lévesque, Mythes et réalités*, edited by Alexandre Stefanescu, VLB Éditeur, Montréal, 2008, p.167 quoting "Levesque Explains Quebec 'Nationalism.' Claims Trend Must Continue, *"The Montreal Star,* June 11, 1963.

[21] Jan Wong, "Get Under the Desk,*"* *The Globe and Mail*, September 16, 2006.

[22] http://onevoicemovement.org/programs/documents/OneVoiceIrwinReport.pdf.

[23] http://www.awrad.org/pdfs/English_tables-Ocotober2010.pdf

[24] Benny Morris, "Bleak House ," *Tablet Magazine*, December 2, 2010, http://www.tabletmag.com/news-and-politics/51926/bleak-house/print/

[25] Ceremony marking the end of the Sabbath.

[26] Three of four main branches of Judaism accept homosexuality. The Reform and Reconstructionist movements accept gay and lesbian rabbis and also perform same sex marriages. The Conservative or Masorti movement permits the ordination of homosexual rabbis but leaves the question of same sex marriage to the discretion of each rabbi. Finally, the Orthodox movement is obviously more strict (no openly gay rabbis or same sex marriage) but the most liberal Orthodox rabbis accept the homosexual individual. For the most recent declaration by the Orthodox Rabbinate, see: http://statementofprinciplesnya.blogspot.com . Even the most renowned ultra-Orthodox Rabbi in the U.S., Rabbi Shmuley Boteach, recently wrote a relatively liberal article on the subject: Shmuley Boteach, "My Jewish Perspective on Homosexuality, " *The Wall Street Journal*, October 15, 2010. http://online.wsj.com/article/SB10001424052748704361504575552203494330686.html

[27] *L'Arche*, May 2010, No. 624, p.53.

[28] Book of Ruth 1:16.

[29] http://religions.pewforum.org/reports

[30] This number includes people going from one Protestant church to another. If those are not included, the number is 28 percent, which still represents more than a quarter of the American population.

[31] A convert to Judaism is called the son or daughter of Abraham. For a convert has the greatest test of all; the convert is the potential Jewish soul that has been born to non-Jewish parents. The convert is the one that has to stand on the other side, to break away from how he or she was raised and educated and say, "No matter what you think, I know my soul, and I am a Jew". http://www.chabad.org/theJewishWoman/article_cdo/aid/439373/jewish/Pleased-to-Meet-Me.htm

[32] Book of Ruth 1:16.

[33] http://www.circumcisemetheplay.com

[34] For my entire speech see: http://www.parl.gc.ca/HousePublications/Publication.aspx?Mode=1&Parl=37&Ses=1&DocId=1385149&Language=E#Int-189609

[35] Nadeau was defeated in 2011.

[36] Libby Davies gets her party in trouble almost every time she talks about the Middle East. For example, during an anti-Israel demonstration on June 5, 2010, she went as far as to question Israel's very legitimacy by saying that the occupation started in 1948 (the year of Israel's creation): http://www.youtube.com/watch?v=utXDAha_vGg . Not only does this not help the Palestinians, it is counterproductive, radicalizes segments of the population and puts its proponent outside the international consensus, according to which the only possible solution is two states, one Jewish and one Arab, living side by side in peace. Davies was forced to retract this but did not withdraw her support for BDS (boycott, divestment and sanctions) against Israel. Canada needs a strong, progressive voice on foreign affairs. This kind of statement by Libby Davies can only hurt the NDP in its desire and quest to be that voice.

[37] To have a sense of the diversity - religious, political, linguistic, etc. - of the Quebec Jewish community through some of its members, see: Julie Châteauvert et Francis Dupuis-Déri, *Identités mosaïques, Entretiens sur l'identité culturelle des Québécois juifs*, Boréal, 2004.

[38] The majority of facts found in this chapter come from Joe King, *Les Juifs de Montréal, Trois siècles de parcours exceptionnels*, Éditions Carte Blanche, Montréal, 2002, which I read in the French translation by Pierre Anctil. I highly recommend this book to anyone interested in learning more about the history of the Jews of Quebec.

[39] Rémi Maillard, *René Lévesque, Si je vous ai bien compris, vous êtes en train de dire à la prochaine fois...*, Les Éditeurs Réunis, 2009 quoting from *La Presse*, April 26, 1980.

[40] Guy Wagner-Richard, *Le cimetière juif de Québec Beth Israël Ohev Sholom*, Septentrion, Quebec, 2000, p. XVIII.

[41] The Hart family would also play an important role in one of Quebec's major religions: hockey. One member of the Hart family led the Montreal Canadiens to two Stanley Cups in 1930 and 1931. As well, the Hart Trophy, given by the National Hockey League to the Most Valued Player to his team, was named in honour of another member of the same family.

[42] Guy Wagner-Richard, *Le cimetière juif de Québec Beth Israël Ohev Sholom*, Septentrion, Quebec, 2000, p. XVII.

[43] Sylvie Taschereau, "Nouveau regard sur les relations judéo-québécoises: le commerce comme terrain d'échanges, 1900-1945," *Juifs et Canadiens français dans la société québécoise*, Septentrion, Sillery, 2000, p.36.

[44] Ibid. at p. 37.

[45] On this subject, see the book by Simon Belkin, *Le mouvement ouvrier juif au Canada*, translated from yiddish to French by Pierre Anctil, Éditions Septentrion. See also Bernard Dansereau, "La place des travailleurs juifs dans le mouvement ouvrier québécois au début du XXè siècle," *Juifs et Canadiens français dans la société québécoise*, Septentrion, Sillery, 2000.

[46] Pierre Anctil, Ira Robinson et Gérard Bouchard, *Juifs et Canadiens français dans la société québécoise*, Sillery, Éditions Septentrion, 2000, p.154.

[47] Jacques Rouillard, *Les travailleurs juifs de la confection à Montréal (1910-80)* http://www.lltjournal.ca/index.php/llt/article/viewFile/2642/3045 .

[48] Charles Lewis, "Jewish imports: Why so many of Canada's rabbis are from the United States ," *National Post*, October 16, 2010 http://life.nationalpost.com/2010/10/16/jewish-imports-why-so-many-of-canada%E2%80%99s-rabbis-are-from-the-united-states/ .

[49] René Lévesque, *Attendez que je me rappelle...*, Éditions Québec/Amérique, Montréal, 1986, pp.132-134. Pierre Godin, *René Lévesque, un enfant du siècle*, Boréal, Montréal, 1994, pp 166-171.

[50] http://www.youtube.com/watch?v=qbcUAFbXGBI&feature=player_embedded.

[51] http://www.jewishfederations.org/page.aspx?id=216011

[52] Lysiane Gagnon, "L'avocate du diable," *La Presse*, October 16, 2010, Cahier Plus, p.7. http://www.cyberpresse.ca/opinions/201010/15/01-4332886-lavocate-du-diable.php

[53] David Ouellette. "Un accord de paix israélo-palestinien ne réglera pas tout," *La Tribune*, April 30, 2010 http://www.cyberpresse.ca/la-tribune/opinions/201004/30/01-4275806-un-accord-de-paix-israelo-palestinien-ne-reglera-pas-tout.php .

[54] This phenomenon is well illustrated by the fact that the *seder* – the traditional Passover meal – is still finished today by the words 'Next year in Jerusalem'.

[55] The Dreyfus Affair divided France at the end of the 19th-beginning of the 20th century. Captain Alfred Dreyfus, a Jew, was wrongly convicted of spying for Germany. It took years to overturn the conviction.

[56] This map and the following one come from the web site of the Israeli Ministry of Foreign Affairs http://www.mfa.gov.il/MFA/Facts+About+Israel/Israel+in+Maps/Israel+in+Maps.htm#prestate .

[57] Mallman, Klaus-Michael et Cuppers, Martin, *Nazi Palestine: The Plans for the Extermination of the Jews in Palestine*, Enigma Books and United States Holocaust Memorial Museum, New York, 2010; Herf, Jeffrey, *Nazi Propaganda for the Arab World*, Yale University Press, New Haven, 2009. French Television ARTE also broadcast an excellent documentary on the subject on December 9, 2009: *La croix gammée et le turban - La tentation nazie du Grand mufti*. Finally, see the chapter on the Mufti in Tarek Fatah, *The*

Jew Is Not My Enemy, Editions McClelland & Stewart, Toronto, 2010, pp.38-77.

[58] Sam Roberts, "Declassified Papers Show U.S. Recruited Ex-Nazis," *The New York Times*, December 11, 2010 http://www.nytimes.com/2010/12/12/us/12holocaust.html and Jordana Horn, "Nazism, Islam shared common enemies – the Jews," *Jerusalem Post*, December 15, 2010, http://www.jpost.com/International/Article.aspx?id=199451 .

[59] The best summary of this episode, in my opinion, is found in Allis and Ronald Radosh, *A Safe Heaven, Harry S. Truman and the Founding of Israel*, Harper Perennial, New York, 2009, pp.207-244.

[60] Paul Giniewski, *Le contentieux israélo-arabe*, Cheminements, 2007, p. 109, quoting the BBC, May 15, 1948. See also: http://www.bankingonbaghdad.com/archive/ReformJudaism2004V33N2/black.shtml .

[61] Dore Gold, *The Fight for Jerusalem,* Washington, Regnery Publishing, 2007, p.135 quoting Trygve Lie, *In the Cause of Peace*, New York, MacMillan, 1954, p.174.

[62] Amos Elon, *The Israelis, Founders and Sons*, Bantam Books, New York, 1971, p.4.

[63] The well-known Palestinian American activist and professor Edward Said went as far as to say "[t]he whole of Palestinian nationalism was based on driving all Israelis out." See: Harvey Blume, "Setting the Record Straight," *The Atlantic*, September 22, 1999 http://www.theatlantic.com/past/docs/unbound/interviews/ba990922.htm .

[64] Italian author and journalist Giulio Meotti called this terror campaign, as used in his book's title: *A New Shoah, The Untold Story of Israel's Victims of Terrorism*, Encounter Books, New York, 2010.

[65] Aluf Benn, "What happened on September 13," *Haaretz*, July15, 2009 http://www.haaretz.com/print-edition/opinion/what-happened-on-september-13-1.280031 , Aluf Benn, "Olmert's plan for peace with the Palestinians ," *Haaretz,* December 17, 2009 http://www.haaretz.com/print-edition/news/haaretz-exclusive-olmert-s-plan-for-peace-with-the-palestinians-1.1970 and http://www.cicweb.ca/scene/wp-content/uploads/2011/02/Olmert-in-autobiography-tells-of-peace-negotiations-Yedioth-Aharonoth1.pdf

[66] Peter Goodspeed, "A Palestine that might have been," *The National Post*, January 29, 2011 http://www.canada.com/story_print.html?id=4188585&sponsor= .

[67] http://www.awrad.org/pdfs/English_tables-Ocotober2010.pdf

[68] Charles Krauthammer, "Land without peace: Why Abbas went to the U.N.", *The Washington Post*, September 29, 2011 http://www.washingtonpost.com/opinions/land-without-peace-why-abbas-went-to-the-un/2011/09/29/gIQACaoI8K_story.html)

[69] Ben Dror Yemini, "The Arab Apartheid," *The Daily Telegraph*, May 18, 2011 http://my.telegraph.co.uk/actuality/realdeal/15813560/the-arab-apartheid-ben-dror-yemini/ .

[70] The United Nations Relief and Works Agency for Palestine Refugees.

[71] Kenneth Bandler, "Time to start planning for resettlement," *Miami Herald*, October 20, 2010, http://www.miamiherald.com/2010/10/20/1881772/time-to-start-planning-for-resettlement.html.

[72] On this subject, see the excellent website of Palestinian Media Watch http://www.palwatch.org

[73] Yohai Livshitz, 18; Yonatan Yitzhak Eldar, 16; Yonadav Haim Hirschfeld, 19; Neria Cohen, 15; Segev Peniel Avihail, 15; Avraham David Moses, 16; Roee Roth, 18; Maharta Taruno, 26.

[74] Nadav Eliyahu Samuels.

[75] Ethan Bronner, "Poll Shows Most Palestinians Favor Violence Over Talks", *The New York Times*, March, 19, 2008, http://www.nytimes.com/2008/03/19/world/middleeast/19mideast.html .

[76] Agence France-Presse, "Le Fatah a demandé à Israël d'attaquer le Hamas," December 20, 2010 http://fr.canoe.ca/infos/international/archives/2010/12/20101220-125917.html .

[77] See the Report of the Standing Committee on Foreign Affairs and International Development of Canada's House of Commons titled: Ahmadinejad's Iran: A threat to peace, human rights and international law, which was published in December 2010. http://www2.parl.gc.ca/Content/HOC/Committee/403/FAAE/Reports/RP4835870/403_FAAE_Rpt03_PDF/403_FAAE_Rpt03-f.pdf

[78] Ibid.

[79] Of note is the unanimous motion voted in the House of Commons on the subject of Iran on October 27, 2009:http://www.parl.gc.ca/HousePublications/Publication.aspx?DocId=41 77807&Mode=1&Parl=40&Ses=2&Language=E

[80] "L'Iran et les Arabes : l'éclairage de WikiLeaks," *Le Monde*, http://www.lemonde.fr/ idees/article/2010/11/30/l-iran-et-les-arabes-l-eclairage-de-wikileaks_1446803_3232.html.

[81] Human rights activists in Iran have reached the same conclusion. See for example the article by Canadian of Iranian origin Nazanin Afshin-Jam , "Human Rights Activists Must Work To Halt Iran's Nuclear Weapons Program, Too," *The Huffington Post*, October 15, 2010 http://www.huffingtonpost.com/nazanin-afshinjam/human-rights-activists-mu_b_764343.html .

[82] http://www2.parl.gc.ca/HousePublications/Publication.aspx?DocId=2333186&Mode=1 &Language=F

[83] Judy Wasylycia-Leis had previously tabled a similar bill. That bill had died before being adopted by Parliament.

[84] To read the debates, go to: http://www2.parl.gc.ca/HousePublications/Publication.aspx? Language=E&Mode=1&Parl=37&Ses=2&DocId=1113051

[85] Except, of course in Quebec, where the legal system is based on the civil law.

[86] This agreement was first signed in 1997 by a PQ government led by Lucien Bouchard. It was renewed and extended in 2007 and further expanded in 2008.

[87] http://www.mdeie.gouv.qc.ca/index.php?id=84&no_cache=1&tx_ttnews%5Btt_ news%5D=1685&tx_ttnews%5BbackPid%5D=122&tx_ttnews%5Bpointer%5D=3&cHa sh=8198767f4f

[88] Conversations with the author, July 2, 2010 in Jerusalem.

[89] Numbers do not lie: 72% of French-speaking BC residents speak English at home, so do 74,4% of French-speaking Franco-Saskatchewans, 69% of Franco-Albertans, 55,5% of Franco-Manitobans and 41,8% of Franco-Ontarians. Even in Acadia, the linguistic transfer rate is about 10%.

[90] For an explosive essay on the subject of Jewish assimilation in the American context, see: Alan Dershowitz, *The Vanishing American Jew*, Touchstone, 1997.

[91] For a great book on anti-Semitism in Great-Britain, see Anthony Julius, *Trials of the Diaspora*, Oxford University Press, 2010.

[92] On Sweden, see Ronald Lauder, "Even a tolerant country cannot tolerate intolerance," *The Globe and Mail,* August 14, 2010 http://www.theglobeandmail.com/news/opinions/ even-a-tolerant-country-cannot-tolerate-intolerance/article1672437 and Donald Snyder, "For Jews, Swedish City Is a 'Place To Move Away From'," *The Forward*, July 7, 2010 http://www.forward.com/articles/129233.

[93] http://www.tou.tv/une-heure-sur-terre/S2009E21

[94] Broadcast on RDI.

[95] Research by Noah Shack and David Ouellette on the subject.

[96] http://www.ahlul-bayt.org/main/links

[97] Now deceased.

[97a] Cairo Conference Report Back, United Steelworkers of America Building, 25 Cecil St. Tacuto, Friday April 27, 2007

[97b] Ali Mallah's Speech on Al-Quds Day, Al-Mahdi Islamic Centre, October 20, 2006

[98] Jonathan Kay, "Canadian Arab Federation official spreads conspiracy theory that Norway attack was Israel's handiwork", *The National Post*, July 26, 2011 http://fullcomment. nationalpost.com/2011/07/26/president-of-canadian-arab-federation-spreads-conspiracy-theory-that-norway-attack-was-israel%E2%80%99s-handiwork/ .

[99] Joe Friesen, "More than 300 people linked to suspected case of citizenship fraud," *The Globe and Mail*, February 1, 2010 http://www.theglobeandmail.com/news/national/more-than-300-people-linked-to-suspected-case-of-citizenship-fraud/article1451454 .

[100] http://classic-web.archive.org/web/20071124041309/www.palestinehouse.com/hamil-ton.declaration.html

[101] http://www.memritv.org/clip/en/678.htm

[102] http://www.memri.org/report/en/0/0/0/0/0/0/389.htm

[103] http://web.archive.org/web/20080403003138/www.palestinehouse.com/habash.htm

[104] http://web.archive.org/web/20080128023436/http:/www.palestinehouse.com/index.html

[105] http://www.youtube.com/watch?v=CJzJe6DxtHQ

[106] http://www.tadamon.ca/about-us/information

[107] Ibid.

[108] Ibid.

[109] http://www.tadamon.ca/post/926

[110] http://www.tadamon.ca/post/822

[111] http://web.archive.org/web/20071016203200/ajlm.org/savants.php

[112] http://www.ccmmontreal.com/index.php?option=com_content&task=blogsection&id=4&Itemid=35

[113] "Protest opener peaceful," *The Gazette*, November 20, 2004, p.A1; "Riot cops move in to quell protest," *The Gazette*, April 27, 2002, p.A4.

[114] "Plenty of rage to go around," July 29, 2003;"Le mouvement altermondialiste se prépare pour Cancun," *La Presse*, p.A1, August 2, 2003, p.B3.

[115] Edmond Omran is also one of the leaders of the Fondation canado-palestinienne du Quebec who in May 2011, called for "Montréal, c'est la troisième Intifada!" (Montreal, it is the third intifada). Not a great example of support for a peaceful resolution of the Arab-Israeli conflict.

[116] Hélène Buzetti, "La bienveillance, paravent fiscal? ," *Le Devoir*, March 2, 2010 http://m.ledevoir.com/politique/canada/284154/la-bienfaisance-paravent-fiscal .

[117] http://www.radio-canada.ca/apropos/lib/v3.1/pdf/revision_sur_une_heure_sur_terre_du_16_jan08.pdf

[118] http://www.canadianislamiccongress.com/mc/media_communique.php?id=814

[119] http://www.montrealmuslimnews.net/transcript.htm

[120] http://www.canadianislamiccongress.com/opeds/article.php?id=1687

[121] I do not include here the Canadian Muslim Congress, whose members I met the first time when they testified in front of a Parliamentary Committee I was sitting on, in favour of same-sex marriage. Since then, they have often made headlines with their liberal and pro-secularism positions. See: http://www.muslimcanadiancongress.org .

[122] Khan, as soon as his career was over at *La Presse*, officially joined a pro-Palestinian advocacy group, confirming the partiality he had shown under the guise of political analysis.

[123] Quoted in Jean-Luc Allouche, *Les jours redoutables, Israël-Palestine: la paix dans mille ans*, Denoël Impact, 2010, p.45.

[124] "UN says no massacre in Jenin," *BBC*, August 1, 2002 http://news.bbc.co.uk/2/hi/middle_east/2165272.stm .

[125] http://spme.net/cgi-bin/articles.cgi?ID=6539 .

[126] http://www.parl.gc.ca/HousePublications/Publication.aspx?DocId=4580527&Mode=1&Parl=40&Ses=3&Language=E .

[127] http://fmc-cmf.com/index.php?id=112 .

[128] http://www.macnet.ca/about .

[129] "Richard Nadeau honoré par la communauté libanaise et musulmane," *Radio-Canada*, September 3, 2010 http://www.radio-canada.ca/regions/ottawa/2010/09/03/005-richard-nadeau-honore.shtml .

[130] http://www.irfi.org/articles2/articles_3151_3200/muslim%20author%20speaks%20out%20against%20'islamo-fascism'html.htm .

[131] For more on the subject of Jewish anti-Zionism, see British lawyer Anthony Julius' excellent essays: "Jewish Anti-Zionism Unravelled: The Morality of Vanity (Part 1)," *Z Word*, March 2008 http://www.z-word.com/z-word-essays/jewish-anti-zionism-unravelled%253A--the-morality-of-vanity-%2528part-1%2529.html and "Jewish Anti-Zionism Unravelled: Questioning Antisemitism (Part 2)," *Z word*, April 2008, http://www.z-word.com/z-word-essays/jewish-anti-zionism-unravelled%253A-questioning-

antisemitism-%2528part-2%2529.html .

[132] http://www.youtube.com/watch?v=R-r04SQ97_Q .

[133] 2007 FC 1025.

[134] Robin Sheppard, *A State Beyond the Pale, Europe's Problem With Israel*, Weidenfeld & Nicolson, September 10, 2009, p.105.

[135] Pierre-André Taguieff, *La nouvelle propagande antijuive*, Presses Universitaires de France, Paris, 2010, p.362.

[136] See for example http://www.investigativeproject.org/article/789 by terrorism expert and former CSIS agent David Harris.

[137] See the excellent article by Terry Glavin, "The Cairo Clique: Anti-Zionism and the Canadian Left*, "* April 2008, http://z-word.com/z-word-essays/the-cairo-clique%253A-anti-zionism-and-the-canadian-left.html .

[138] Jehad Aliweiwi et al., "Don't be silenced by extremists," *The Toronto Star*, February 28, 2006 http://www.muslimcanadiancongress.org/20060228.pdf .

[139] See http://www.ledevoir.com/2008/10/03/208854.html , *La Presse* editorial by Mario Roy, titled "Les modérés," October 4, 2008 and "Le cri d'alarme de trois musulmans" by Jacques Brassard , October 16, 2008 edition of *Le Quotidien*.

[140] Much information included here comes from research done by David Ouellette.

[141] Amir Khadir, "Oussama ben Laden, ami de la famille Bush", *La Presse,* December 14, 2001, p.A15.

[142] "Que l'Assemblée nationale rappelle, à la suite de la mort d'Oussama Ben Laden qui a orchestré les attentats du 11 septembre, que le Québec a été et continuera d'être un allié de l'ensemble de la communauté internationale en matière de sécurité et plus particulière-ment face à la menace terroriste;

Qu'elle salue la persévérance et la détermination des États-Unis et de ses alliés dans la recherche d'une plus grande sécurité à l'échelle mondiale; Qu'elle souligne l'importance de demeurer vigilant et réitère son appréciation de la contribution des Québécoises et des Québécois déployés en Afghanistan, notamment dans la lutte continue contre le terrorisme".

[143] Paul Journet, "Motion sur ben Laden: Khadir contre tous," *Cyberpresse*, May 10, 2011, http://www.cyberpresse.ca/international/dossiers/ben-laden-est-mort/201105/10/01-4398035-motion-sur-ben-laden-khadir-contre-tous.php?utm_categorieinterne=trafficdriver s&utm_contenuinterne=cyberpresse_BO2_quebec_canada_178_accueil_POS1 .

[144] http://www.assnat.qc.ca/fr/travaux-parlementaires/assemblee-nationale/39-1/journal-debats/20100601/18481.html#_Toc263339582 .

[145] http://www.assnat.qc.ca/fr/video-audio/AudioVideo-22517.html .

[146] Amir Khadir, "Hamas et Hezbollah? Des 'obscurantistes'!," December 22, 2010, http://www2.lactualite.com/jean-francois-lisee/amir-khadir-hamas-et-hezbollah-des-obscuran-tistes/6975 .

[147] Lysiane Gagnon, "Khadir le fanatique," *La Presse*, December 21, 2010, http://www.cy-berpresse.ca/chroniqueurs/lysiane-gagnon/201012/20/01-4354210-khadir-le-fanatique.php

[148] Pierre-André Normandin, "Une représentante de Québec solidaire appuie le Hezbol-lah," *Le Soleil*, July 29, 2006.

[149] The following day, Québec Solidaire dissociated itself from Lewis.

[150] The coalition included the following groups: Alternatives, AQOCI, CISO, Comité de solidarité de Trois-Rivières, Comité pour la justice sociale, COPHAN, CSN, CSQ, FFQ, FNEEQ, FTQ, Handicap international, Solidarity with Palestinian Human Rights, Tadamon.

[151] http://www.csq.qc.net/index.cfm/2,0,1676,9656,2323,0,html?action=display&BoxID=1 3689&LangID=2&KindID=2&complete=yes

[152] Mario Roy, "La hiérarchie des causes," *La Presse*, July 3, 2010, http://www.cyber-presse.ca/place-publique/editorialistes/mario-roy/201006/30/01-4294645-la-hierarchie-des-causes.php .

[153] On this subject see: Caroline Fourest, *La Tentation obscurantiste*, Grasset; Alexis Lacroix, *Le socialisme des imbéciles (quand l'antisémitisme redevient de gauche)*, Édi-

tions de La Table Ronde; Pierre-André Taguieff, *La nouvelle judéophobie*, and *Prêcheurs de haine* both Éditions Mille Et Une Nuits. In English, see Paul Berman, *Flight of the Intellectuals*, Melville House, April 2010.

[154] Freddy Eytan, *Sarkozy, le monde juif et Israël*, Éditions Alphée-Jean-Paul Bertrand, 2009, pp.176-177.

[155] See Chapter 22.

[156] Gérard Bouchard, *Les rapports avec la communauté juive: un test pour la nation québécoise* in Juifs et *Canadiens français dans la société québécoise*, Septentrion, Sillery, 2000, pp.14 and 25.

[157] TVA Nouvelles, "Les Québécois francophones mal-aimés au Canada," January 27, 2010 http://lcn.canoe.ca/lcn/infos/national/archives/2010/01/20100127-153157.html .

[158] Elizabeth Thompson, "Cultural split exists in attitude to Jews," *The Gazette*, November 8, 2010 http://www.montrealgazette.com/health/Cultural+split+exists+attitude+Jew s/3792919/story.html .

[159] Pierre Anctil, "Parcours divergents et réalités communes," *Juifs et Canadiens français dans la société québécoise*, Septentrion, Sillery, 2000, pp.183-184.

[160] Pierre Anctil et Gary Caldwell, *Juifs et réalités juives au Québec,* Institut québécois de recherche sur la culture, 1984, p.313.

[161] Pierre Anctil, "Parcours divergents et réalités communes," *Juifs et Canadiens français dans la société québécoise*, Septentrion, Sillery, 2000, p.184.

[162] Many of the articles cited below were later deleted in whole or in part by Vigile, following an article that appeared in *La Presse* about their anti-Semitism.

[163] http://www.vigile.net/+-Canada-colonie-sioniste- .

[164] http://www.vigile.net/+-Colonie-sioniste-Quebec- .

[165] http://www.vigile.net/-Annapolis-croisee-des-chemins-ou- .

[166] http://www.vigile.net/L-horreur-de-Gaza .

[167] Ibid.

[168] http://www.vigile.net/Les-mechants-mots-antisemitisme-et .

[169] http://www.vigile.net/Lise-Noel-et-Gaza .

[170] http://www.vigile.net/Lettre-a-mes-concitoyens,33851 .

[171] http://www.vigile.net/Vigile-et-Judeoscope-le-profilage .

[172] In French: " il me vient parfois des arrière-goûts de meurtre contre monsieur Juif ".

[173] http://www.vigile.net/L-antisemitisme-d-Adrien-Arcand .

[174] http://www.vigile.net/La-verite-a-propos-des-Juifs-de .

[175] http://www.vigile.net/Le-lobby-juif-est-responsable-de-l .

[176] http://www.vigile.net/Mouvement-Nationaliste .

[177] Joel-Denis Bellavance, "Un site souverainiste accusé d'antisémitisme," *La Presse*, March 16, 2011, http://www.cyberpresse.ca/actualites/quebec-canada/politique-quebecoise/201103/16/01-4380099-un-site-souverainiste-accuse-dantisemitisme.php . See also Joseph Facal, "Les mauvaises fréquentations," March 21, 2011, http://www.josephfacal.org/les-mauvaises-frequentations/ .

[178] Beaudoin resigned from the Parti Québécois in June 2011 for unrelated reasons .

[179] On the Bouchard-Taylor Commission, see also Chapter 20.

[180] http://tva.canoe.ca/emissions/je/reportages/16935.html .

[181] Jan Harold Brunvald, *The Jewish Secret Tax, Encyclopedia of Urban Legends*, Reprint, New York, New York, W.W. Norton & Company, pp.222-223.

[182] Caroline Touzin and Laura-Julie Perreault, "Accommodements raisonnables: Bouchard-Taylor: mythes et réalités", *La Presse*, November 26, 2007.

[183] There are only 17 kosher restaurants in Quebec, all on the Island of Montreal, out of 18,077 restaurants in Quebec according to the Association des Restaurateurs du Quebec.

[184] For a great book on the subject of kosher food, see Sue Fishkoff, *Kosher Nation, Why More and More of America's Food Answers to a Higher Authority*, Schocken, New York, 2010.

[185] See also Gérard Bouchard and Charles Taylor, *BUILDING THE FUTURE A Time for Reconciliation*, abridged report of the Consultation Commission on Accommodation Prac-

tices Related to Cultural Differences, Gouvernement du Quebec, p.20: "No authoritative comprehensive study currently exists on the topic. However, we do have at our disposal testimony and partial but reliable overviews that clearly establish that a) the interest that businesses display in kosher certification reflects marketing strategies that cover a portion of the United States; b) the additional costs that consumers must assume are very minimal; c) kosher certification may require companies to modify certain production procedures, e.g. additional washing, but not to modify the composition of their products; and d) rabbis do not profit by certification." http://www.accommodements.qc.ca/documentation/rapports/rapport-final-abrege-en.pdf .

[186] For a short but excellent article on the connection between anti-Semitism and anti-Zionism, see: Robert S. Wistrich, "Quelques réflexions sur l'antisémitisme contemporain," in *Diversité canadienne*, volume 8:4, Autumn 2010, p.5.

[187] "Studied under its ideological/political dimension, anti-Zionism can be recognized by its reasoning, which leads to the legitimization of the destruction of Israel, one way or another – by force or indirectly, with either the creation of a bi-national State or the returns of all the Palestinian 'refugees' (including their descendants) on Israeli territory. For the radical anti-Zionists, the objective of the final destruction of Israel can be unconscious or clearly stated. In every case however, the elimination of Israel is the logical conclusion of a diabolizing argument against Israel and which by systematically condemning the decisions and political actions of the Jewish State, leads to making Israel one state too many - the only State in the world to be so treated. Radical anti-Zionism's premise is that Jews cannot form a national community with a territory and a State. This is discriminatory against the Jewish State: it is the only people to whom a national State life is negated." Pierre-André Taguieff, *La nouvelle propagande antijuive*, Presses Universitaires de France. Pris. 2010, p. 57.

[188] http://www.european-forum-on-antisemitism.org/working-definition-of-antisemitism/english .

[189] http://www.ldh-toulon.net/spip.php?article372 .

[190] www.bdsquebec.org .

[191] To see the true nature of this movement, see: http://www.youtube.com/watch?v=tnpilMYsR0I .

[192] Meanwhile, high calibre French intellectuals were harshly criticizing the very idea of boycott against Israel in the French daily Le Monde: http://www.lemonde.fr/idees/article/2010/11/01/le-boycott-d-israel-est-une-arme-indigne_1433857_3232.html .

[193] http://qic-cqi.org/IMG/pdf/09_29_2010_Masuku.pdf .

[194] See for example: http://www.nationalpost.com/opinion/disgrace+CUPW/3661471/story.html, One speaker at Canadian Union of Postal Workers sponsored anti-Israel conference admits support for terror, another heads organization that threatened South African Jews, http://eyecrazy.blogspot.com/2010/10/one-speaker-at-canadian-union-of-postal.html and Jonathan Kay, CUPW's radical politics and anti-Israel bigotry are a disgrace to letter carriers, *The National Post*, Full Comment, October 12, 2010. http://fullcomment.nationalpost.com/2010/10/12/jonathan-kay-cupws-radical-politics-and-anti-israel-bigotry-are-a-disgrace-to-letter-carriers. This is without mentioning the numerous Facebook and Twitter exchanges on the subject.

[195] Lawrence Summers, a senior Clinton and Obama Administrations official, said when he was the president of Harvard University, that BDS was "anti-Semitic in effect, if not intent".

[196] See: http://www.tuliponline.org/?p=1901 .

[197] http://www.spme.net/cgi-bin/articles.cgi?ID=7322 .

[198] Julie Wiener, "UNRWA Head: Don't Boycott Israel," *The Jewish Week*, November 16, 2010, http://www.thejewishweek.com/features/new_york_minute/unrwa_head_dont_boycott_israel .

[199] http://www.blocquebecois.org/bloc.aspx?bloc=3fb92a9c-d849-4147-8954-90d76dc9d676 .

[200] Taïeb Moalla, "Khadir refuse de débattre d'une motion adéquiste," *Le Journal de*

Québec, February 2, 2011.
http://lejournaldequebec.canoe.ca/journaldequebec/politique/provinciale/archives/2011/02/20110209-134449.html .

[201] http://www.crif.org/index.php?page=articles_display/detail&aid=22376&artyd=2 .

[202] Noémi Mercier, "Amir Khadir, un rebelle au salon bleu," *L'Actualité*, vol. 36, no. 4, March 15, 2011, Amir Khadir *"peut devenir très émotif sur la question palestinienne. Ça lui demande un effort pour se maîtriser:"*

[203] http://www.jcpa.org/phas/phas-sharansky-f04.htm .

[204] Stéphane Gendron, "Bienvenue au Canada," *Le Journal de Montréal*, June 1, 2010, !http://lejournaldemontreal.canoe.ca/journaldemontreal/chroniques/stephanegendron/archives/2010/06/20100601-065306.html .

[205] His fellow *Journal de Montréal* columnist Richard Martineau took him to task a few days later: Richard Martineau, "Histoire de bateaux", June 7, 2010. http://martineau.blogue.canoe.ca/2010/06/07/histoires_de_bateaux#comments

[206] Jean-Michel Nahas, "Stéphane Gendron est déçu et frustré," *Journal de Montréal* , June 20, 2007 http://argent.canoe.ca/infos/quebec/archives/2007/07/20070726-071243.html .

[207] Supra, note 202.

[208] Pierre Foglia, "Nous ne sommes pas antisémites," *La Presse*, June 5, 2010 http://www.cyberpresse.ca/chroniqueurs/pierre-foglia/201006/04/01-4287102-nous-ne-sommes-pas-antisemites.php?utm_categorieinterne=trafficdrivers&utm_contenuinterne=cyberpresse_B13b_pierre-foglia_3264_section_POS1 .

[209] Pierre Foglia, "Les géants," *La Presse*, August 12, 2010 http://www.cyberpresse.ca/chroniqueurs/pierre-foglia/201008/11/01-4305832-les geants.php?utm_categorieinterne=trafficdrivers&utm_contenuinterne=cyberpresse_B40_chroniqueurs_373561_accueil_POS2.

[210] See Emmanuel Poncet, "Edgar Morin, 82 ans, sociologue, penseur de la complexité," *Libération*, May 13, 2004.

[211] Howard Jacobson, "Anti-Zionism - facts (and fictions)", *The Jewish Chronicle,* July 28, 2010 http://www.thejc.com/comment-and-debate/comment/36256/anti-zionism-facts-and-%EF%AC%81ctions .

[212] Sharon Begley, "The DNA of Abraham's Children," *Newsweek*, June 3, 2010, http://www.newsweek.com/2010/06/03/the-dna-of-abraham-s-children.print.html. See also Nicolas Wade, "Studies Show Jews' Genetic Similarity," *The New York Times*, June 9, 2010 http://www.nytimes.com/2010/06/10/science/10jews.html?hpw and Robert Adler, "Scattered Seeds: Two New Studies Trace Jewish Genetic History," *Suite101.com*, June 9, 2010 http://humangenetics.suite101.com/article.cfm/scattered-seeds-two-new-studies-trace-jewish-genetic-history and Alex Joffe, "The DNA Speaks," *Jewish Ideas Daily*, December 20, 2010 http://www.jidaily.com/dna/e .

[213] This does not mean that Jews are a race. If it were the case, I could clearly not be Jewish. What it does mean however is that the Jewish nation was indeed born in the Middle East and that its Diaspora shares the same roots. This does not prevent conversion to Judaism a millennia-old phenomenon, well codified by Jewish Law.

[214] Nicolas Wade, "Studies Show Jews' Genetic Similarity," *The New York Times*, June 9, 2010, http://www.nytimes.com/2010/06/10/science/10jews.html .

[215] Pierre Anctil, "René Lévesque et les communautés culturelles," *René Lévesque, Mythes et réalités*, sous la direction d'Alexandre Stefanescu, VLB Éditeur, Montréal, 2008, p.181.

[216] Gérard Bouchard et Charles Taylor, Fonder l'avenir, *Le temps de la conciliation, rapport abrégé de la Commission de consultation sur les pratiques d'accommodements reliées aux différences culturelles*, Gouvernement du Quebec, p.83. http://www.accommodements.qc.ca/documentation/rapports/rapport-final-abrege-fr.pdf .

[217] Manon Cornellier, "La réflexion du Bloc sur la citoyenneté déborde les rangs souverainistes," *Le Devoir* June 14, 1999.

[218] Ibid.

[219] Joseph Facal, *Quelque chose comme un grand peuple*, Boréal, Montréal, 2010, p.53.

[220] Michel David, "La carte identitaire," *Le Devoir*, June 22, 2010 http://www.ledevoir. com/politique/quebec/291375/la-carte-identitaire .

[221] Indeed, even in English Canada, the issue of multiculturalism is being questioned. See for example an editorial of October 8, 2010 in *The Globe and Mail* titled *"Strike multiculturalism from the national vocabulary"* http://www.theglobeandmail.com/ news/national/time-to-lead/multiculturalism/editorial-strike-multiculturalism-from-the-national-vocabulary/article1748958 and a November 7, 2010 *Toronto Star* column titled *"The failed promise of multiculturalism "* http://www.thestar.com/opinion/editorialopin-ion/article/886854--persichilli-the-failed-promise-of-multiculturalism.Countries like Germany (Agence France-Presse, "Le modèle multiculturel allemand totalement échoué selon Merkel,"*Cyberpresse.ca*, October 16, 2010 http://www.cyberpesse.ca/international/ europe/201010/16/01-4333212-le-modele-multiculturel-allemand-a-totalement-echoue-selon-merkel.php) and Great Britain: (Jason Groves, "We need to b a lot less tolerant towards Islamic extremists': Cameron calls for immigrants to respct British core values," *The Daily Mail*, February 17, 2011 are also questioning the virtue of multiculturalism.

[222] On this subject, see Bruce Bawer's books *While Europe Slept,* Broadway Books (2006) and *Surrender* Anchor Books (2009).

[223] Mario Roy, "Liberté, sécurité, prospérité," *La Presse*, October 23, 2010 http://www. cyberpresse.ca/place-publique/editorialistes/mario-roy/201010222/01-4335121-liberte-se-curite-prosperite.php .

[224] On this subject, see the interesting column by Richard Martineau titled *"Catholique non-croyant"* on November 1, 2010 http://martineau.bloguecanoe.ca/2010/11/01/ catholique_non_croyant#comments .

[224a] Robert Dutrisac, "Le projet de loi 94 inquiète les juif orthodoxes", Le Devoir, 21 octobre 2010, http://www.ledevoir.com/societe/education/298472/le-projet-de-loi-94-inquiete-les-juifs-orthodoxes

[225] http://www.eyeontheun.org/browse-year.asp?ya=1&s=1&ua=1&tp=1&tpn=Resolution .

[226] http://www.un.org/News/fr-press/docs/2010/ECOSOC6419.doc.htm .

[227] http://www.un.org/womenwatch/daw/daw/index.html .

[228] Judith Lachapelle, "Femmes, séismes et manœuvres politiques," *La Presse*, April 21, 2010 http://www.cyberpresse.ca/international/201004/21/01-4272589-femmes-seismes-et-manoeuvres-politiques.php .

[229] "La Libye élue au Conseil des droits de l'Homme," *Le Monde*, May13, 2010 http:// www.lemonde.fr/international/article/2010/05/13/a-libye-elue-au-conseil-des-droits-de-l-homme-de-l-onu_1351318_3210.html .

[230] http://www.webcitation.org/5dViuhEdA .

[231] http://daccess-dds-ny.un.org/doc/UNDOC/GEN/G10/140/88/PDF/G1014088. pdf?OpenElement .

[232] http://www.terrorism-info.org.il/malam_multimedia/English/eng_n/pdf/hamas_charter. pdf .

[233] Jared Malsin, "UN expert Richard Falk: PA told me to quit," *Ma'an News Agency*, March 9, 2010, http://www.maannews.net/eng/ViewDetails.aspx?ID=267176 .

[234] http://www.interlinkbooks.com/product_info.php?products_id=1326 .

[235] Eli Lake, "UN Officials Calls for Study of Neocons' Role in 9/11," The New York Sun, April 10, 2008, http://www.nysun.com/news/foreign/un-official-calls-study-neocons-role-911 .

[236] Natasha Mozgovaya, Shlomo Shamir and Reuters, "Ban Ki-moon condemns UN Palestinian human rights official for backing 9/11 slurs," *Haaretz,* January 25, 2010 http:// www.haaretz.com/news/international/ban-ki-moon-condemns-un-palestinian-human-rights-official-for-backing-9-11-slurs-1.339181et Agence France-Presse, "Ban critique un Rapporteur de l'ONU pour des propos sur le 11 Septembre," January 25, 2011 http:// www.24heures.ch/depeches/communales-2011/ban-critique-rapporteur-onu-propos-11-septembre .

[237] For more about the UN, I suggest you visit the web site of UN Watch at www.unwatch. org, whose director is Montreal-born Hillel Neuer, a young, smart, rigorous and eloquent

man.

[238] http://www.un.org/News/Press/docs/2006/sgsm10796.doc.htm .

[239] Joseph Facal, "La fabrique de la haine," September 30, 2009 http://www.josephfacal. org/la-fabrique-de-la-haine .

[240] See for example the excellent analyses produced by the Jerusalem Center for Public Affairs at http://jcpa.org/JCPA/Templates/showpage.asp?DBID=1&LNGID=1&TMID=84 &FID=452&PID=131 .

[241] A. Mounier-Kuhn, "Ancienne haut-commissaire aux Droits de l'homme Mary Robinson commente les dossiers les chauds de ce début d'année," Le Temps, Feb. 4, 2009.

[242] "Israel's bombardment of Gaza is not self-defence – it's a war crime," The Times, January 11, 2009 http://www.timesonline.co.uk/tol/comment/letters/article5488380.ece .

[243] "Goldstone walks a fine line in an ancient war zone," Business Day, August 4, 2009, http://www.businessday.co.za/articles/Content.aspx?id=77618.

[244] Tehiya Barak, "Judge Goldstone's dark past," Ynetnews, May 6, 2010, http://www. ynetnews.com/articles/0,340,L-3885999,00.html .

[245] Anshel Pfeffer and Dana Harman, "UN report co-author: Hamas fired 2 rockets before Gaza op," Haaretz, February 11, 2010, http://www.haaretz.com/hasen/spages/1149044. html .

[246] Taguieff, Paul-André, La nouvelle propagande antijuive, Presses Universitaires de France, Paris, 2010. p.37.

[247] Richard Goldstone, "Reconsidering the Goldstone Report on Israel and war crimes," The Washington Post, April 1, 2 11, http://www.washingtonpost.com/opinions/reconsidering-the-goldstone-report-on-israel-and-war-crimes/2011/04/01/AFgl11JC_story.html . See also: Ethan Bronner and Isabel Kershner, "Head of U.N. Panel Regrets Saying Israel Intentionally Killed Gazans," The New York Times, April 2, 2011, http://www.nytimes. com/2011/04/03/world/middleeast/03goldstone.html?_r=1 .

[248] David Bernstein, "Human Rights Watch Goes to Saudi Arabia," The Wall Street Journal, July 15, 2009 http://online.wsj.com/article/SB124528343805525561.html .

[249] Egypt and Iraq.

[250] Robert L. Bernstein, "Rights Watchdog, Lost in the Mideast," The New York Times, October 19, 2009 http://www.nytimes.com/2009/10/20/opinion/20bernstein.html .

[251] Nicholas D. Kristof, "The World Capital of Killing," The New York Times, February 6, 2010 http://www.nytimes.com/2010/02/07/opinion/07kristof. html?scp=4&sq=kristof&st=cse and Nicholas D. Kristof, "The Grotesque Vocabulary in Congo," The New York Times, February 6, 2010 http://www.nytimes.com/2010/02/11/ opinion/11kristof.html?scp=4&sq=kristof&st=nyt .

[252] In August 2010, the leader of Amnesty International's Finnish branch Frank Johanson called Israel a 'scum State' on his web site http://www.jpost.com/International/Article. aspx?id=185846 .

[253] On this subject, see the excellent article by Melanie Phillips, The moral blindness of the "human rights" industry, February 16, 2011, http://www.spectator.co.uk/melaniephillips/5777877/the-moral-blindness-of-the-human-rights-industry-thtml .

[254] The remains of the soldiers (together with a kidnapped Israeli civilian) were exchanged for 436 prisoners and the remains of 59 armed men in January 2004.

[255] http://www.cbc.ca/world/story/2010/11/19/f-rifa-macdonald-lebanon-hariri.html .

[256] http://www.stl-tsl.org/en/media/press-releases/2-09-2011-a-public-service-announcement-by-the-special-tribunal-for-lebanon

[257] This changed somewhat in August 2010, however, the new statute gives Palestinian refugees the same rights as foreign workers in Lebanon. This does not actually change the situation much as access to the professions is often dependent on reciprocity agreements between Lebanon and the workers' country of origin. As there is no Palestinian State, such a reciprocity agreement is impossible. See: http://www.google.com/hostednews/ap/article/ ALeqM5gG-zpmVkw-1nfyIUVZsjsAy8s2wgD9HLB7000 and Le Monde with Reuters, "Le Liban octroie des droits civiques aux Palestiniens," August 18, 2010 http://www. lemonde.fr/proche-orient/article/2010/08/18/le-liban-octroie-des-droits-civiques-de-base-

aux-palestiniens_1399982_3218.html .

[258] http://www.google.com/hostednews/afp/article/ALeqM5hQgEbOn5jFd44coMyjIDf-Jt2FvQ .

[259] A report financed by the European Union, released on December 14, 2010, comes to the same conclusion: Simona Sikimic, "Living conditions of Palestinian refugees worse than believed – study," *The Daily Star*, December 15, 2010 ,http://www.dailystar.com.lb/article.asp?edition_id=1&categ_id=1&article_id=122554#axzz18AfNl3Gg .

[260] Thomas Abgrall, "Liban, Ahmadinejad accueilli en héros," *La Presse*, October 14, 2010, p.A31.

[261] "Nasrallah: No peace in Middle East as long as Israel exists," *Haaretz*, September 11, 2008, http://www.haaretz.com/news/nasrallah-no-peace-in-middle-east-as-long-as-israel-exists-1.253594 .

[262] Amos Harel and Avi Issacharoff, *34 Days: Israel, Hezbollah, and the War in Lebanon*, Palgrave Macmillan, New York, 2008, p.102-103.

[263] Ibid. p. 98.

[264] http://en.g8russia.ru/docs/21.html .

[265] http://sisyphe.org/spip.php?breve671 .

[266] http://www.melaniephillips.com/diary/?p=1291 .

[267] Amal Saad-Ghorayeb, *Hizbullah; Politics and Religion*, London, Pluto Press, 2002, p.170.

[268] http://www.camera.org/index.asp?x_context=7&x_issue=11&x_article=1158

[269] http://www.liberal.ca/newsroom/speeches/speech-to-the-inter-parliamentary-coalition-for-combating-anti-semitism .

[270] "Wikileaks: Les liens entre Téhéran et le Hezbollah," *Le Monde*, November 29, 2010, http://www.lemonde.fr/international/article/2010/11/29/teheran-a-utilise-des-ambulances-pour-passer-des-armes-au-hezbollah_1446273_3210.html .

[271] Thanassis Cambanis, "Stronger Hezbollah Emboldened for Fights Ahead," *The New York Times*, October 6, 2010, http://www.nytimes.com/2010/10/07/world/middleeast/07hezbollah.html?_r=1 .

[272] George Malbrunot, "Dans le secret des caches du Hezbollah," *Le Figaro*, October 25, 2010 http://www.lefigaro.fr/international/2010/10/25/01003-20101025ARTFIG00681-dans-le-secret-des-caches-d-armes-du-hezbollah.php .

[273] See for example: "Lebanon hails militants freed in prisoner swap," *CNN*, July 17, 2008, http://www.cnn.com/2008/WORLD/meast/07/16/israel.swap/index.html and "Kuntar receives a hero's welcome," *The Jerusalem Post*, July15, 2008, http://www.jpost.com/Home/Article.aspx?id=107755 and "Hezbollah celebrates swap with Israelis," *The New York Times*, July 16, 2008.

[274] Jonathan D. Halevi, "Talking to Hamas? - Increasing Expressions of Genocidal Intent by Hamas Leaders Against the Jews," *JCPA*, Vol.10, No.19, January 3, 2011 ,http://www.jcpa.org/JCPA/Templates/ShowPage.asp?DRIT=1&DBID=1&LNGID=1&TMID=111&FID=379&PID=1861&IID=5576&TTL=Talking_to_Hamas?_%E2%80%93_Increasing_Expressions_of_Genocidal_Intent_by_Hamas_Leaders_Against_the_Jews .

[275] http://www.terrorism-info.org.il/malam_multimedia/English/eng_n/html/hamas_e133.htm and http://www.crif.org/index.php?page=articles_display/detail&aid=22731&artyd=121. See also: "Hamas confirms losses in Cast Lead for first time," *The Jerusalem Post*, November 1, 2010 http://www.jpost.com/MiddleEast/Article.aspx?id=193521 and Evelyn Gordon, "Hamas Finally Admits Most Gaza Fatalities Were Combatants, Not Civilians," *Commentary*, November 1, 2010 http://www.commentary-magazine.com/blogs/index.php/evelyn-gordon/379742 .

[276] Sabrina Tavernise and Anderw W. Lehren, "A Grim Portrait of Civilian Deaths in Iraq," *The New York Times*, October 22, 2010, http://www.nytimes.com/2010/10/23/world/middleeast/23casualties.html?_r=2 . See also: Evelyn Gordon, "WikiLeaks and the Gaza War," *Commentary*, October 25, 2010 http://www.commentarymagazine.com/blogs/index.php/evelyn-gordon/377631.

[277] With the exception of the Parti Québécois MNA Monique Richard and Québec Solid-aire MNA Amir Khadir.

[278] See: http://qic-cqi.org/spip.php?article169 and http://www.youtube.com/watch?v=eXgMbZwUBeI .

[279] Rima Elkouri,"Sus au terrorisme intellectuel," *La Presse*, January 18, 2009, http://www.cyberpresse.ca/chroniqueurs/rima-elkouri/200901/17/01-818631-sus-au-terrorisme-intellectuel.php.

[280] Richard Martineau, "Feu l'objectivité," *Journal de Montréal*, January 22, 2009 http://www.canoe.com/infos/chroniques/richardmartineau/archives/2009/01/20090122-090200.html .

[281] For an excellent BBC documentary on the subject, see: http://www.youtube.com/watch?v=SXrzF0IOQYE and http://www.youtube.com/watch?v=Nfo91FQVr7M.

[282] http://www.qic-cqi.org/spip.php?article208 .

[283] http://palwatch.org/main.aspx?fi=676&fld_id=676&doc_id=2337 .

[284] Mario Roy, "Un plan simple," *La Presse*, June 5, 2010, http://www.cyberpresse.ca/place-publique/editorialistes/mario-roy/201006/04/01-4287033-un-plan-simple.php?utm_c ategorieinterne=trafficdrivers&utm_contenuinterne=cyberpresse_BO40_editoriaux_199_accueil_POS2 .

[285] Richard Hêtu, "Est-ce ainsi que les pacifistes agissent?," *Cyberpresse*, May 31, 2010 http://blogues.cyberpresse.ca/hetu/2010/05/31/est-ce-ainsi-que-des-pacifistes-agissent/?utm_categorieinterne=trafficdrivers&utm_contenuinterne=cyberpresse_blo-guesaccueilcp_BO3_accueil_ECRAN1POS2 and http://www.youtube.com/watch?v=bU12KW-XyZE&feature=player_embedded .

[286] http://www.terrorism-info.org.il/malam_multimedia/English/eng_n/html/ipc_e130.htm.

[287] http://www.mfa.gov.il/MFA/HumanitarianAid/Palestinians/Humanitarian_aid_flotilla_transferred_Gaza_1-Jun-2010.htm .

[288] http://ht.ly/1T5PL .

[289] http://www.cicweb.ca/scene/2010/06/israel_aid_to_gaza/ .

[290] Gabin Ribinowitz, "Israël allège le blocus de Gaza," *Agence France-Presse*, June 20, 2010, http://www.cyberpresse.ca/international/moyen-orient/201006/20/01-4291791-israel-allege-le-blocus-de-gaza.php?utm_categorieinterne=trafficdrivers&u tm_contenuinterne=cyberpresse_B13b_moyen-orient_291_section_POS4 .

[291] http://www.cicweb.ca/scene/2010/06/gaza-facts/ The CIC's source was the very credible *CIA World Fact Book*: https://www.cia.gov/library/publications/the-world-factbook .

[292] "Chemicals used in making explosives caught at West Bank checkpoint," *Haaretz*, December 29, 2007, http://www.haaretz.com/news/chemicals-used-in-making-explosives-caught-at-west-bank-checkpoint-1.236148 .

[293] http://www.mfa.gov.il/MFA/HumanitarianAid/Palestinians/Legal_aspects_Gaza_aid_26-May-2010.htm and Section 67A of the San Remo Manual on International Law Applicable to Armed Conflicts at Sea.

[294] http://www.navy.forces.gc.ca/cms/4/4-a_fra.asp?id=504 .

[295] http://news.globaltv.com/canada/Canadian+navy+fights+terrorism/2782546/story.html .

[296] http://www.middle-east-online.com/english/?id=44055 .

[297] http://www.turkel-committee.gov.il/index.html

[298] http://www.un.org/News/dh/infocus/middle_east/Gaza_Flotilla_Panel_Report.pdf

[299] Branch of Islam founded in the 19th century that has about 20 million adherents.

[300] Jane Perlez, "Pakistani Taliban Carried Out Attack on Lahore Mosques, Police Say," *The New York Times,* May 29, 2010, http://www.nytimes.com/2010/05/30/world/asia/30pstan.html .

[301] "Female suicide bomber kills dozens in Iraq," *BBC*, February 1, 2011 http://news.bbc.co.uk/2/hi/middle_east/8490819.stm .

[302] http://www.google.com/hostednews/afp/article/ALeqM5j3hkp5QaMaIGyTFmFG77iN-PHWkcQ .

[303] Mohamed Sifaoui, "Aux promeneurs du samedi et à leurs copains d'une certaine gauche," January 11, 2009, http://www.mohamed-sifaoui.over-blog.com/article-26644084.html . (Translation).

[304] Burak Bekdil, "Why is Palestine a 'Second Cyprus' for Turks?," *Hurriyet Daily News*,

A Quebec Jew

June 3, 2010, http://www.hurriyetdailynews.com/n.php?n=why-is-palestine-8216a-second-cyprus8217-for-turks-2010-06-03 .

[305] This led the Qatari Head of State to say, on February 23, 2010, that Israelis can't be blamed for mistrusting Arabs. JSSNews, "L'Emir du Qatar: "Israël doit être félicité pour toujours vouloir la paix," December 1, 2010 http://jssnews.com/2010/12/01/lemir-du-qa-tar-israel-doit-etre-felicite-pour-toujours-vouloir-la-paix and "WikiLeaks cables: You can't blame Israel for mistrusting Arabs, says Qatari ruler," *Haaretz*, November 30, 2010, http://www.haaretz.com/news/diplomacy-defense/wikileaks-cables-you-can-t-blame-israel-for-mistrusting-arabs-says-qatari-ruler-1.328061

[306] On the justification of the Israeli demand for such recognition by the Palestinians, see: Michael B. Oren, "An End to Israel's Invisibility," *The New York Times*, October 13, 2010 http://www.nytimes.com/2010/10/14/opinion/14oren.html .

[307] To compare, there are 26 officially Muslim States on the planet. There are also 18 officially Christian States (mainly in Europe). But there is only one Jewish State. Moreover, the accusation that Israel is a racist State by nature because it defines itself as a Jewish and democratic is even more ridiculous when one realizes that this accusation usually comes from states in the Arab/Muslim world and their allies. Consider the official names of some of those countries: Libya (Great Socialist People's Libyan *Arab* Jamahiriya), Syria (Syrian *Arab* Republic), Egypt (*Arab* Republic of Egypt), Iran (*Islamic* Republic of Iran), Emirates (United *Arab* Emirates), in addition to those States that are named after a family, like *Saudi* Arabia and the *Hashemite* Kingdom of Jordan.

[308] http://en.wikipedia.org/wiki/List_of_Arab_members_of_the_Knesset .

[309] On the subject of Christian growth in Israel, see: Benny Avni, "Bethelem's Exodus," *The New York Post*, December 23, 2009 http://www.nypost.com/p/news/opinion/opedcolumnists/bethlehem_exodus_jH6iVNuar-sPLBceXPzHO6I .

[310] "Le calvaire des chrétiens," *Le Point*, No.1999, January 6, 2011, p.42.

[311] http://www.theisraelproject.org/atf/cf/%7B84dc5887-741e-4056-8d91-a389164bc94e%7D/20101213_CHRISTMAS_PRESS_KIT_UPDATED-PRINT.PDF.

[312] http://cjcuc.com/site/2010/06/08/cjcuc-statement-on-christians-in-the-middle-east .

[313] Irshad Manji, "Modern Israel is a far cry from old South Africa," *The Australian*, February 9, 2007, http://www.theaustralian.com.au/news/opinion/irshad-manji-modern-israel-is-a-far-cry-from-old-south-africa/story-e6frg6zo-1111112964516 . Edward Said, "Israel-Palestine: a third way," *Le Monde Diplomatique* (English translation), September 1998, p. 6.

[314] Edward Said, "Israel-Palestine, une troisième voie", *Le Monde Diplomatique,* août 1998, http://www.monde-diplomatique.fr/1998/08/SAID/10786

[315] Jacob Dayan, "Yes, Israel's a democracy", *The Los Angeles Times*, May 27, 2010, http://www.latimes.com/news/opinion/opinionla/la-oew-dayan-20100527,0,4680781.story.

[316] Alain Dieckhoff, Centre d'études et de recherches internationales, CNRS, *Sociologie et sociétés*, Vol. XXXI, No 2, Fall 1999, quoted by Fabien Ghez and Liliane Messika, *La Paix impossible?*, L'Archipel, Paris, 2006, p.489-490.

[317] http://content.ksg.harvard.edu/leadership/index.php?option=com_content&task=view&id=511&Itemid=115 .

[318] Brian Henry, "Shiny happy Israelis," *The National Post*, August 17, 2010 http://fullcomment.nationalpost.com/2010/08/17/brian-henry-shiny-happy-israelis .

[319] Jackson Diehl, "Why Palestinians want to be Israeli citizens," *The Washington Post*, January 12, 2011 http://voices.washingtonpost.com/postpartisan/2011/01/_one_of_the_givens.html and http://pechterpolls.com/?p=317.

[320] Tarek Fatah, *The Jew Is Not My Enemy*, McClelland & Stewart, Toronto, 2010, pp.95-96 and 179-180.

[321] Chaim Levinson,"Top rabbis move to forbid renting homes to Arabs, say 'racism originated in the Torah'," *Haaretz*, December 7, 2010, http://www.haaretz.com/news/national/top-rabbis-move-to-forbid-renting-homes-to-arabs-say-racism-originated-in-the-torah-1.329327 .

[322] "Peres: Rabbis' petition against renting to Arabs creates moral crisis in Israel," *Haaretz*, December 8, 2010, http://www.haaretz.com/news/national/peres-rabbis-petition-against-renting-to-arabs-creates-moral-crisis-in-israel-1.329505 .

[323] Barak Ravid and Chaim Levinson, "Netanyahu slams top rabbis' call to forbid renting homes to Arabs," *Haaretz*, December 7, 2010, http://www.haaretz.com/news/national/netanyahu-slams-top-rabbis-call-to-forbid-renting-homes-to-arabs-1.329384 .

[324] Lidor Grave-Lazi, "Rabbis sign petition against religious discrimination," *The Jerusalem Post*, December 14, 2010, http://www.jpost.com/JewishWorld/JewishNews/Article.aspx?id=199360 .

[325] Jack Khoury and Eli Ashkenazi, "Public outcry ensues after rabbis tell Jews not to rent to Arabs," *Haaretz,* October 21, 2010, http://www.haaretz.com/print-edition/news/public-outcry-ensues-after-rabbis-tell-jews-not-to-rent-to-arabs-1.320336 .

[326] http://cicweb.ca/media/news_101210.cfm .

[327] "These are not the values of Israel," February 28, 2011, http://www.cjnews.com/index.php?option=com_content&task=view&id=20506&Itemid=86 .

[328] "PA court: Sale of Palestinian land to Israelis is punishable by death," *Haaretz*, September 20, 2010, http://www.haaretz.com/news/diplomacy-defense/pa-court-sale-of-palestinian-land-to-israelis-is-punishable-by-death-1.314735 .

[329] On this subject, see the Israeli Declaration of independence: http://www.mfa.gov.il/mfa/peace%20process/guide%20to%20the%20peace%20process/declaration%20of%20establishment%20of%20state%20of%20israel .

[330] See the article: "Israel is only place I can live openly gay" by Mike Hamel, president of the Israeli gay rights group Aguda in the March 10, 2010 edition of the *Ottawa Citizen*. http://www.ottawacitizen.com/opinion/Israel%20only%20place%20live%20openly/2664530/story.html .

[331] Mario Roy, "La hiérarchie des causes," *La Presse*, July 3, 2010, http://www.cyberpresse.ca/place-publique/editorialistes/mario-roy/201006/30/01-4294645-la-hierarchie-des-causes.php .

[332] See s.25 (2) of Bulgaria's constitution : http://www.parliament.bg/en/const .

[333] See: http://www.citizensinformation.ie/categories/moving-country/irish-citizenship/irish_citizenship_through_birth_or_descent .

[334] See s.116 of the German constitution : https://www.btg-bestellservice.de/pdf/80201000.pdf .

[335] See: http://athens.usembassy.gov/uploads/7z/Z4/7zZ4A6EyE4dMjph5dNxFew/citizenship_code.pdf http://athens.usembassy.gov/uploads/7z/Z4/7zZ4A6EyE4dMjph5dNxFew/citizenship_code.pdf .

[336] http://en.wikipedia.org/wiki/Right_of_return .

[337] See chapter 1, s.4 of the Palestinian Basic Law. http://www.palestinianbasiclaw.org/2003-amended-basic-law .

[338] Jeffrey Goldberg, "Is Israel Still A Democracy?," *The Atlantic*, January 17, 2011, http://www.theatlantic.com/international/archive/2011/01/is-israel-still-a-democracy/69377.

[339] This is the same Arab League that, in April 2011, was continuing to support Syria's bid for a seat on the UN Human Right Council despite its massacre of hundreds of pro-democracy protesters. Colum Lynch, "Civilian massacres don't disqualify Syria from joining Human Rights Council," *Foreign Policy (online)*, 27 April 2011 http://turtlebay.foreignpolicy.com/posts/2011/04/27/ongoing_civilian_massacres_dont_disqualify_syria_from_seat_on_human_rights_council

[340] Of course to include "Palestine" here is an error as there has never been a state of Palestine.

[341] Rami G. Khouri, "The Arab State : durable and vulnerable," *The Daily Star*, May 15, 2010 http://www.dailystar.com.lb/article.asp?edition_id=10&categ_id=5&article_id=114876 and http://www.theglobeandmail.com/news/opinions/the-paradoxical-arab-world/article1576423 .

[342] Ibid.

[343] http://www.idrc.ca/fr/ev-160226-201-1-DO_TOPIC.html .

[344] Jean Mohsen Fahmy, "La tragédie occultée des chrétiens en pays musulmans," *Le Devoir*, March 16, 2010 http://www.ledevoir.com/international/actualites-internationales/285020/la-tragedie-occultee-des-chretiens-en-pays-musulmans .

[345] www.state.gov/g/drl/rls/irf/2008/108492.htm .

[346] The Bahá'is' world centres are in Haifa and Acco in Israel.

[347] See the Report of the Standing Committee on Foreign Affairs and International Development titled "Ahmadinejad's Iran: A threat to peace, human rights and international law," tabled in December 2010. http://www2.parl.gc.ca/HousePublications/Publication.aspx?DocId=4835870&Mode=1&Parl=40&Ses=3&Language=E .

[348] Serge Truffault, "Les chrétiens d'Orient – Le désarroi," *Le Devoir*, January 11, 2010 http://www.ledevoir.com/international/actualites-internationales/280813/les-chretiens-d-orient-le-desarroi .

[349] For an interesting articles on the Copts' situation in Egypt, see: Moheb Zaki, "Egypt's Persecuted Christians," *The Wall Street Journal*, May 18, 2010 http://online.wsj.com/article/SB10001424052748703745904575248301172607696.html?mod=WSJ_latest-headlines and Raymond Ibrahim, "Egypt Cuts a Deal: Christians Fed to Muslim 'Lions'," Hudson Institute, October 18, 2010 http://www.hudson-ny.org/1608/egypt-christians-lions.

[350] http://la-croix.com/afp.static/pages/101128151821.zsdcm5pg.htm .

[351] "Le calvaire des chrétiens," *Le Point*, No.1999, January 6, 2011, p.42.

[352] http://www.state.gov/g/drl/rls/irf/2006/71431.htm .

[353] www.state.gov/g/drl/rls/irf/2008/108481.htm .

[354] Constitutional Declaration 2011.

[355] ttp://www.egypt.gov.eg/english/laws/constitution/default.aspx .

[356] "Le calvaire des chrétiens," *Le Point*, No.1999, January 6, 2011, p.42.

[357] Imad Boles, "Egypt – Persecution, Disappearing Christians of the Middle East," *Middle East Quarterly*, Winter 2001, pp.23-29.

[358] Agence France-Presse, "Les chrétiens égyptiens débutent 2011 dans le sang," *La Presse*, December 31, 2010 http://www.cyberpresse.ca/international/afrique/201012/31/01-4356554-les-chretiens-egyptiens-debutent-2011-dans-le-sang.php?utm_categorieinterne=trafficdrivers&utm_contenuinterne=cyberpresse_vous_suggere_4356581_article_POS1. See also: "Égypte: un attentat fait 21 morts devant une église d'Alexandrie," *Le Monde*, January 1, 2011 http://www.lemonde.fr/afrique/article/2011/01/01/un-attentat-fait-21-morts-devant-une-eglise-d-alexandrie_1460063_3212.html#ens_id=1460085 .

[359] Reuters, "Sécurité renforcée en Egypte sur fond de tensions religieuses," *L'Express*, May 9, 2011, http://www.lexpress.fr/actualites/2/monde/securite-renforcee-en-egypte-sur-fond-de-tensions-religieuses_990818.html .

[360] Jacques Julliard, "Chrétiens persécutés : l'Occident fait l'Autruche," *Le Nouvel Observateur*, October 2010, http://hebdo.nouvelobs.com/sommaire/edito-et-chroniques/101334/la-chasse-aux-chretiens.html .

[361] *Tefillin* are two small black boxes with black straps attached to them. Jewish men are required to place one box on their head and tie the other one on their arm each weekday morning. *Tefillin* are biblical in origin, and are commanded within the context of several laws outlining a Jew's relationship to God. "And you shall love the Lord your God with all your heart, with all your soul, and with all your might. Take to heart these instructions with which I charge you this day. Impress them upon your children. Recite them when you stay at home and when you are away, when you lie down and when you get up. Bind them as a sign on your hand and let them serve as a frontlet between your eyes" (Deuteronomy 6:5-8). http://www.jewishvirtuallibrary.org/jsource/Judaism/tefillin.html

[362] Ronen Medzini, "No yarmulkes allowed in Jordan," *Ynetnews*, October 28, 2010 , http://www.ynetnews.com/articles/0,7340,L-3976092,00.html .

[363] On this subject, see Salim Mansur, "Disgusting silence on church bloodbath," *The London Free Press*, November 6, 2010 http://www.lfpress.com/comment/columnists/salim_mansur/2010/11/05/15992756.html.

[364] "Jour après jour : l'exode des chrétiens d'Orient," *Le Monde,* http://www.lemonde.fr/

idees/article/2010/11/02/jour-apres-jour-l-exode-des-chretiens-d-orient_1434238_3232. html .

[365] http://www.crif.org/index.php?page=articles_display/detail&aid=22921&artyd=108. See also: Ron Csillag, "Christianity arguably the most persecuted religion in the world," *The Toronto Star*, December 4, 2010, http://www.thestar.com/news/insight/article/901492- -thrown-to-the-lions

[366] http://www.cidcm.umd.edu/mar/assessment.asp?groupId=65202 .

[367] Ghez, Fabien et Messika, Liliane, *La Paix impossible?*, L'Archipel, Paris, 2006, p.472.

[368] "PA Court : Sale of Palestinian land to Israelis punishable by death," *Haaretz*, September 20, 2010 http://www.haaretz.com/news/diplomacy-defense/pa-court-sale-of-palestin- ian-land-to-israelis-is-punishable-by-death-1.314735 .

[369] Oren Dorell, "PLO ambassador says Palestinian state should be free of Jews," *USA Today*, September 13, 2011, http://www.usatoday.com/news/world/story/2011-09-13/ palestinian-israeli-jews-future-state-israel-PLO/50394882/1 .

[370] For examples of this, see the Palestinian Media Watch's website: http://www.palwatch.org .

[371] http://www.jcpa.org/JCPA/Templates/ShowPage.asp?DRIT=3&DBID=1&LNGID= 1&TMID=111&FID=624&PID=0&IID=741&TTL=The_Development_of_Arab_Anti- Semitism .

[372] http://www.forcedmigration.org/guides/fmo018 .

[373] Khaled Abu Tomeh, "Palestinians no longer welcome, says Lebanese Mufti," *The Jeru- salem Post*, June 16, 2011, http://www.jpost.com/MiddleEast/Article.aspx?id=225297.

[374] For an excellent article on Arab discriminations against Palestinians, see: Ben Dror Yemini, "The Arab Apartheid," *The Daily Telegraph*, May 18, 2011 http://my.telegraph. co.uk/actuality/realdeal/15813560/the-arab-apartheid-ben-dror-yemini/.

[375] http://www.unhcr.org/refworld/topic,4565c2252,4565c25f5f,49749cfcc,0.html .

[376] http://hdr.undp.org/fr/rapports/regional/etatsarabes/RBAS_ahdr2002_EN.pdf , p.3.

[377] Pierre-Antoine Donnet, Agence France-Presse, "ONU Femmes : l'Iran écarté du conseil, l'Arabie Saoudite élue," *Cyberpresse*, November 10, 2010 http://www. cyberpresse.ca/international/moyen-orient/201011/10/01-4341263-onu-femmes-liran- ecarte-du-conseil-larabie-saoudite-elue.php?utm_categorieinterne=trafficdrivers&u tm_contenuinterne=cyberpresse_lire_aussi_4341508_articl e_POS3 As popular Quebec commentator Richard Martineau wrote, it is as if Dracula was elected to the board of the blood bank of Canadian Red Cross.

[378] Alan Dershowitz, "Let's have a real apartheid education week," *The Winnipeg Jew- ish Review*, February 23, 2011, http://www.winnipegjewishreview.com/article_detail. cfm?id=761&sec=1&title=Let's_Have_a_Real_Apartheid_Education_Week_ .

[379] Agence France-Presse,"Émirats arabes – battre sa femme, oui, mais sans laisser de trace," *Le Devoir*, October 19, 2010, http://www.ledevoir.com/international/proche- orient/298282/emirats-arabes-battre-sa-femme-oui-mais-sans-laisser-de-trace .

[380] See what Freedom House has to say on the status of women in the Arab world: www. freedomhouse.org/template.cfm?page=163 .

[381] For the interview of Nathalie Morin's mother with Denis Lévesque on LCN, see: http:// videos.lcn.canoe.ca/video/68768665001/levesque-emission-du-25-fevrier-2 .

[382] Fabien Ghez and Liliane Messika, *La Paix impossible?,* L'Archipel, Paris, 2006, p.449.

[383] Ibid, p. 450.

[384] Ibid, p. 465.

[385] For interesting reports on this phenomena, see the report by the *Australian Broadcast- ing Corporation* at: http://www.youtube.com/watch?v=Iq5J1M2dNlU and this one on CNN: http://www.youtube.com/watch?v=iVRvQtGTv-s&sns=fb.

[386] "Daughter raped by brothers, murdered by mother," *World Net Daily*, November 18, 2003, www.worldnetdaily.com/news/article.asp?ARTICLE_ID=35663 .

[387] http://news.bbc.co.uk/2/hi/middle_east/1874471.stm. According to Wikipedia, the "abaya "is a long over garment, essentially a robe-like dress worn by some women in parts of the Islamic world. http://en.wikipedia.org/wiki/Abaya

[388] Mathieu Szeradzki, "Pour Ahmadinejad, 'il n'y a pas d'homosexuels en Iran'," *Rue 89*,

September 25, 2007, http://www.rue89.com/2007/09/25/pour-ahmadinejad-il-ny-a-pas-dhomosexuels-en-iran .

[389] www.iranian.com/BTW/2005/August/London/index.html .

[390] http://fr.wikipedia.org/wiki/Droits_des_personnes_LGBT_en_%C3%89gypte http://www.amnesty.org/fr/region/egypt/report-2009 or http://www.hrw.org/en/news/2008/02/14/egypt-spreading-crackdown-hiv-endangers-public-health .

[391] See s.4 http://www.palestinianbasiclaw.org/2003-amended-basic-law .

[392] http://www.pcpsr.org/domestic/2001/conste1.html.

[393] Roee Nahmias, "MK Ganaim calls for Islamic caliphate in Israel," *Ynetnews,* October 5, 2010, http://www.ynetnews.com/articles/0,7340,L-3887468,00.html .

[394] http://cicweb.ca/media/news_100312.cfm .

[395] John Ivison, "Layton hopes Israel issue disappears," *The National Post,*http://www.nationalpost.com/opinion/columnists/story.html?id=b634b778-e525-4190-8117-9a89adf22725.

[396] http://www.liberal.ca/fr/newsroom/media-releases/17617_declaration-du-chef-liberal-michael-ignatieff-sur-la-semaine-contre-lapartheid-israelien.

[397] http://www.liberal.ca/newsroom/speeches/speech-to-the-inter-parliamentary-coalition-for-combating-anti-semitism/

[398] UNHCR, *Refworld,* "South African Archbishop Desmond Tutu visits Osnaburgh Ojibway Reserve in northwestern Ontario. He says that Canada's treatment of its Native people is similar in many ways to South Africa's treatment of blacks under the system of apartheid". http://www.unhcr.org/refworld/country,,,CHRON,CAN,,469f3877c,0.html .

[399] Frank James, "Jimmy Carter Apologizes For Criticizing Israel," NPR, December 23, 2009, http://www.npr.org/blogs/thetwo-way/2009/12/jimmy_carter_apologizes_for_cr.html; Ron Kampeas, "Carter offers Jewish community 'Al Het'," JTA, December 21, 2009, http://jta.org/news/article/2009/12/21/1009832/carter-offers-jewish-community-al-het;

[400] Caroline Fourest, *La dernière utopie : menaces sur l'universalisme,* Grasset, 2009, p.95.

[401] Sarah-Maude Lefebvre, Agence QMI, "Intégrer les immigrants au travail," May 2, 2010 http://www2.canoe.com/infos/quebeccanada/archives/2010/05/20100502-145105.html .

[402] Pita Aatami and Maggie Emudluk, "Les leaders inuits lancent un cri du coeur," *Le Soleil,* March 18, 2010, http://www.cyberpresse.ca/le-soleil/opinions/points-de-vue/201003/18/01-4261904-les-leaders-inuits-lancent-un-cri-du-coeur.php .

[403] Louise Leduc, "La situation des jeunes autochtones inquiète," *La Presse,* June 26, 2010, http://www.cyberpresse.ca/actualites/quebec-canada/sante/201006/26/01-4293487-la-situation-des-jeunes-autochtones-inquiete.php.

[404] Caroline Montpetit, "Le racisme au Québec, un certain déni," *Le Devoir,* February 23, 2010 http://www.ledevoir.com/societe/actualites-en-societe/317403/le-racisme-au-quebec-un-certain-deni .

[405] Daniel Amar, *Le triangle des solitudes, dans, Une réalité méconnue : les Juifs au Québec,* Cap-aux-Diamants, No.105, pp.33-36

[406] Jeremiah 29:5-7.

Richard Marceau

Other Éditions du Marais Publications

Essays

Achille, Théodore E. *Les Haïtiens et la double nationalité.* 56 p. ISBN 978-2-9809556-6-2

Bensoussan, David. *Anthologie des écrivains sépharades du Québec* .656 p. ISBN 978-2-923721-13-2

Elbaz, André E. *La tentation de l'occident, itinéraire d'un juif Maghrébin.* 378 p. ISBN 978-2-9809556-8-6

Étienne, Gérard. *La femme noire dans le discours littéraire haïtien.* 306 p. ISBN 978-2-9809556-9-3

Étienne, Gérard. *Le créole une langue.* 414 p. ISBN 978-2-923721-10-1

Marceau, Richard. Juif, une histoire québécoise. 346 p. 978-2-923721-22-4

Nerson, Annette. *Une âme dépareillée tome I Guerre et vie. Lettres d'Annette Espinas Nerson à sa mère, Jeanne Gide-Espinas 1940-1963. Établissement du texte et préface d'Evelyne Nerson-Meron.* 384 p. ISBN 978-2-923721-02-6

Piquion, Henri J. & Prophète, Jean L. *Paul Eugène Magloire (1907-2007) La République était belle sous était belle sous l'empire.* 124 p. ISBN 978-2-9809556-7-9

Régnoux, Philippe. *Nous tracerons des horizons.* 172 p. ISBN 978-2923721-20-0

Sansaricq, Bernard. *Le pouvoir de la foi.* 396 p. ISBN 978-2-9809556-4-7

Poetry

Benayoun-Szmidt, Yvette. *Échos de souvenance.* 70 p. ISBN 978-2-923721-14-9

Étienne, Gérard. *Lettre à Montréal.* (Texte, CD interprété par Philippe Régnoux). ISBN 978-2-923721-18-7

Étienne, Gérard. *Natania.* 116 p. ISBN 978-2-923721-01-9
Feuerwerker, Hillel. *Feuille de route.* 70 p. ISBN 978-2-9809556-1-7

Leger, Dyane & Savoie Paul. *L'incendiaire.* 74 p. ISBN 978-2-923721-04-0

Redouane, Najib. *Le Blanc de la parole.* 70 p. ISBN 978-2-923721-00-2

Redouane, Najib. *Ce soleil percera-t-il les nuages.* 74 p. ISBN 978-2-923721-06-4

Richard Marceau

Redouane, Najib. *Lumière fraternelle*. 70 p. ISBN 978-2-923721-05-7

Redouane, Najib. Ombres confuses du temps. 74p. ISBN 978-2-923721-17-0

Redouane, Najib. *Paroles éclatées*. 70 p. ISBN 978-2-9809859-3-5

Redouane, Najib. *Songes brisés*.70 p. ISBN 978-2-9809859-4-2

Young, Lélia. *Aquarelles, la paix comme un poème*. 68 p. ISBN 978-2-9809556-3-1

Young, Lélia. *Réverbère*. 80 p. ISBN 978-2-9809859-2-8

Fiction

Bensoussan, Fiby. *De Marrakech à Montréal*. 178 p. ISBN 978-2-923721-12-5

Étienne, Gérard. *Un ambassadeur macoute à Montréal*, 2ᵉ édition. 228 p. ISBN 978-2-923721-19-4

Étienne, Gérard. *Le Nègre crucifié*. Préfaces 2ᵉ édition Franck Laraque, 3e édition Gérard Étienne, Lexique Max Manigat, Postface 4ᵉ édition Keith Louis Walker, Dartmouth College. 198 p. ISBN 978-2-9809859-6-6

(Aussi disponible aux Éditions Métropolis à Genève et en Haïti aux Presses Nationales d'Haïti.)

Étienne, Gérard. *La Reine Soleil Levée*. 200 p. ISBN 2-7601-1974-2

Étienne, Gérard. *Vous n'êtes pas seul*. 186 p. ISBN 978-2-9809556-5-5

Gallego, André Gérôme .*Le Fennec*. 398 p. ISBN 978-2-923721-15-6
Kattan, Naim. *Le premier amour de Daniel*. 58 p. ISBN 978-2-923721-07-1

Lacasse, Lise. *Les Battants*. 258 p. ISBN 978-2-923721-03-3

Lacasse, Lise. *Pour qui tu te prends ma fille*. 308 p. ISBN 978-2-923721-16-3

Lasry, Pierre. *Don Juan et les moulins à vent*. 304 p. ISBN 978-2-9809859-5-9

Theater

Étienne, Gérard. *Monsieur le président*. 132 p. ISBN 978-2-9809859-1-1

Kattan, Naïm. *Avant la cérémonie*. 128 p. ISBN 978-2-9809556-0-0

De Paola, Paolo. *Donald, sa muse. 112 p.* Traduit de l'anglais par Janik Tremblay. ISBN 978-2-923721-09-5

De Paola, Paolo. *Soleil Rose*. 142 p. ISBN 978-2-923721-08-8

Toumi, Alek Baylee. *Madah-Sartre*. 164 p. ISBN 978-2-923721-11-8

In English

Black, Ayanna. *Invoking the spirits*. 68 p. ISBN 978-2-9809859-0-4

Étienne, Gérard. *Crucified in Haiti*. Translated by Claudia Harry, introduction by Keith L. Walker. 180 p. ISBN 978-2-9809556-2-4

Also available

Feuerwerker, David. *L'émancipation des juifs en France de l'ancien régime au Second Empire*.
ISBN 2-226-00316-9

To be published

Étienne, Gérard. *Une femme muette* ,2ᵉ édition. Roman

Étienne, Gérard. *Le Bacoulou2.Roman*

Grysman, Rabbi Charles. Essai

Latour, François. *Regard sur Haïti*. *Essai*

Nerson, Annette. *Une âme dépareillée tome II. Enfer et bonnes intentions. Essai*

Redouane, Najib. *Peu importe. Poésie*

Toumi, Alek Baylee. *Albert Camus entre la mère et l'injustice. Théâtre*

Young, Lélia. *Lettres au pied du lit*. Nouvelles

Young, Lélia. *Regard sur des textes francophones*. Essai

Young, Lélia. *Failles*. Poésie

Young, Lélia. *Le désert*. Théâtre

www.editionsdumarais.ca